BELIEF AND AGEING

Spiritual pathways in later life

Peter G. Coleman and colleagues, University of Southampton

This edition published in Great Britain in 2011 by

The Policy Press
University of Bristol
Fourth Floor
Beacon House
Queen's Road
Bristol BS8 1QU
UK

Tel +44 (0)117 331 4054
Fax +44 (0)117 331 4093
e-mail tpp-info@bristol.ac.uk
www.policypress.co.uk

North American office:
The Policy Press
c/o International Specialized Books Services (ISBS)
920 NE 58th Avenue, Suite 300
Portland, OR 97213-3786, USA
Tel +1 503 287 3093
Fax +1 503 280 8832
e-mail info@isbs.com

British Library Cataloguing in Publication Data
A catalogue record for this book is available from the British Library.

Library of Congress Cataloging-in-Publication Data
A catalog record for this book has been requested.

ISBN 978 1 84742 459 4 paperback
ISBN 978 1 84742 460 0 hardcover

Cover design by The Policy Press
Front cover: image kindly supplied by www.istock.com
Printed and bound in Great Britain by TJ International, Padstow
The Policy Press uses environmentally responsible print partners.

Contents

Foreword

Judith Phillips

Spirituality is a neglected area for public discussion, yet a crucial aspect for many older people in later life. Reviewing life and its meaning from the perspective of later life is often missing in academic texts on ageing and older people. Yet spiritual needs increase with age and spirituality can be a crucial support to many, particularly during transitions associated with later life such as bereavement.

This book redresses that omission. It deals with the terminology around spirituality, religion and belief; it stresses older people's views throughout; it looks at spirituality from a multi-faith perspective and couches this within different cultural, religious and social contexts. With an increasing emphasis on Islam and alternative meaning systems, it addresses both contemporary debates alongside historical accounts.

To fit in with the 'Ageing and the Lifecourse' series it takes a lifecourse approach, looking at the diversity of beliefs and different faiths that an older person may have witnessed over their lifetime. It also challenges the tendency to view old age as an isolated, separate or static phase of life and emphasises the interrelationship between different phases of life and continuities across the lifecourse.

Preface

This book is based on the contributions of very many people. Some have also been main or co-authors of particular chapters and I am very grateful to them for their excellent collaboration in the making of this book: Amina Begum, Marie Gianclli, Saba Jaleel, Marie Mills, Ignat Petrov, Peter Speck, John Spreadbury and Peter Wilkinson. Others have contributed to the studies reported through sharing in the data collection, helping in the study design, and generally developing the thinking necessary to conduct such studies. I mention in particular previous students and colleagues: Abdulaziz Aflakseir, Roxana Carare, Elizabeth Forbes, Sacha Guglani, Victoria Hui, Christine Ivani-Chalian, Julia Lyubchenko, Andrew McCulloch, Fionnuala McKiernan, Maureen Robinson, Anita Saigal and Andrea Yap. Others have given help and encouragement at important times and/or shared significant data with us. These are too many to name but we would like to mention at least the following persons: Cyriaque Bigirimana, Georgiy Chystiakov, Grace Davie, Francis Davis, Brian Dyas, Sandro Lagomarsini, Rob Merchant, John Owen, Andrei Podolskij, Colin Pritchard, Euan Sadler, David Sillince, Eleanor Tarbox, Ben Wilkinson and David Voas.

Although I have been critical in this book of the neglect of the study of religion and spirituality by gerontologists in the UK, I am grateful to many colleagues in the British Society of Gerontology who have encouraged me to persist in work in this field, particularly to Chris Phillipson, but also to, among others, Simon Biggs, John Bond, Ricca Edmondson, Malcolm Johnson, Sally Richards, John Vincent, Alan Walker and Tony Warnes. I also gladly acknowledge the support of Age Concern England and Help the Aged (now joined together as Age UK) for this topic, and especially Ann Webber and Gerry Burke, and also the encouragement of fellow members of the Christian Council on Ageing, and especially Mannes Tidmarsh and Albert Jewell. I should also like to acknowledge research grant awards from the Economic and Social Research Council, the Leverhulme Trust, the Nuffield Foundation and the University of Southampton, and the support of diverse colleagues in the last organisation.

Last but not least, we want to thank all the older interviewees who have been so generous with their time and have provided the bulk of the material of this book. All names used in the text are fictitious, but I should like to dedicate this book to the first person I interviewed on the subject of belief and ageing over 40 years ago. Her name was Alice Haimes. She was especially encouraging to me. I thank her in person but also as a representative of all the other older people who have contributed to the making of this book.

Peter G. Coleman
Southampton, August 2010

ONE

Ageing and belief

Peter G. Coleman

Belief, spirituality and meaning

This is a book intended to make some contribution to filling what has become a large gap in the study of ageing, especially in the UK. We have learned so much in the last half century about the biological, social and psychological processes involved in human ageing, but we have neglected the spiritual dimension. This neglect is the more surprising when one takes into account that the later stages of life raise fundamental questions about the purpose and meaning of life, for example finding justification for continued living in states of diminished physical or social functioning (Howse, 1999; Polivka, 2000). In the not so distant past most older people sought and received answers to such questions from the ordinary wisdom present within their culture and provided largely by religious bodies whose presence was pervasive throughout the culture. But western society is now increasingly fragmented, and individuals often have to search for their own answers in relative isolation from one another. They are much less likely to draw strength or take refuge in collective beliefs about the meaning of life and suffering.

The title of this book emphasises belief. This is a deliberate choice, because the concept of belief, although not without its difficulties, is less complex than either spirituality or religion. Life is unimaginable without belief. We may like to think that our actions are for the most part based on secure knowledge but a little reflection would show how small the domain of our knowledge is compared with our belief. Beliefs, explicit and implicit, in regard to small and large matters, and of varying degrees of rationality, underpin all our actions. Action without belief is not conceivable. It is merely behaviour, response in relation to stimulus. To act is to be purposeful and beliefs give us purpose. When events threaten our beliefs we either change them or seek to support them by looking to other evidence that might sustain them. Beliefs can be mistaken, whereas knowledge that is mistaken is not knowledge at all. So although true knowledge is hard to attain, beliefs are common and an essential part of ordinary living.

Beliefs determine what we value as goals and objectives in life. Our particular attention in this book is to the denotative use of the term belief, as in 'belief in my son', 'belief in democracy' or 'belief in God', that is where belief is directed to a person, set of ideas or an abstract principle as a source of guidance in the choice of goals and decisions that we make. These beliefs provide orientation and direction for our lives at difficult or unclear moments. To whom or what should we look? What principles should shape our thoughts and actions? Writing in the closing years of the Second World War, seeing the disasters that had resulted from the mass adoption by European nations of totalitarian and racist beliefs, Martin D'Arcy (1945) felt strongly the need for more profound reflection on the rationality of beliefs. At the same time he wanted to demonstrate the rationality of Christian religious belief. New ideologies had threatened to overthrow centuries of European culture and its emphasis on belief in the dignity and worth of all human lives regardless of status and background. Since then new challenges have arisen and our often casually assumed societal beliefs need constant questioning. The value of constant economic growth, for example, is an important belief that is widely held by those in political power and that has major consequences not only for the future of society but of the planet itself, yet it is insufficiently questioned.

Beliefs about the nature of humankind, its purpose and destiny, and its relationship with the world and universe in which it is embedded, are increasingly referred to as spiritual beliefs. Use of the word 'spiritual' appears to have lost its original tethering alongside religion and to have come to refer to a search for connection (the underlying root meaning of the word 'religion') with and/or belonging to whatever powers, forces or principles are considered to underlie the universe we live in. Spiritual practice is understood as the appropriate response to this awareness of connection. The relatively new use of the substantive term 'spirituality' has also gained in popular usage in the West and appears to have achieved this at the expense of religion. Indeed it often seems to be chosen precisely in order to avoid the negative connotations that surround the concept of religion, particularly relating to its rules and regulations.

Religious decline is a palpable fact of contemporary Western European culture, although, as we will see, this decline is more variable and complex than has often been assumed. In its retreat it has left a vacuum that needs filling. This absence has been particularly strongly felt in some areas of healthcare, especially in psychiatry and nursing (Paley, 2007). These are areas of life where the practical relevance of dealing with issues of meaning and belonging in the face of suffering, alienation and death are everyday occurrences. Responding to spiritual needs has become a major area of nursing practice and education in recent years. But there may be better alternative choices to the use of the term 'spiritual'. For example 'meaning-based' needs may be a more accurate and less ambiguous term with which to refer to human experience of needing to justify continued existence in the face of the pain that life can bring.

Yet, paradoxically, the language of spirituality may be chosen in preference to more secular terminology precisely because of its overlap with religion and its reference to that aspect of human nature that goes beyond itself. This has obvious advantages for the user. It allows for slippage between religious and secular discourse. The religious connotation can be accepted or ignored. But it also leads to ambiguity. A number of writers in the field of pastoral care have commented on this lack of clarity. For example, James Woodward, a minister of the Church of England who has much experience of dealing with the pastoral needs of older people, comments:

> Over the last 20 years ... I have come to share the belief that the word spirituality runs the danger of becoming a vague and diffuse notion, functioning like 'intellectual Polyfilla', which changes shape and content conveniently to fill the space its user has devised for it. (Woodward, 2008: 69)

Ambiguity may be convenient in certain settings, as for example in healthcare settings where hospital chaplains may wish sometimes to appear to be providing religious ministry and at other times not. But it also has disadvantages for those for whom the remaining religious connotations of the term 'spiritual' are off-putting. This is a persistent problem often encountered, particularly in care of older people. Of course this may in time be resolved by the disappearance altogether of the religious connection from understanding of the word spiritual. That this is a real possibility is shown by the widening inclusion criteria for deployment of the term. A good example is Michael Hogan's reference to the well-known biologist and atheist Richard Dawkins (Dawkins, 2006) as a 'deeply spiritual man' (Hogan, 2010: 14). How can this be, since Dawkins has emerged as one of the most articulate and determined opponents of religious influence in the early 21st century?

Hogan perceives Dawkins as attempting to provide crucial life guidance to people who may still be in thrall to religious considerations. In his writings he is not just trying to prove the incorrectness of religious belief but trying to show people the benefits of atheistic ways of approaching life and its problems. He would like them to put their belief and trust in science and in humankind's rational capacities. In a very real sense he is trying to promote life-sustaining beliefs. In the context of his own discussion of spiritual development Hogan invites Dawkins to stand back a little from the object of his hostility and to discriminate the positive from the negative functions of religious thought and behaviour. Dawkins emphasises the latter but gives insufficient acknowledgement to the former, such as the capacity that religious belief can implant to endure hardship and remain resolute in the pursuit of goals. Hogan argues that most if not all of these positive functions can be subsumed by the term 'spiritual' and are not exclusively tied to religious beliefs. He raises the prospect that these qualities can be promoted and can flourish in a post-religious world. In a very real sense spirituality would then have replaced religion.

However, writing about this subject at this point in time, I think it is impossible to avoid the continuing ambiguity in the use of the term 'spiritual'. There will undoubtedly be many occasions throughout this book when the word is used where the religious connotation is clearly present. But there will also be occasions where it is not. Moreover, there will be many occasions, as in the second sentence of this introductory chapter, where the ambiguity is deliberate. These are circumstances where one does not wish to exclude religious belief, but at the same time one does not want to focus exclusive attention on it. Despite the ambiguity it is probably better to follow the current trend in the use of the word than referring to expressions such as sources of ultimate or existential meaning that would read more awkwardly.

However, there will be many pages of this book where the word 'spiritual' will not appear and this will be for another reason: that this is a book about ageing that intends, in accord with the philosophy of the series to which it belongs, to give space to older people's own views and ways of expression. In the current enthusiasm about spirituality it is insufficiently recognised that the widespread use of the word 'spiritual' as an adjective is new, and that the abstract term 'spirituality' would have been regarded as highly unusual 50 and even 25 years ago. As will be illustrated in Chapter Two, it was rare for older people in Britain in the 1970s to employ these terms at all, and even today it is relatively uncommon for persons in their 70s, 80s and older to use them.

This is a good example of the kind of generational shift in discourse that poses genuine problems for communication between younger and older people. The latter may be as unused to the new and rapidly developing terminology in the field of spirituality as they are to the language of new technology, and be at the least bemused and at worse made suspicious by the change of usage.

There are now the beginnings of a literature specifically on spirituality and ageing. An excellent example is Atchley's recent examination of the importance of spiritual life as people age, which is based on his own increasing focus on the subject in the latter part of his career as a gerontologist in the US. His thought has been strongly influenced by eastern philosophical and religious concepts and is therefore not representative of the dominant Christian character of much US research on ageing and belief. His aim seems not to describe how current American older people experience spirituality within their lives but rather to explore ways of thinking about this newly recognised aspect of ageing and its implications for the future of ageing. He regards spirituality as a sensitising concept drawing attention to a person's sense of relationship to a greater whole. But, as he admits himself (Atchley, 2009: 63), the use of the term 'spiritual' to refer to a category of inner experience only began to take hold in the US in the 1950s. Older people who reached adulthood before that time are still unlikely to apply the term to themselves. Therefore generational comparisons between the currently young-old and old-old are not appropriate.

Our stance in the present book is rather to begin with what older people tell us themselves about their beliefs, whether religious, spiritual or neither, and in particular what they say about how these beliefs support them in understanding and coping with life's challenges. Our focus is on belief in action, referred to in the context of older people's actual daily lives, rather than spirituality as a normative developmental characteristic of subjective experience as persons grow older.

Religion, spirituality and ageing

By contrast with the changing and often ambiguous character of spirituality the concept of religion provides a more clearly definable object of study. This is because religion, as a culturally regularised system of human action and behaviour, can be observed. Its uses of symbols and rituals connect the society or group or individual who practise them to the powers of supreme importance that are considered to underlie or rule the experienced world. These symbols as well as the powers to which they refer are often described by a special discriminating term such as 'sacred' or 'transcendent'.

Religion appears to have played a central part in human history (and prehistory). Over the last three centuries many intellectuals, especially in Europe, have predicted a declining influence of religion on world affairs as scientific investigation provides increasing explanation for much physical phenomena, but events do not bear this out. Europe in fact remains the 'exceptional' or 'distinctive' case in this regard (Davie, 2002). For the greater part of humankind religion continues to provide more satisfying explanations for issues affecting the perceived meaning and purpose of life, which science does not address.

Indeed the US, for the last half century the leading exponent of western culture, has remained a very religious country. Although there are in the US as in Europe signs of a shift towards spiritual rather than religious discourse, the religious culture there has adapted well to the changes. From its foundation the US has fostered pluralism in religious belief, and this encourages the creation of new forms of Christian church organisation alongside traditional churches. Whereas Europeans of a Christian background often show their new-found autonomy in the religious realm by not going to church, Americans are more likely to search for a more suitable form of church community in which to experience shared belief (Dillon and Wink, 2007: 205-14).

Distinct religions have developed in different parts of the world and, in general, despite having changed in some respects and sometimes been superseded, have shown great stability over long centuries of history. What these traditional religions have in common is a belief in a transcendent reality usually filled with supernatural beings with which communication, connection and even identification or co-inherence is possible.

Problems of definition do exist, and may be particularly apparent at a time of change as at present. When does the individual practice of a belief in a transcendent reality become a religion? Evidence for the existence of a new religion would include being shared by a sufficient number of people and being organised in such a way as to be consistently recognised by fellow members and by the rest of society. We are currently living through a time of religious change in the UK. Not only is the presence of non-Christian major world religions becoming stronger, but the dominance of the Christian tradition on British culture is under threat from new forms of belief sometimes associated with an attempted recovery of pre-Christian pagan religions.

Unfortunately even in the early days of growth of gerontological study in the 1950s and 1960s religion, including belief, was a neglected subject. This probably has to do with the discomfort and reluctance of a subject claiming to be a science of objectively measurable bodily functioning and behaviour to focus on the more subjective realms of life. It also reflected the anti-religious bias (see Levin, 1994; Baumeister, 2002) of the academic establishment, and perhaps too their assumption that religion was of declining importance. Spirituality, so far as it was considered, was still seen to be dependent on religion (Atchley, 2009: 30). But in retrospect it seems a major omission to have neglected the sociology and psychology of ageing and spiritual belief, particularly when it should have been very evident from anthropological studies that religion has always played an important role in older people's lives. The lack of earlier databases limits what we can conclude about changes with age over the last half century, particularly within the UK and the rest of Europe.

Most of the data available from the early post-war years were collected by David Moberg, a sociologist who pioneered work in this field in the US and who has also made major recent contributions (Moberg, 2001a). Even in the 1950s the US was a much more religious society than much of Western Europe. One of Moberg's interests was whether people became more religious with age. His cross-sectional age comparisons suggested so but were open to interpretation in terms of cohort or generational differences. However, the fact that he has continued to find similar cross-sectional findings over many years, and thus with successive cohort groups, is more convincing evidence in favour of developmental change with age (but see further Chapter Four).

Spiritual development is also a theme of some of the few notable psychologists who have sought to formulate theories of development with age, the most influential of whom being Erik Erikson ([1950] 1963). His theory of successive life tasks to be completed is explicitly intergenerational in character and this gives it a special almost cyclical character. The sense of trust that young children need to acquire in order to begin their development is reinforced at the end of life by their grandparents' need for their own sense of completion to acknowledge the goodness of life, which he describes in terms of 'integrity'. When one considers that he was writing in the immediate post-war years, Erikson now appears to have been surprisingly sanguine about the harmony between human society and individual development. Culture itself, he thought, provided the necessary institutions to promote human development, the basis of which was religion, which provided the secure grounds for acquiring a sense of trust. Older people's integrity confirmed the validity of this belief.

It is interesting to note that Lars Tornstam, one of Erikson's most recent successors as a developmental theorist of ageing and whose work has been influential within care practice (Tornstam, 1996), has formulated a contrary pessimistic view on the interaction between society and individual development (Tornstam, 1999). He sees the achievement of 'gerotranscendence' as an intrinsic process leading to disengagement from the self and a spiritual process of absorption in the greater whole of life, but regards the active role of society in this process as solely negative. Tornstam, it should be noted, is writing in a Northern European context, largely devoid of a strong religious presence. In his perspective older persons are drawn to seek wisdom, but often in isolation, and in spite of the world around them.

Belief in action

Like a number of other researchers working in this field, such as Kenneth Pargament (Pargament, 1997), we consider that belief is best studied in context, and in the ensuing chapters we give examples of research studying religious and non-religious belief in later life in various European contexts, but principally in the UK. Because we are dealing predominantly with samples of older people brought up within a Christian culture, their experience, both positive and negative, of the presentation and practice of Christian faith, will inevitably colour much of what is discussed in this book. However, in Chapter Eight we will consider the growing influence within Europe of other great world faiths.

Any person's belief system has to be understood in context, as a heritage not only of their personal experience but of that of the experience of their family, community, nation and race. Important historical events, such as the religious wars of the 17th century and later, have shaped European attitudes to religion. Adherence to different branches of Christianity does not only reflect different personal convictions about aspects of faith and religious practice, but also tribal and regional loyalties. Nevertheless, underlying the various uses to which religion is put is a search for what is of supreme importance – the 'sacred' – and the wish to incorporate it in one's own life, and that of one's family and community. It is interesting that 'the search for the sacred' is Pargament's own definition of spirituality, one among many competing definitions. For him spirituality is the core of religion, which he defines as 'a search for significance in ways related to the sacred' (Pargament, 1997: 32). This search is life long but it is understandable if it is intensified in the last stage of life.

We begin in Chapter Two with an examination of the religious context of ageing in UK since the 1960s, making use of data on interviews with older people that we have collected over the last 40 years. Although the 1960s intensified the challenge to conventional religion, we shall show that diversity of belief has long been a characteristic of the British population. Orthodox Christian belief was held by only a minority of the population even in the immediate post-war years. Our data illustrate the various ways older people have witnessed to their beliefs over the last 50 years and the influence that holding or not holding on to a Christian faith has had for particular individuals. The data also demonstrate that spiritual and religious beliefs constitute an increasingly variegated element among older people as well as in the rest of society.

Collecting information on people's use of belief is not straightforward. It is probably one of the most difficult areas of experience for people to articulate adequately what they think and feel. Often metaphor and alternative symbolic forms of communication are preferable to standard verbal propositions. Religion itself makes much use of non-verbal ritual. Questionnaires are of limited value, and even qualitative research is handicapped by its usual focus on the written word. It is important to pay attention to other features of communication. Above all it is necessary to provide the time and opportunity for people to articulate as best they can the nature of their spiritual beliefs and to allow for different modes of expression. Diary expression and even newer contemporary formats such as 'blogging' are also useful sources of data. The quality and genuine interest of attention for the person that the researcher communicates is of vital importance in interviewing, as well as skills in listening and recording. Chapter Three discusses such issues, which relate not only to research methods in this area but also to pastoral care and communication.

Chapter Four considers the important issue, already mentioned, of spiritual development with age. If it is true that people's spiritual needs intensify with age, this should be better recognised and catered for by religious as well as other bodies concerned with older people's well-being. As it is, older people's spiritual needs tend to be rather neglected, not least by religious ministers, who can appear sometimes over-focused on evangelisation to younger people. The question of developmental change can only really be settled by longitudinal study and across successive generations of persons growing older. The little evidence we have of this nature from the UK suggests large variation. For some people religious belief and practice does become important or re-emerge. But loss of faith and disillusionment with religious ministry seem to have been characteristic of many people entering their 70s and 80s in the changing British society of the 1980s. Other types of spiritual development, of the kind Erikson and Tornstam describe, are harder to spot. Case studies of different types of trajectories of belief set these religious histories in the context of actual life experience.

A key experience of later life, with the capacity both to weaken as well as strengthen spiritual belief, is bereavement. Bereavements mount in number as people age, but the most distressing experience next to death of a child is loss of spouse or partner. In the nature of things bereavement is inevitable for one or the other partner. A central attachment link is broken. Chapter Five considers the role of belief in this experience of loss in later life. We attempt to elucidate by means of case illustrations those aspects of Christian faith and practice that appear to be particularly beneficial. These include the opportunities for engagement in religious ritual and the opportunities that religious organisations provide for shaping a new identity following loss of spouse. The doctrines of Christianity and the consolation provided by key passages in the Bible are also important resources to which bereaved persons can turn.

Chapter Six takes a contrasting perspective on coping with loss in old age with a further case study examination of those who have rejected religious beliefs but have found adequate substitutes in secular and philosophical systems of thought. We examine the origins and character of the alternative meaning systems that they have been able to construct. There is evidence that uncertainty in matters of belief is associated with greater mental distress in the face of difficulties, and that therefore agnosticism, although arguably a more rational state of mind (Kenny, 2006), may have distinct disadvantages for the holder. But little or no direct comparison has been made among religious believers, agnostics and atheists. The chapter refers to a case comparison study of older British Humanists and strong religious believers facing different types of stressful experience in later life. This illustrates the value of a securely grounded view of life and its meaning, whether spiritual in content or not.

Expression of religious beliefs has provided some of the most distinctive aspects of human culture. British religious history has given it a mixed religious culture, predominantly Christian, but of mixed Catholic and Protestant elements, which sometimes lie uneasily together and are still cause for conflict. However, tolerance for pluralism of belief is more widespread. Britain is now again more involved with its place in Europe, after a centuries-long interlude focusing on running a world empire. European religious history is extremely complex. Its variety provides the opportunity for comparative perspectives on belief and ageing. Recent increased migration has brought greater acquaintance with different forms of Christianity within Eastern Europe, and also a greater appreciation of the suffering of religious believers under repression by Communist governments. In Chapter Seven studies conducted in Eastern and Southern Europe are used to illustrate both the persistence of religious belief under persecution, often thanks to the stubborn witness of older people, and the significance, for the family as well as for the community, of religious memories.

Migration from other parts of the world has introduced into the UK yet other forms of Christianity, for example Pentecostalism particularly among the African and Caribbean immigrants, and has enlarged the presence of the other great faiths. Prior to the 1950s only Judaism had a notable presence. But now Islam, Hinduism, Sikhism, Buddhism, Baha'i and a number of other faiths are also not only present but offer alternative religious pathways to British people, especially as they age. Chapter Eight examines some of the consequences for the UK of this greatly increased religious pluralism. Although numbers are relatively small, the impact of these new faiths can be expected to increase. In Chapter Eight we consider attitudes to ageing within some of the world's great faiths, with special attention given to Islam. We report studies on older Muslims that illustrate the need for health and social service personnel, in particular, to be better aware of the religious needs and perceptions of different faith groups.

Chapter Nine draws together the main points of this book in observations on the changing context of belief, the importance of finding meaning in life, and possible future trends in spiritual exploration. Belief, it is argued, will become an increasingly important feature of identity because it is more likely to be chosen and willed rather than assumed.

We have tried throughout the book to let older people's voices themselves be 'heard' as they attempt to explain their beliefs. We hope that their willingness to let themselves be heard will encourage other researchers to listen more closely to this often hidden but important aspect of life, which contributes greatly to the person's overall sense of well-being in the later years.

TWO

The changing social context of belief in later life

Peter G. Coleman

In this and the following chapters we shall aim to cite generously from the transcripts of recordings we have made of older people speaking about their beliefs. We have attempted neither to improve the language used nor to hide the very real difficulties people often encounter in putting their beliefs into words. This is one reason perhaps for the social sciences' neglect of spiritual discourse. It is hard to analyse, and appropriate methods of qualitative analysis may not yet have been developed. But the importance of spiritual discourse is indicated by its frequent proximity to expressions of personal well-being.

We have also included at the beginning of every chapter an introduction to the relevant subject matter. The change of style from more academic analysis to reportage of people's freely expressed attitudes will be evident to the reader. But we have hoped thereby to bring alive the place of belief in people's lives. We begin with a chapter which includes analyses of some of the first interviews that the present author and colleagues conducted on the subject of belief in the aftermath of the social changes of the 1960s, often regarded as a watershed in the evolution of religious and spiritual attitudes in the west.

The 1960s revolution against authority

Although there are various ways to characterise the social revolution that began 10 to 15 years after the end of the Second World War, the changes in attitudes that swept through western culture in those years can now be seen to have had a lasting influence on many areas of social life. One of the principal areas affected in Britain and elsewhere was religious allegiance. Indeed some commentators, such as Callum Brown (2001), argue that the processes of secularisation in Britain did not properly take hold until the 1960s. According to this view, although decline in allegiance to Christianity may have begun in the aftermath of the First World War as a reaction to the horrors of that war and the inability of the churches to oppose the mass slaughter that occurred, this did not impose lasting damage on the Christian character of the country. Christian values as a socialising force remained strong both through and after the Second World War. The changes of the 1960s were of an altogether different order and have provided a much more serious threat to the influence of Christianity on social values. Brown in fact suggests that there is a strong association between the sexual and the religious revolution. For example, the contraceptive pill changed women's attitude to sexuality and to child rearing. At the same time part of the basis for the strong support women drew from the churches and gave back to them in return was weakened (we shall come back to the important subject of gender differences in religiosity a little further on).

It is important to note that Britain was not the only European country that experienced religious upheaval in this period. Its near neighbour the Netherlands experienced probably even greater changes and over a shorter period, changing from a very religious (and religiously authoritarian) society to a liberal one in a period of little more than 15 years. The presence on the streets of male clergy and religious men and women with their distinct dress and habits, still so prevalent in the Catholic south of the country in the late 1950s, had vanished by the early 1970s (when the present author was working there). Partly this was due to the implementation of reforms in the Catholic Church allowed by the Second Vatican Council. But it also appeared to reflect Dutch society's wish to abandon past habits and put the new freedoms they were now allowed into action. Affiliation to Christian churches dropped from 76% of the population in 1958 to 40% in 1999 (Houtman and Mascini, 2002), the lowest proportion in Western Europe.

In an intriguing study Houtman and Mascini (2002) collected and analysed data on various age groups in the Netherlands in order to test the thesis both of 'rationalisation' and of 'individualisation' as explanations of declining religious belief and practice. The evidence strongly refutes the former, which would suggest that declining religious belief has relatively little to do with an increase in the scientific mindset advocated by atheists such as Dawkins. Indeed an emphasis on scientific and rationalistic thinking as well as on religious belief appears more common in older than younger people. Faith in both religion and scientific authority appears to have declined. What the evidence does support is an increase in forms of spiritual belief and non-religiosity in younger generations. This seems to reflect a move on the part of younger generations towards emphasising personal life experience as the touchstone of belief, and a distrust and dislike of external authority especially relating to moral rules and regulations. Such attitudes have only intensified in recent years as a result of the failures of church authority, demonstrated most of all by the Roman Catholic child abuse scandal which has affected a number of European countries as well as the US.

The evidence from this study provides strong support for the individualism thesis of British sociologists such as Paul Heelas (Heelas, 1996). Houtman and Mascini also draw interesting parallels between New Age Spirituality, with its emphasis on holism, spiritual transformation (that is, reincarnation) and syncreticism, and the gnosticism of the early Christian era, which also emphasised the primacy of personal experience and induction into that experience by elite groups, and which the Church authorities engaged in long but eventually successful combat in the early centuries of its existence. It is probably no coincidence that alternative writings about Jesus, the so-called Apocryphal Gospels, which were excluded from the canon of officially sanctioned Biblical material after the Christian

Church became a major recognised institution within the Roman Empire, have gained renewed interest in recent years. They appeal to the inquisitive mind that is suspicious of official sources. Religion that emphasises external authority has become distinctly less popular in much of Western Europe. Individuals want to make up their own mind without being overly (or at least consciously) influenced by external sources of persuasion and authority.

The generational divide in religious attitudes

During the 1960s decline in attendance at religious services began to be noticed in many parts of Western Europe. A particularly striking phenomenon in Britain was the disappearance of the Sunday school, an institution characteristic of British social life on Sundays and to which great importance has been attributed in the development of British culture and social mores (Davies, 2004). Sunday schools also undoubtedly had a huge role in creating religious literacy in the population, a literacy that has disappeared to a surprising degree. Understanding of the significance of major Christian festivals, even of Easter itself, has been greatly eroded.

The end result of this rapid historic decline is a division in knowledge and attitudes between generations. People in their 60s and older were brought up with a substantial religious education, and a respect for religious authority, whereas their children and grandchildren have had both a very different (and many would argue less substantial) religious education and have been taught to be more critical of all forms of authority. The large baby boom generation of those born after the Second World War and particularly in the 1950s and 1960s ceased to receive Sunday school education. At the same time they benefited from the expansion of higher education following the Robbins report of 1963. A longitudinal study of a sample of the 'advance guard' of the baby boom generation – those born in March 1946 – has shown that of the 87% who had been brought up with a faith a quarter had given up their original religious affiliation by the time they had reached adulthood in the 1970s. Educational factors are associated with these changes. Loss of religious affiliation was particularly related to obtaining higher education qualifications, especially in the social sciences, psychology and philosophy (Wadsworth and Freeman, 1983).

However, there is a danger in exaggerating the changes in religious beliefs brought about among those educated in the 1960s, and hence the differences between generations. Analysis of various survey data on traditional and non-traditional religious beliefs does show evidence for changes occurring after the 1960s but also some surprising constancies both of belief and disbelief (Davie, 2000). Data that we do have from the 1940/50s show that some of the most distinctive features of Christian belief, such as belief in God as a person, belief in Jesus as Son of God, and belief in life after death, were not as high then as we might imagine. For example, Gallup polls showed that belief in a personal God was expressed by less than half of the British population in the post-war years, and has now declined to less than a third. On the other hand, belief in Christ's resurrection seems to have remained relatively stable at around half of the population, and belief in some form of life after death has in fact increased in recent years, separate from belief in God, particularly among young people (Davie, 2006; Voas, 2010; see also the University of Manchester website 'British Religion in Numbers' www.brin.ac.uk).

Data on non-traditional beliefs are more limited but do not show marked change over the last half century, apart from belief in ghosts, which appears to have doubled from 15% to 31% in the period from mid to end 20th century. Belief in reincarnation, a typical feature of eastern religion, has been held fairly constant by around one quarter of the British population since the 1970s, and belief in the capacity to foretell the future by around one half of the population over the same period of time. Taken together these figures do suggest a distinct influence of the 1960s on British beliefs but also that Britain has not been a uniformly orthodox Christian country for a much longer period of time. It is perhaps significant that even detailed social history accounts of the post-war period have surprisingly meagre references to religion and minimise its relevance to public life (Kynaston, 2007; Kynaston, 2009), although this may be another reflection of past academic neglect of and bias against religion.

Gender, religion and ageing

Gender also appears to be a very important factor in religious attitudes. Women's greater religiosity makes social gerontology's neglect of religion even more surprising when one considers that women form a clear majority of the older population in the UK and most developed societies. Research data collected in western cultures, but also more recently in an eastern society (Japan), consistently show women to express stronger religious beliefs than men (WHOQOL-SRPB Group, 2006; Krause et al, 2010). This not only applies to traditional religions but also to membership of new types of spiritual organisations (Houtman and Mascini, 2002).

This gender difference is still poorly understood, but a social psychological explanation might suggest that it is related to the greater vulnerability, dependency and absence of control experienced by women throughout life, with social factors building on biological differences. In turn women have been socialised to experience and express a greater neediness. In a religious context this heightened awareness of dependency also allows for and encourages a readier acknowledgement of the person's need for help from a higher power. Women also express stronger needs for social relationships and bonds. However, the accelerating social and sexual changes of the 20th century have given them greater independence. According to this view their declining willingness from the late 1950s onwards to accept the authority of the Christian churches and to rely on them for socialising and controlling male behaviour (a point that Brown lays particular stress on) has been a principal factor in changing Britain's religious character.

However, this change has not been sufficient to affect the basic gender ratio in religious behaviour. Women outnumber men by a ratio of three to two in most Christian churches in the west (Woodhead, 2004). Linda Woodhead (2004) comments on the apparent paradox of the greater female attraction to Christianity with its masculine bias evident not only in the figure of its founder Jesus Christ and its traditional male clergy, but also in its patriarchal conception of God, and even in its account of the secondary creation of woman out of man in the Genesis story. She offers an explanation in terms of the Christian emphasis on 'feminine' values such as love, self-sacrifice and humility. As a result the Christian Church has always been an environment in which women could feel at home, more so in fact than the great majority of men, who, if they did not have active roles within the church community as priests, servers and wardens, were also placed in a passive role.

The gender difference in church congregations is also partly of course explained by the greater number of older women than older men in the population as a whole. As we will see in Chapter Four church services attract more older than younger people. This chapter will also explore the idea of a gender cross-over effect in later life whereby men become more willing to accept their passivity and seek accommodation rather than confrontation whereas women tend to lose previous inhibitions they may have had when asserting needs for inclusion and for greater control over their lives. This may be related to older men's greater acceptance of religious faith and older women's increased tendency to voice criticism. It is important to understand the spiritual needs of older men and women, and in particular those of the present generation, within the perspective of their very different life experiences and trajectories.

Interviewing older people on their religious beliefs in the 1970s

Although little or no data were collected in Britain and other parts of Europe specifically about older people's religious attitudes in the post-war years, it is possible to document the impact of the 1960s from interviews conducted as part of other studies. Particularly useful in this respect are data collected from the late 1960s to early 1980s in London and Southampton on older people's attitudes to social change (Coleman, 1972; McCulloch, 1985; Coleman and McCulloch, 1985, 1990; Coleman, 1986).

These studies were conducted in sheltered housing schemes and therefore need to be interpreted with some caution as representative of the British older population of the time. Data on attendance at religious services indicate that well under one half reported attending regularly in the immediate post-war years, a period regarded as one of increasing church attendance. Of those who had been regular attenders a good proportion, almost half, indicated that they could no longer go either because of disability, the greater distance from their church since they had moved into sheltered housing, or lack of transport. The importance of church attendance to them was evident in many of their replies. Some greatly missed no longer being able to go, others appreciated the transport they received from family and friends that enabled them to attend, and some received visits at home from clergy. There were also examples of older people who attended more since they retired, for example one woman who previously could not attend church because her work as a caretaker had precluded going to church on Sundays.

A recent decline in churchgoing in the general population was mentioned by some of the participants, some of whom reflected on the factors involved. Mrs Stanton, for example, a widow of 87 years, was one of those fortunate to be taken each Sunday to her local Baptist church by her son and his family. Praying was one of the quiet activities she enjoyed in her daily life, alongside reading. She described herself as "living with God". She stressed how she believed not because she was "afraid" but because she "loved God". She regretted that her own husband had not wanted to go to church, and this had led her to consider the reasons for developing faith. She thought the decline in church attendance in England reflected people's greater freedom in matters of belief. It was not the absence of teaching that was responsible, rather the reception given to it. Belief in God was both a gift and a response. She pondered other people's failure to respond, especially given the comfort that faith gave her:

> "I don't understand people who don't believe, although they don't understand it you see, they don't take notice. If you were to tell them that you really knew Him they would think you were potty. No, they haven't the least idea. It's no good you trying to tell them, especially those people that don't ever think about it …they say you should talk to people about it but they don't want to listen.
>
> "It was really her [Mrs Stanton's mother] that sent us when we were little. Then I must say she left it to us whether we did or whether we didn't, but I always did go … I was the only one in the family though, the others never did.
>
> "My husband never stopped me going or anything like that but he wouldn't go. I know when I was baptised I thought perhaps that would make him think more seriously but it didn't. You see, you can't make people think unless they really believe and know God. Because there's nothing in it to them. They can't make out what you're talking about if they don't see God as you do. See, he's not living for them.
>
> "It's up to their feelings. I didn't have any influence. My mother never talked to us about religion, but she did make me go to church and Sunday school, so I got it there. And it appealed to me you see, but my sisters didn't take any notice of it. Out of all the people in these flats, there's only one person that I know that goes to church, funny isn't it?"

The greater freedom to attend or not was picked up by other residents. There had been considerable social pressures on people to attend even in the remembered past. Not attending could even affect chances of employment, in much the same way as attending church damaged prospects in communist states. Surveillance existed, even if not so systematically organised as in Eastern Europe. As one male participant commented:

> "If you didn't go to church you had to give account of yourself: 'Where were you on Sunday? If it goes on like this we shan't employ you.'"

In societies with social, cultural or politically enforced norms about religious worship, with pressure to attend or not to attend, actual presence at services is a poor guide to actual belief. Also in later life, when restricted health and mobility and lack of transport opportunities can conspire to make attendance difficult, belief can continue to be expressed in other ways. For many older people in the 1970s and 1980s the media, and particularly television, were providing welcome opportunities to follow religious services without the need to travel. A survey in Southampton in the late 1970s showed that 88% watched religious services on TV or listened to religious broadcasts on the radio, whereas only 33% attended church services (Coleman et al, 2004). Prayer and reading of religious texts were perhaps the strongest indicators of religious faith. Indeed some people interviewed in these studies indicated that they expressed their faith solely by means of prayer.

Mrs Ditton, a widow of 96 years, was a good example of faith expressed though belief in prayer, even though she appeared never to have attended church regularly since becoming an adult. Her beliefs nevertheless had helped her deal with a series of devastating blows. Four of her brothers had been killed in the First World War. She said her own mother had been "broken" by these losses. Mrs Ditton's own husband had been invalided out of the army after being badly gassed, and because he left the army hospital to which he had been brought against orders he was not entitled to receive any pension. His appeals were refused. He was ill for the remaining 16 years of life, and Mrs Ditton had to bring up six children by going out to work herself. But she said that it was in this period that her belief grew in the power of God's help to be obtained through prayer. God, she was sure, had given her the strength to survive misfortune.

When her husband returned from the First World War unable to work and without a pension it was suggested that she place her children in a home, put her husband in a hospital, and go into service herself:

> "I said no, not while I've got a pair of hands, and I went and brought all mine up. I went hungry and cold for them. I am not religious but I do believe in God. Because I had nothing to eat and we were hungry, I knelt down in a chair and prayed to God."

Help was not immediately forthcoming, not even from the church, but it did come in an unexpected way:

> "The parish wouldn't help me, and the MP said he could only give me half a ton of coal because my husband disobeyed the laws of the hospital. That's the truth. My sister went up the road, she went to the back doors of the shops ... and she got me a rabbit and also some vegetables and things to make custard and I think that was the answer to my prayer. And I've believed in that ever since. If you ask you get, not in the way you ask, but you get, and that's what makes me as I am today. Of course I had to work very hard. Those that I worked for, they used to give me clothes for the children and help me in that way. And I think it was the answer to my prayer and that's what I believe in."

Subsequent life events contained some further hard knocks. Mrs Ditton had been bombed out of her house in the Second World War, and her second husband also incurred serious injury and subsequent disability after falling off a roof while working. A son's death and a burglary had been more recent events that she had to bear. But in each case she had experienced help from God, which she attributed to her belief:

> "I always have believed, because I have had hardships and I've prayed and I've had help and I think that's how it is. ... I still believe in God and I pray for everybody in my prayers at night: the sick, the wounded, everybody, which I think is only right, but people don't think of that today. I don't go to church because I can't, but I have the service on here in my room and sing with them. ... Otherwise I don't worry about nothing. Whatever has got to come, I always feel the Lord is beside me and he'll guard me, that's how I look at it. I'm not religious, but I do believe in trust, and I don't think he'll let anything happen to me that way. ... I travelled by plane to Canada [to see her son]. I put myself in the hands of God that he will help me and I got back safe, and I think that is the best way. But you've got to have that belief and trust, you can't just think it, you've got to have it."

Despite her denial of being "religious" (by which she probably meant attending religious services) she had sufficient religious education to speak with confidence not only on the help that can be obtained by prayer but also about other beliefs that she held. Not all of this was necessarily in accord with standard church teaching. For example, she attributed the devil with considerable power over the world:

> "This world is ruled by the devil. If you read in your Bible you know it's true. That's why there's all this wickedness. And it was destroyed once through wickedness and if it's not very careful ... That's what the

war was with all the bombing. ... Look at all these things happening. That's not the work of the Lord is it, oh no. The devil's in all of us, those with tempers and all. Mine are in the Salvation Army, and my four little grandchildren, if I see them in a temper I tell them, I say 'now don't lose your temper because there's the devil working you.' In the Bible it doesn't say he was to be properly in control, but that he was going to rule the world, he was given it."

Personal expression of gratitude, in particular to answered prayers, was a characteristic of a number of other members of these studies. For example, a partially sighted widower of 77 years attributed his healing to God, and wanted to give thanks for this:

"I still believe there is a God. I still believe there is one. There must be one. I was completely blind altogether a while back. Well, I'm still paralysed up my left side now, but not so much. I used to have to go round on sticks or elbow crutches. In the end I couldn't go out at all. ... I still think there must be a God or I wouldn't have got like this."

Social change, war and questioning of belief

However, there were also many older people interviewed in these studies who indicated that their previous belief in God as a benevolent power in control of the world had been shaken by events they experienced, including the wars, but also the social changes of the 1960s. The latter may seem surprising given the death and destruction, and effects of unemployment and poverty that this generation had experienced earlier in the century, not to mention the mass murder of Jewish people and others on the continent of Europe, which they could not have failed to register. Surely these had been greater evils than the new patterns of behaviour that emerged in the UK in the 1960s? But for many older people the changes within everyday life in their own local communities seemed to have had a more damaging effect on morale.

Decline in moral standards, especially poor parenting, and the resulting bad behaviour of young people, as well as loss of common courtesies, are a shared feature of interviews with older people recorded at this time (Seabrook, 1980). This was associated in many people's minds with loss of religious influence in society and in some with a feeling that God was no longer in control.

In particular, older men interviewed at this time were inclined to refer to religion in terms of a "disciplining force" that in the past had "kept the country together" but no longer did so. Some criticised the churches themselves for allowing this loss of control to have taken place. Women on the other hand were more inclined to express disturbed bewilderment at the state of society, which led to questioning of previously held norms and values (Coleman and McCulloch, 1990). For some women the distress experienced at the force of social change had been enough to shake their own religious faith. Out of a sample of 47 older people living in Southampton and interviewed in depth on the subject of social change in the early 1980s, nearly all (n=44) had been brought up in the Christian faith, but more than a third (n=16) said that they no longer believed or were unsure about the religious teaching that they had received in their youth. Moreover, the vast majority (n=38) acknowledged that the way society had changed had made it more difficult to hold on to religious beliefs (McCulloch, 1985).

Media presentation on the television in particular had an important role in disturbing their peace of mind:

> Interviewer:"Do things that you read and hear today make it difficult for you to believe?"

> Participant:"Yes, you can't believe when you see those little children suffer.You can't believe there is a God can you? You see those little children suffer. It's terrible."

Mrs Sowerby seemed to be at a point of crisis in this respect. She was 80 years of age, living in sheltered housing, and had two children whose families she saw regularly. However, she felt she spent much of her time alone, relied on her happy memories, and expressed negative opinions about young people's behaviour. In particular she was concerned about what kind of future they would have. This anxiety had begun to affect her own beliefs:

> "I don't know what the world's going to become, what it's going to be like in a few years' time. ... It's getting beyond belief. ... There are times when I've wondered even if I was in the right direction. ... I think it's everything that's happening today you see. It makes you wonder."

She had even become concerned about death and her previous unquestioned beliefs in God and an afterlife:

> "I sometimes wonder if there are such places. That's recently, recently that's come into my brain. ... Things you read in the paper. Certain things, it makes you wonder.You even wonder if there's a God. ... My people, they're horrified, they can't understand what's happened to me."

For other people interviewed religion had lost its significance for reasons directly associated with changes in personal circumstances. This applied particularly to those who appreciated religion for its community and family building potential. Outside of that context its importance withered. Such was the case for Mr Jewell, a widowed Jewish participant, a furrier from the East End of London. When interviewed in the early 1970s at the age of 71 years he had still been positive about the role of religion in society:

"I think it is important to be a little bit on the religious side, because
having that at the back of your mind, it gives you a little bit of
conscience, doing right or doing wrong, but a person that hasn't got
a religion can do wrong and still think they are doing right."

His son had married a gentile girl, and although he would have liked her to have
converted, and at this time was still hoping that the children would be brought
up in Jewish, he considered their happiness to be the most important thing.
However, his son's divorce five years later affected him badly. By the early 1980s
he was feeling more lonely, and his religious life had disappeared. He said he had
"used to like the Jewish faith" and especially taking part in its celebrations. But
now that his brother and sisters had died, and feeling that he had no family of
his own, "religion did not mean anything" to him any more.

Although the social changes of the 1960s appear to have had an influence on
people's readiness to question previous ways of behaving grounded in religious
teaching, it remains true that the great wars of the first part of the 20th century had
already shaken people's belief in God. Many of the men interviewed in the studies
of the 1960s and 1970s were First World War veterans and had direct experience
of the pointless slaughter in France and Belgium while fighting against an enemy
that proclaimed the same God in its similar religious services. Religion had been
omnipresent during the war but had also appeared curiously passive in the face
of such horror. Many men, but also some women in these studies, commented
on how experience of war in their lifetime had affected belief in a good God:

"You can't expect people to believe there's a God up there when
you've got bombing night after night. You remember so and so, they
were killed in the blitz. And all this, well, it makes people disillusioned."

A number of eloquent testimonies of how the war had made them think differently
about what and who they should believe were given by veterans of the First World
War (Coleman, 1986). For example, Mr Norton had been through the Great War
from start to finish, and it dominated his reminiscences and indeed much of his
conversation. There were still elements of traumatic memory recall in his speech
and clearly he had suffered a lot in the aftermath of the war, having to endure the
night sweats and conditioned reactions to danger cues as sudden noises. It had left
him also with lasting suspicion of authority figures in the church and state who
had acted in concert against the interests of the common person:

"They [the politicians] did very well out of the war ... the big steel
people. So did the clergy too. 'Praise the Lord my dear Augusta, we've
won a battle, such a muster. Ten thousand Germans sent below. Praise
God from whom all blessings flow!'"

He himself had come from a Quaker family and respected his own father's search for truth, but had come to the view that it was only science and the disciplined use of reason that could help humans from self-destruction. The problem was too complex for simple answers. Human competition for the means of life was too ingrained. But the religious leaders, like the politicians, only served to keep people in ignorance of the true situation, and did not encourage people's reasoning. Religion for him was a particular obstacle to progress because it prevented proper analysis of human behaviour and sentimentalised thought rather than identifying the conditions that promoted good actions. He was contemptuous of religion's hypocrisy and ineffectiveness:

> "They start the day with prayers and end up calling each other bastards. ... What gets me are these jaspers going about saying, 'Love your neighbour.' You shouldn't do anything of the sort! ... You've got to teach them how to adapt themselves, live in harmony with their neighbours, not love them at all, take them for what they are. ... Animal heredity plays a big part. Darwin was right, we're all near to the ape."

He believed that it should be possible to form a "natural religion" in which human intelligence could be harnessed to counteract the self-seeking motivation that dominated human behaviour and the struggle for life. But it had to be based on proper analysis of human behaviour. There was no meaning or purpose to life to be found as the result of some special revelation; it had to be created on the growing awareness of a common humanity and what would happen if we did not impose some control on human behaviour. This also led him to some striking anti-libertarian conclusions, for instance on restricting rights to marriage and procreation.

Exploration of new forms of spiritual belief

Like Mr Norton a number of other informants in studies on social attitudes in the 1960s and 1970s were searching for new forms of commitment and belief compatible with the changes they had experienced in their lifetimes. This exploration had led them away from their religion of origin to a more personally owned set of beliefs. This process could continue until very late life. McCulloch (1985) noted one 91-year-old widow in his study who described her own philosophy of life as both religious and political and displayed a continuing interest in current affairs. She remarked how society was becoming more "civilised" in some ways (for example by abolishing the death penalty and banning corporal punishment) but less in others. On the whole she thought people were becoming less thoughtful and principled in their attitudes to life. Other participants were more impressed, and some even overwhelmed, by recent changes in thought and behaviour, and were exploring tentatively what implications and opportunities there might be for themselves in the new type of society that was emerging.

One of the most striking examples of self-exploration instigated in part by access to new forms of belief was Mrs Parsons, who was interviewed over six years as part of a study on the functions of reminiscence (Coleman, 1986). She reported spending much time in introspection and claimed to have learned a lot from looking back on her life. She had also attained a new form of serenity in the process. Her life had contained a good deal of hard experiences. She had witnessed the cruelty of her father, who had physically abused her mother; had cared both for a sick son, her only child, who was born with deformed kidneys and died at the age of 15 years, and subsequently for her husband, to whom she had been very closely attached, through a long painful illness; and had experienced long years of loneliness after the latter's death. It was only recently, at the age of 76 years, she claimed, that she had achieved the inner peace that was now such a striking feature of the face she presented to the world. She had come to understand and accept a lot of what had happened in her life without rancour or overmuch regret.

When first interviewed in 1969 she spoke about another regular visitor who was a follower of the Maharishi Mahesh Yogi's method of transcendental meditation (TM), derived from Hindu practice. This was the time of growing interest in eastern spirituality, and the encounter of the Beatles with the Maharishi in London (at which the present author was also present!), followed by their journeys to India to learn meditation. Hindu beliefs in karma and in reincarnation made sense to Mrs Parsons. She interpreted them in hopeful ways that allowed for progressive improvement over successive lifetimes:

> "Perhaps the experience I've had in this life, if I were born again, I might be born with a better understanding, you see what I mean, having experienced my failures in this life. I do certainly believe that we go on, I don't believe we just die and that's an end of us. I do believe that there's something after this, but what form it takes of course we don't know."

Although she had rejected the traditional teachings of Christianity, in particular belief in a personal God, with which she had been brought up, she now had a stronger belief in a spiritual force or power which could be called upon in need. Clearly this belief was of great importance to her. It reflected her own experience of life and the worries that had beset her and that she now felt she could counteract:

> "I can't think of God, as God – as he's pictured to us. I know, mind you, that there's some powerful force at work, but I can't think of God as the church teaches him, do you see what I mean? ... but I do believe that there's someone or something very powerful that does guide us. But to be able to pick out any one of those millions of people and say, you know, to know all about us and all our troubles and all our worries, it's impossible, isn't it really, don't you think so? Of

all the millions in the world, millions and millions of people, and yet he knows, according to the church, God knows each one of us, but I can't think that. But I think when we pray, if we do pray earnestly enough, we can call something into our environment. Yes, that helps us. I do think that whether by praying we pick something up or we contact something, I don't know, but I do think that we do contact something when we pray very earnestly. It seems as if we have got to get into such a state of mind that we can reach whatever it is that is God, or whatever it is that is this power."

She also believed in life after death, and the vivid dreams about both her son and her husband after their deaths had meant a lot to her:

"I believe and I think that when our loved ones do die I think that there is another life and I think that they are still around to influence and guide us."

Mrs Parsons had to work out her own views on these matters, and was not easily going to accept what she was told by others. Indeed she became sceptical of the Maharishi himself and had made this clear to her other visitor:

"She said he was trying to help the world to think differently and think in the right channels. I said to her why doesn't he start in his own country, India is in such a bad state … and she said, 'Oh well, he wants the world to get the message first and then help would come to India'. And if that was me, and I was the Maharishi, I should help my own country first, wouldn't you? After all, charity begins at home, doesn't it?"

I continued to meet her and correspond with her over the following seven years, on more than one occasion meeting her other visitor who practised TM. In a letter Mrs Parsons wrote to me shortly before she died, she mentioned again the chronic problems that she had with dermatitis of the hands and the benefits that she had thought that she had obtained from seeking help from a psychic healer. She also referred to the meditation that she practised, distinguishing it explicitly from TM, referring to it in her own words as "a spiritual meditation". Interestingly, this is the only use of the word 'spiritual' that I have come across reviewing material from interviews with older people in this period, and is another indication of how Mrs Parsons was in her own quiet but determined way ahead of the times.

Another striking example of independent belief in the same study was provided by Mrs Manners. She had found a way of reconciling Christian belief with spiritualism, experience of which had clearly helped her counter fear of death, which had been an ever-present fear in her life from childhood onwards. Her mother had died while she was still an infant, her brother had been killed in the

First World War, and she had lost her own son soon after birth. She knew the Christian injunction against raising the dead, but the séances she had experienced from her mid-40s onwards had changed her views and brought her much consolation. She also was prepared to challenge traditional Christian thinking in other ways. For example, like Mrs Parsons she had adopted a view of personal development over successive lives:

> "There's another thing I've never been able to accept, that Christ died on the cross, that we were told he takes all our sins, and that it doesn't matter how wicked you've been in life, as long as you say I'm sorry before you die all your sins are forgiven you. … I think that whatever mistakes we make here, and at some future date and some future life, we should be given the opportunity to put them right, and I think we will have to put them right."

One conclusion that can be drawn from this consideration of interview material collected 30–40 years ago is that many of the salient elements in current discourses about belief, religion and spirituality were already present in some older people's thoughts and conversations in the 1970s: in particular the foregrounding of personal experience (and personal interpretation of that experience) rather than the authority of church teaching. In the arguments of Mr Norton one can see close similarities with a 'Dawkins'-like emphasis on rational and scientific humanism. One can also perceive the beginnings of the influence of eastern spirituality and a more personalised approach to prayer and conception of God. Although the word 'spirituality' had not come into common usage a more individualised and heterodox approach to religious belief was evident in the lives of at least some older people, such as Mrs Parsons and Mrs Masters. In addition, this period was marked by a great deal of disapproval by older people of social change. Although still present – and perhaps common to the experience of ageing in any rapidly changing society – the acerbity of that criticism has largely subsided. Perhaps it is because we are that much further away from the massive changes of the post-war period, and it is now precisely the baby boomer generation – those who were the recipients and principle beneficiaries of the revolution of the 1960s – who are now growing old. They have expectations of a continually changing world – one they think they will still be able to influence for the better.

Religion, spirituality and non-religiosity in the early 21st century

The return of religion to a prominent place in world affairs has been a surprising feature of the late 20th and early 21st centuries. Although this is largely seen as a result of the involvement of the US and its allies in conflicts in the Middle East, which has reawakened negative memories among Muslims of the era of the Crusades, it has also indicated the importance of religion to personal and cultural identity. In addition, perhaps unexpected by religious as well as by secular authorities, there has been the partial replacement of religion in some western societies such as the UK not by an increase in rational humanism but by the still poorly conceptualised phenomenon of personal spirituality (Heelas and Woodhead, 2005). However, as we shall see, the extent of this transfer of allegiance has perhaps been exaggerated. There appears to be a growth also in the phenomenon of 'non-religiosity', separate both from religious/spiritual belief and from atheism.

The concept of spirituality is now commonplace and outside of a religious context often chosen in preference to religion as a means of identifying persons' belief systems. Its use has become so widespread that it is worth remembering just how recently it has emerged in its current form. In the 1950s the associations of the word 'spiritual' were solely religious ones, with the practice of prayer, piety and mysticism (Sheldrake, 1992). Even in the 1980s the term was still understood predominantly in a religious context, and often an exclusively Christian one. An important Christian textbook published in that period and titled *The Study of Spirituality* (Jones et al, 1986) was entirely Christian in its scope and did not feel it necessary to apologise for this fact. The *Handbook of Christian Spirituality* written 20 years later (Sheldrake, 2005) has had to be more explicit about its subject matter.

It has only been in the 1990s and increasingly in the first decade of the 21st century that the term has become popular in the New Age movement and marketable to a wide audience (Carrette and King, 2005). There are still those who would defend its previous more restricted use in the context of belief in God (Fawcett and Noble, 2004), but resisting popular trends in language use is rarely successful. 'Spirituality' appears to be the language of current preference, whereas the previously used term 'mysticism' has strong medieval and Christian connotations. When applied in a Christian context they both appear to refer to the same subject matter, but the language of spirituality has now escaped its Christian associations and indeed strong links to any particular religion.

However, it can also be argued that the set of attitudes that have grown around so-called New Age spirituality do in themselves have some of the characteristics common to a new religion. Indeed some sociologists, such as Lynch (2007), refer to a new 'progressive' belief which is seen as emerging out of four contemporary concerns: 'the desire for an approach to religion and spirituality that is appropriate for modern, liberal societies, the rejection of patriarchal forms of religion and the search for religious forms that are authentic and liberating for women, the move to re-sacralize science (particularly quantum physics and contemporary theories of cosmology), and the search for a nature-based spirituality that will motivate us to try to avert the impending ecological catastrophe' (Lynch, 2007: 10). Whether such 'progressive spirituality' will establish itself as a new religion and become a shared identity over and above people's religions of origin remains to be seen. However, consideration of this possibility helps to throw into relief the essential unifying and meaning-making qualities of religious movements.

We will be exploring European variation in belief in Chapter Seven, but it is worth noting here that the European Union has resisted pressure (including from the Pope and new more religious entrants such as Poland) in recent years to acknowledge the special place of Christianity in its history and heritage (Davie, 2006). It has also adopted the new language of spirituality. Particularly indicative of the new context of belief are the conduct and results of the Eurobarometer values survey of 2005. This offered the possibility of belief in a spirit or life force as distinct from belief in God and belief in none. The former obtained a particularly high response in the UK (40%), as well as in the Netherlands and the Nordic countries. Belief in a personal God remained strongest (above 80%) in Eastern Europe, especially in Greece and Cyprus, Poland and Romania, but also in Portugal. By contrast, lack of any type of spiritual belief only reached above 30% in France. Overall this would support the view that spiritual belief is gaining at the expense of traditional religious belief, and that pure materialistic atheism is still rare.

However, as Lynch admits, the British population shows only a limited enthusiasm for this new type of 'spirituality' as a replacement for religion. The vast majority neither profess religious commitment nor the new agenda of spirituality except in highly diluted forms. Paley (2007), commentating on the trend in the UK towards incorporation of spiritual care into the role definition of nurses, argues that this is something for which neither nurses nor patients in Britain are properly prepared. Religious and spiritual beliefs are specific and need to be ministered to by those skilled in counselling on the territory of those beliefs (that is, religious chaplains and eventually their secular atheist equivalents). Counselling at the level of some common denominator of belief in there being 'something there' appears altogether too bland. Where there is a more homogeneous and developed religious world view, as perhaps is the case in the US, nurses who also share this understanding can indeed assist chaplains in identifying and responding to religious and spiritual need, but this is generally not the case in the UK. What may be regarded as praiseworthy in the US may be regarded as an unprofessional intrusion in the UK. Indeed objections have been raised in the UK to nurses offering to pray with patients. Nevertheless, skilled 'non-denominational' hospital chaplaincy services are increasingly providing important leadership in this difficult new field of work (Cobb, 2005; Speck, 2005; Mowat, 2008).

This major difference between the UK and the US deserves further elaboration. For example, Paley cites the work of Norris and Inglehart (2004) in this context. When asked 'How often, if at all, do you think about the meaning and purpose of life?' 58% of people in the US say often, whereas in the UK the figure is 25%. It may be hard for those involved in the religion vs atheism debate to accept, but there does seem to be present in the British population a substantial degree of 'non-religiosity' that is distinct not only from religion and the new spiritual movements but is also not identifiable with atheism. Rather it reflects a disregard and disinterest in questions of belief and ultimate meaning. As indicated in the work of Houtman and Mascini (2002), already mentioned earlier in the chapter, the same seems to be true of the Netherlands. The increase in New Age spirituality in the population only accounts for a proportion of the loss of traditional religious belief. As many, even more, may have moved towards a position of non-religiosity.

In its best-articulated form non-religiosity appears to equate with agnosticism, which for some, again notably British, commentators appears to be the only 'reasonable' position since both theism and atheism make over-strong claims on our sense of reason and our means of proof (Kenny, 2006). An interesting question is whether agnosticism is itself a form of belief or rather the negation of belief, the inability or unwillingness to make a commitment. It certainly represents a refusal to make a choice in the area of religious and spiritual belief, and would appear unsatisfactory if the issue at stake is thought to be important. But probably for most contemporary agnostics the inability to believe is not seen to have serious consequences. We will return to this issue in Chapter Six.

Since the 1970s church attendance in the UK has declined further. The substantial survey analyses of Alasdair Crockett and David Voas demonstrate continuing declines over successive age cohort groups right up to the beginning of the 21st century (Crockett and Voas, 2006). The most recent survey (Tearfund, 2007) indicates that 15% of adults report attending church services at least monthly, and 59% report never attending. On the other hand, as many as 72% of the UK population identified themselves as 'Christian' in the 2001 national census. Although this figure is disputed by the British Humanist Association, on the grounds that the question 'What is your religion?' was asked in a context of ethnicity and was biased towards a religious answer, the discrepancy between church attendance and affiliation needs further interpretation. There are competing claims in this regard. For example, Grace Davie in her thesis of 'believing without belonging' (Davie, 1994) argues that whereas few people are committed to regular attendance at Christian churches, the majority want church services to continue, also on their behalf, and to be available to them at special times, at life transitions and at important occasions in public life. David Voas and Alasdair Crockett (Voas and Crockett, 2005), on the other hand, argue for progressive changes in affiliation as much as attendance, the former in consequence of the latter, and related substantially to failure of transmission of religious attitudes by parents to their children.

Although there seems to be a measure of agreement that an attitude of non-religiosity captures the stance of the most substantial part of the present British population, new currents of religious and spiritual belief are making themselves felt. Certain groups of Christian churches, particularly the Pentecostal, Charismatic and Evangelical, appear to be bucking the trend of decline. This is partly a result of immigration to the UK of Christians from the Caribbean and from Africa. Immigration is also increasing the numbers of those belonging to other major world faiths, particularly Islam. Although the influence on the indigenous population is small so far in terms of actual religious conversion, the context in which people think about religion and belief is inevitably changing as a result of the greater salience of religion (Davie, 2006). Choices which might have seemed counter-cultural not many years ago have now become feasible.

Older people's religious and spiritual beliefs at the beginning of the 21st century

To what extent do British older people share in these trends? Are they influenced by new religious and spiritual movements? Have they also become less religious? Are they equally unconcerned about issues of meaning and purpose? Or does ageing and the increasing awareness of death make it less easy to avoid existential angst about the human condition? We do now at last have more quantitative as well as qualitative data to answer such questions, although they are far from extensive and only provide limited answers.

Evidence from surveys consistently shows higher attendance levels and other indicators of religious belief in older adults. As already mentioned in Chapter One, the fact that these differences have been found consistently over the last 50 years in the US have led some commentators, such as Moberg (2001b), to claim them as evidence for developmental change with age. However, because of its declining rates of religiosity such evidence on its own cannot be used to make the same claim in the UK. Indeed in the British Social Attitudes Survey the numbers of people over the age of 60 years reporting to be Christians decreased from 74% to 66% whereas those reporting no religion increased from 20% to 29% over the period 1991 to 1998, which would accord with the theory of gradual secularisation of the population. On the other hand, other religious indicators such as belief in God or a higher power, belief in an afterlife, and at least monthly frequency of church attendance, and of prayer remained stable or slightly increased (at 85%, 48%–49%, 30%–33%, and 56% respectively) in the same period of time (Sadler, 2009). This would suggest some stabilising of religious and spiritual belief among the older population.

A survey in 2009 of the beliefs of members of an older adults' participant pool at the University of Southampton, a sample of 254 people over the age of 55 years, shows comparable figures (Spreadbury, 2010): as many as 38% claimed to attend church at least monthly (31% weekly) and 53% to pray at least monthly (30% daily). To the question 'Do you have a religion and if so what is it?' (the form of religious question the British Humanist Association has suggested for the next census), 73% gave a Christian answer, similar to the figures reported by the British Social Attitudes Survey. This sample over-represents those with a higher education, but the evidence on associations between education and religion already reported (and present within this sample data itself) would lead one to expect lower figures on religiosity as a result. More data on cohort difference and on longitudinal change with age will be reported in Chapter Four, but it suffices here to conclude that up to the present time the older members of the UK population continue to appear substantially more religious in attitude and interest than younger members.

Is there any evidence for a shift on the part of older people, similar to that evident in younger people, away from traditional religious belief to the language of personal spirituality? A recent study by Euan Sadler (2009) on the religious and spiritual views of older people of Black Caribbean and White British origin living in or around the London borough of Lambeth provides a negative answer to this question. Some of the older people he interviewed continued to confuse it with spiritualism, which confirms that the language of spiritualism had been more common in the past than that of spirituality. Most of the participants, however, expressed difficulties articulating the meaning of spirituality because they considered it too abstract a term, and also unhelpful. As one participant said:

> "It's a very sort of elastic concept. It's like Humpty Dumpty. When I use the word it means what I chose it to mean, nothing more, nothing less."

The oldest participants expressed the greatest difficulties with the term, which might suggest a cohort effect. But there was no relationship with educational status. Some of the most educated expressed the most unease:

> "To me it's such a vague term. If you asked me I would go and get out my dictionary and look it up and see what the dictionary says."

Those who could give it a meaning did so in clearly religious terms, as "putting your trust in God" or as "the indwelling spirit of God". One participant expressed this religious sense with emphasis:

> "Spirituality is the gift given to you by God, no-one can give that, only God can give it. It's an indwelling thing inside of you. Your inner thoughts and – if you know what I mean? And the spirit that dwells in you, teaches you how to live your life."

There were a minority in the sample who gave the term a more contemporary meaning, for example "making sense of one's life in relation to higher truths". But most members of the sample were clearly more comfortable with the concept of religion by which they understood a community of shared beliefs and practices. The evidence from this and other studies suggests that the present older population remains distinct from the rest of the population in terms of religious affiliation and preference for religious rather than spiritual belief.

However, contemporary older people in the UK do seem to share with younger people a good part of the contemporary ethos of independence from authority. The result is much heterodoxy of belief, not only as a result of misunderstanding or limited religious education, but also wilful contradiction of established church teaching. The extent of deviation can be quite startling to non-Christian observers. For example, Hui (personal comment) has remarked on a major difficulty, in carrying out comparative research among older believers of different religions, of establishing that people who claim to be Christians in the UK actually believe in orthodox Christian teaching. In her sample of self-identified Christians over the age of 60 years 25% did not believe either in the divinity of Jesus or a personal God to whom they could relate.

These complexities regarding the content of belief have been highlighted in a study of recently bereaved older spouses conducted in the South of England (Coleman et al, 2007), which we shall describe in greater detail in Chapter Four. All the participants had been brought up in England with a Christian education and had attended Sunday school. In terms of general religious indicators the sample seemed quite representative of the UK older population: 70% believed in God or a higher spiritual power, 44% attended church on a regular basis, and 80% prayed when they were on their own.

When interviewed in more detail about their beliefs it became clear that many members of the sample had doubts about basic tenets of the Christian faith. Some could not conceptualise God as a person, preferring to think instead of a powerful life force. But this in turn implied doubts about a loving God. Moreover, the doctrine of the Trinity, of God as a community of persons in relationship, fundamental to the development of early Christian doctrine, was not understood or accepted even by some of those who expressed an otherwise strong faith in God. The beliefs of these people appeared closer in character to that of the Unitarian Church. There was also considerable variation in whether they referred to strengthening, stabilising or weakening of their faith as they grew older. Most said they were at peace with their beliefs, but some said they were not.

A striking characteristic of this sample, and perhaps related to their experience of recent bereavement, was a belief in fate, as a way of explaining what otherwise could not be explained. Often this was expressed in non-orthodox ways, as a set plan for life independent of God's will. For example, Mrs Collier suffered from a debilitating osteoporosis that confined her to a wheelchair. Her childhood had been spent in India, where she had wanted to become a nun. She had happy memories of the Catholic rituals that she had experienced as a child, but her practice had lapsed as an adult and she now had limited contacts with the church. Most of her prayer, she said, consisted of arguing with God and getting angry with Him. She saw God as loving but imperfect:

> "[I see Him] as a loving person but He gets it wrong. … I think, yes, he's still the good God but He gets it wrong, even more now than He did. Oh dear … I argue with Him. … Mucking my life up. I can't get on with doing things, doing things with and for other people, can't even do that now."

More powerful than her belief in God though seemed to be her belief in fate:

> "It's already arranged. It's just going to happen. You can't change it, I
> don't think. Quite a lot of it is just luck. If it wasn't luck you could
> just change it at will. My illness is just bad luck."

Yet the vast majority of this sample of bereaved persons practised some form of
individual prayer. Even those who had very limited religious or spiritual belief
said they prayed. For many this was a great source of comfort and strength. Mrs
Wilkinson was a Methodist but did not go to church. She did not consider the
Bible God's word and questioned even the notion of a perfect God. But she did
pray and appreciated the benefit it gave her:

> "Every night when I go to bed I always thank God for my day, for
> keeping me safe and well, and again in the morning. ... Well if I miss
> a night, I think I've done wrong. But it is important to me to pray
> at night. Even if I miss in the morning, I always pray at night, at the
> end of the day. ...
>   "As you get older so many things happen to your life and you're not
> able to fight it. And that's where your belief comes in. Religion helps
> you to accept it. You wonder, 'Why did I worry, why? You're still here
> at the end of the day'. At the beginning of the day everything can be
> against you. By praying, by the end of the day I feel calm."

Nor was everyone as puzzled by the experience of doubt as some of those
already mentioned. Mrs Cooper, a frail woman of 85 years, also spoke of personal
experiences being determined, but she saw this not as fate but as a personal
destiny from which you learned. She prayed ("I talk to the Lord") and saw God
as a mystery:

> "Yes, a mystery. A good mystery. He's always trying to tell me to, you
> know, to teach me to do things ... I hope one day I shall understand
> it all. ... Well, it is a mystery isn't it, don't you feel that? I think that
> everyone should feel that God's a mystery, because nobody quite
> knows."

As can be appreciated from this brief survey of older people talking about their
religious and spiritual beliefs, it is necessary to approach interviews on this subject
with an awareness and preparedness for potential variation. It is also important to
understand the lifespan antecedents of faith. In Chapter Four we shall illustrate
evidence for the importance of childhood experiences and particularly the
influence of parents' faith on expressions of belief until late in life. But before
presenting this material we shall in the next chapter explain something of
what we have learned about methods of collecting data on personal beliefs and
particularly about interviewing older people in regard to this neglected area of
human experience. We consider that our studies of bereavement in particular have

provided the opportunity to develop a more sensitive methodology for examining belief in context. In Chapters Five and Six we shall present some of our more recent work in the area of belief and coping with loss.

THREE

Listening and enabling the sharing of beliefs and values in later life

Marie A. Mills, Peter Speck and Peter G. Coleman

Interviewing about beliefs and values

Little is written of the inherent practical difficulties in questioning and listening to older people speaking about sensitive issues. For some older people, such matters can include personal beliefs, which may never have been readily discussed before. We also have to bear in mind that thoughts about beliefs and values may never have been fully processed and thus remain difficult to articulate. The older person may fear being judged as foolish, uneducated, or misunderstood. In addition to having a good knowledge of the ageing process, we have found in our research that the researcher, as both listener and collector of data, requires further skills that are not easily identifiable. The qualitative researcher is sometimes seen as a negotiator who is able to collect data using a variety of methods (Strauss and Corbin, 1998; Marshall and Rossman, 2006). The literature discusses methods in some detail, but there is a lack of understanding of the skills necessary to understand the world from another's perspective. The idea that the researcher and the participant, at whatever age, will form a mutually beneficial relationship, certainly in longitudinal projects, is rarely considered.

There is still a tendency for researchers, especially in psychology, to favour quantitative approaches to the study of religion and spirituality. A wide range of questionnaire measures are in use (Hill and Hood, 1999). This no doubt reflects caution about using new research methods in an area which still lacks scientific respect. However, as Coyle (2008) among others has argued, qualitative methods are especially appropriate to researching areas of human experience, such as religion and spirituality, where there is no consensus about the ontological status of the reality being studied. Involvement with an interested interviewer also allows for the teasing out of the meaning of the religious/meaning words used, whereas the meaning of standardised terms employed in survey questionnaires may remain blurred and ambiguous. This advantage is heightened in longitudinal study, where participants over time gain confidence in expressing themselves about an area of life that is acknowledged as important but is often left poorly articulated.

The nature of qualitative longitudinal research is similar to the therapeutic process. Jones (1991: 211) points to the fact that she, together with other researchers, has noted the therapeutic and counselling role of some interviews. The entire research process in qualitative longitudinal research can be seen in this light. For instance, counselling contracts are similar to research agreements with participants, and are also subject to stringent ethical requirements. As far as possible the counsellor makes clear what is expected of the client and, through client expectations of the counsellor, defines the counselling role. Researcher expectations are also made clear to participants and, as in therapy, the participant is free to withdraw from investigation at any time. Further, similar to psychotherapeutic interventions, the researcher/participant relationship has a beginning, middle and an end. Researchers should be sensitive to the possibility that participants can be anxious at the beginning, and may 'tire' by the middle of the investigation. They may also need to express sadness over the ending of this relationship during the final interview.

David Moberg, who has the longest experience of any researcher in this area, argues that the interviewer/researcher cannot adopt a neutral stance (Moberg, 2001b), but must show that they are warmly empathic, non-judgemental and keenly interested in everything they hear. This concept is not new, but bears repeating. It is known that older people in care are more likely to speak about their beliefs to younger less experienced carers, who are seen as more sympathetic to their views (Tobin, 1991). We have built on this, arguing that the listener, as a qualitative researcher, requires extensive interpersonal skills, similar to those required in the counselling profession (Mills and Coleman, 2002; Mills et al, 2002). Randall (2009) suggests that 'to counsel someone is to listen closely to both the content and the form – the substance and the style, the told and the telling – of the stories that they recount about their life'. This can also be said of the qualitative researcher interested in the meaning that older people give to their lives.

Further, even in research that involves no face-to-face contact, it is the quality of the perceived relationship between the researcher and participants which will influence commitment to the research process. This begins at the first point of contact and is especially helpful where there is difficulty in accessing older participants for qualitative studies. Once the various permissions have been granted, encouraging participation requires carefully worded written invitations that display empathy, warmth, and a genuine interest in the person concerned. The importance of this first contact cannot be overemphasised.

We have used this approach throughout several studies, initially looking at how beliefs helped older people adapt to spousal bereavement (study one). This study used a small sample of older spouses who were visited three times in the second year of their bereavement (Coleman et al, 2002). The results of this study were published in *SAGA Magazine*. This led to research into the importance of beliefs in later life, to discover if faith needs were met and to make suggestions for change within churches and other faith communities (study two). In a third study we looked at clergy knowledge and attitudes towards ageing. We found some good levels of support on a practical and social level, but a lack of understanding of the psychological effects that ageing can bring. We suggested that more training in this area would be helpful for clergy to better meet the spiritual needs of older people affected by a stroke or dementia etc (Speck et al, 2006). In this chapter, we will be focusing on the first two studies and the part they played in enabling older people to feel able to express their beliefs. We will also be using the experience gained in these series of studies to highlight the key points we found when collecting data.

Study one involved face-to-face interviews, with study two comprised of letter and postal questionnaires. Questionnaires in both studies required both closed and open responses. Both examples will largely focus on the narratives of participants, their spoken or written words, rather than the conclusions reached in each study, accounts of which can be found elsewhere (Coleman et al, 2002, 2007). Dan McAdams underlines the importance of narrative, particularly with regard to identity and faith: 'to make meaning in life is to create dynamic narratives that render sensible and coherent the seeming chaos of human existence' (McAdams, 1993:166).

Enabling older people to express their beliefs: a practical perspective

When people respond to questions in face-to-face interviews, or via open-ended postal questionnaires, we know that difficult questions require time to answer. Listening to people in later life share experiences and beliefs requires time and patience. In study one, many of the face-to-face interviews lasted well over two hours, highlighting the importance of providing appropriate support for the researcher since this process can be draining for both listener and speaker.

With this in mind, it was found to be beneficial to schedule two interviews a day, the first in the middle part of the morning and the second in early afternoon. No participant felt rushed or overtired, and neither did the interviewer feel overwhelmed. These factors were also considered in study two. Each participant received a maximum of three mailings, rather than one mailing containing all questionnaires, in order to discourage participant fatigue. In this study it was noted that some questionnaires were not suited to older British populations, who found some US measures confusing. Many participants found individual questions in these questionnaires difficult to answer, and in some cases they were only partially completed or ignored altogether.

We recognised a need to develop instruments more suited to older British participants. Comments also indicated that participants felt constrained and irritated by yes/no questions. In some cases they developed their replies on the questionnaires themselves, or in an attached note. We felt that this indicated a need to include space for further comments in future studies of this kind.

Another consideration is that older British populations can have difficulty with the term spirituality because of the connotations with 'spiritualism', which as we noted in the previous chapter was a belief system prevalent in the UK in the interwar period. Levin and Tobin (1995) argue there is a need to create more sophisticated measures in this field. However, these measures should not exclude the value of individual accounts. Case-study methodology lends itself to rigorous qualitative and quantitative analysis (Fishman, 1999; Coleman, 2002). It would seem to make sense to utilise a variety of measures to further explore and encourage the influence of beliefs in later life, given the importance they have for individual well-being, quality of life issues and societal health care resources (Coleman et al, 2002).

As we have said previously, older people can find difficulty in articulating their beliefs but we found that this applied more to those who had weaker or more moderate beliefs. It was easier for those who are/have been religious to talk about present and past beliefs. This also applied to older people who had developed a more philosophical belief system, in that they did not believe in an external power that could influence them (King et al, 2001).

It is sometimes difficult to obtain answers from a person of any age about their beliefs or values. Our experience is that asking such questions as 'What do you think is really important to you at present?' or 'I wonder what it is that gives your life meaning?' to be helpful questions. We have found that asking such questions in a hesitant, accepting and gentle manner encouraged the older person to feel relaxed and less anxious. It also gave them time to think about their answers and not feel rushed to respond. In addition this approach enabled us to enlarge on unclear or enigmatic statements, as the following example illustrates:

AW: "I'm not perfect, nobody's perfect."

Interviewer: "Er, nobody's perfect? Does that apply to everyone?"

AW: "Yes, nobody is, stands to reason."

Interviewer: "And God, what about God? Do you see Him as perfect?"

AW: "No, nobody is. They can't be."

Older people express their beliefs in different ways. One of our participants, a person of strong spiritual beliefs, saw the city view from her bedroom window as a source of delight: "so much happening, yet it never changes". Another saw life as something to be endured without fuss: "you came back from the war; you just got on with it".

Later in this chapter we give further examples of the variety of ways in which participants expressed their beliefs and values both in general and in daily life. Their stories suggest the many, rich and different ways in which older people perceive and value meaning in their lives.

Belief narratives in later life

Atkinson (1991: 11) argues that 'telling our stories is an act of transcending the personal and entering the realm of the sacred'. Moreover a personal narrative is inextricably interlinked with life and meaning (Sarbin, 1986). Taylor (2001: 1) suggests that 'our greatest desire, greater even the desire for happiness, is that our lives mean something'. Further, disclosing one's beliefs or moral narrative about the self to an understanding other encourages the development of meaning and understanding (Vitz, 1990).

Case study accounts of how older people reveal their beliefs illuminate both their diversity and how they are shaped by life experiences. They also reflect the relationship between the interviewer and the subject. In the study of spousal bereavement in later life, all participants were interviewed after the first year of bereavement. They were interviewed three times over the following year. Not all participants were believers, but all had beliefs that enabled them to make sense of the world, prior to their bereavement. Their adaptation to this major loss was determined by the strength of belief, whether beliefs were strongly religious or philosophical. The following three case studies illuminate this observation and are chosen because they illustrate the three significant groupings within the study sample. These comprised those who held philosophical rather than religious beliefs, those who questioned their beliefs, and those with a strong religious belief.

Case study one concerns 'William Jones' who had no religious or spiritual beliefs. As his words show, his belief was philosophical in that he made sense of his life without a belief in any power outside of self (King et al, 2001). The second case study is of 'Norman Creech' who questioned his weak or low beliefs, and the third case study is that of 'Ella Bright' who held unquestioning strong beliefs.

William Jones

Mr Jones illustrates the adaptive nature of a strong belief, whether it is philosophical, strongly religious and/or spiritual. He found it difficult to speak about his beliefs as he declared that he did not believe in religion. However, his explanation of some of his life experiences and the meanings he attached to those experiences clearly showed the strength of his philosophical beliefs and values.

He was 82 years old at our first meeting, a very tall spare man, with a forthright but pleasant manner. He and his wife had two children. One child, a son, had died 16 years previously in a road accident. He was very close to his daughter Sarah and her husband, together with their two children. At the time of the first interview he said that one had rung him that morning, saying with some pride "He's 6ft 7!" He also had three great grandsons.

He was a man who chose his words carefully. He did not like to display his emotions. He was in the police force for many years. This, he admitted, framed his outlook on life:

"I don't believe in belittling anyone, but 25 years in the police force makes you cynical. You see things, you have to laugh them off, if you know what I mean. ... I suppose in a way it makes you a bit harder, perhaps, than you would normally be. Then, of course, I went through the war."

When asked why he decided to take part in this research he said:

"If people are interested in me, well I'm interested in them. ... I get on with anybody, talk to anybody."

His wife had been ill for many years and had died while on a life support machine. He found the decision to switch off the machine very upsetting:

"That's the saddest part of it as far as I'm concerned, that they just switched her life off like that you know. ... There was nothing they could do. They were frightened she was going to have a heart attack. So was I, you know, I didn't want her to have a massive heart attack and be a cabbage all the rest of her life. The doctor explained it all to us and he said for it was in her interest ... really was ... and that's what was hard to accept."

He felt he had been rather "down" after her death but that he was much better at the time of the first interview. He said he had been determined not to let himself go. He did not want to be like some of his friends. When asked how he had managed this, he said:

"No idea! That's the way I am I suppose."

He was rather scathing about the present interest in talking about one's problems:

"What I can't understand is that ... policeman, or fireman or the soldiers that have to have counselling now, because of their job. They didn't get it during the war and they went through far worse times than what some of these people are going through now."

He thought there was no need for this type of help:

"Well in some places, perhaps, but 90% of the cases no. They play on people don't they? Compensation's what they want, that's what their big aim is these days. Compensation, all the time. ... I mean the average policeman goes to tragic things. I mean things like Hillsborough and other cases like that, it was their job, it's what they're trained to do. ... When I hear of all these people now that, that go for counselling because they've been to a road accident, and all this sort of nonsense. … What we went through during the war, and the accidents I've dealt with afterwards, I didn't have any counselling, I had to get on and deal with it myself. Never thought about it. I just got on and did it, or I came home and tried to forget it."

He prevented himself from thinking about things too deeply:

Interviewer: "Do you find you get very upset when you're on your own sometimes?"

WJ: "Upset is the wrong word – sad, yes."

Interviewer: "How do you deal with that?"

WJ: "You just have to go through, don't I? I just have to switch it off."

Religion has never played a major part in his life. He described his parents as "slightly religious" and that he did attend a church school. He tended to believe in fate:

"Well, there's no such thing as luck is there? It's just things happen and they happen, don't they? … If you can't see it, you don't believe it, do you?"

He was not overly concerned about this:

"I don't think about it, I mean we're here and that's it as far as I'm concerned. … No, there was a big bang and the world came being and nature took over, and human beings started to live on the earth and that's it as far as I'm concerned. They weren't made by anybody, they just, just occurred in nature."

He agreed nature can be cruel but it was an unthinking cruelty:

"Yes, it can be cruel. On the other hand, what else can it do? If a load of explosives kill people, nothing else that can happen is there? It's just as it is. Nature doesn't know what's going to happen does it? Nature's not a thinking object, it's, it's an object and that's it. If it falls on somebody and kills them, it doesn't know."

During one interview he expounded his lack of belief in God. This was the only occasion. It was unprompted and followed the above open-ended general discussion of the natural forces in life. Possibly the nature of the investigation had caused him to think about the topic and marshal his arguments. His disbelief and questioning of the existence of God rested on the factual evidence presented by the universe.

> "You see, the whole of the, the whole of the thing goes round the fact that God had a son who came to this earth to save humanity. From what? Now, this earth has been in business now for four and a half thousand million years, but religion, the Christian religion's only been going for two thousand years. So, that's a question that ponders in my mind if I think about it. And they say when you die you go to heaven. These little toddlers, do they go to heaven? Do they stay at that age when they go up there? What do they do when they're there? Babies? I don't say I don't never think about it, I do think about it. … I do when I look at the stars. I think about everything else out there. This earth, just a tiny speck of dust and we've got the nerve to believe that there's no other life anywhere else."

William Jones' narrative suggests that his own strong philosophical belief supported little inner dialogue. The existence of the universe supported his beliefs and pragmatic view of the world. Neither did his lack of spiritual or religious beliefs impede his ability to cope and adjust to his bereavement. He was not depressed. Further, he had high meaning in his life and felt that everyone has "some goodness in them".

Norman Creech

The second case study illustrates how careful listening and attending to older people as they explore and express their beliefs can result in a rich narrative that explains the basis for what they believe. In the case of Norman Creech these beliefs were philosophical as well as religious. Further, it demonstrates the fluid nature of beliefs and the internal questioning that occupied participants as they tried to make sense of grievous loss in times of crises.

Mr Creech was 68 years at first meeting, a tall grey-haired man with a pleasant and welcoming personality. He was slightly deaf due to an accident when young and this prevented him from making the Royal Air Force his career. He eventually became an aircraft technician with the Ministry of Defence. At the first interview he had been bereaved for 14 months. He and his wife had two children, a girl and an adopted boy. His daughter was unmarried and his son was divorced. He had a seven-year-old granddaughter, Chloe, to whom he was devoted and he was very involved in her care. He was also devoted to Sunny, his golden retriever. He took her for walks twice a day and she accompanied him when he collected Chloe from school.

He lived in a large council estate about two miles from the city centre. The house was pleasant and comfortable. He owned the property. He had no major financial needs and was still able to afford holidays, run a car and pursue his interests in sport and other leisure activities. He looked a young 68-year-old, with an air of vigour and purpose about him. From the first he was able to speak readily about his life experiences and his emotions. When asked why he had consented to be part of the study he replied that he "felt it had come at the right time". He said that talking about his bereavement would be helpful. He was depressed at the time of the first interview, but not at the time of the final interview. He spoke of his wife's sudden death:

> "She had a massive heart attack out there. She was sat here [he pointed to a chair in the room]. And because I don't do crosswords and stuff, she loved to do her 'Take a Break', you know, the *Take a Break* magazine? And when she was stuck, you know, she used to ask me to do it and she'd fill in the end of it so she could send it away. Never did win anything … and she got up and went in, took the magazine in there [pointed to dining room], because we've got a bureau in there and she was going to get a stamp and an envelope and a pair of scissors and cut it up. And she hadn't been gone no more than 20 seconds, and I was sat where you were and reading the Sunday paper. It was Sunday, 7 o'clock at night and I heard a funny noise, and the old dog, the old dog was sort, well near enough, and I said, 'What's up Mum?' and no answer, and the dog went out over there and dog come back all funny, wagging the tail and what not. And so I got up. She'd had a massive heart attack and she'd sat … and the noise I heard was where she fell back against the bureau and on the floor. So I immediately called … she had the third one, is it the third valve? And there was nothing we could do. So in one way looking back I was glad it was like that. … But it leaves you with such an empty … as though you're cut in half you know, you wonder where the half has gone."

Interviewer: "How did you make sense of it?"

NC: "I don't, you know."

Interviewer: "You think you will make sense of it?"

NC: "You look back a lot. This is why faith, is a, this is why … you'll have to excuse me." [He became upset.]

Mr Creech expressed no belief in religion, or an afterlife:

> "Well, we were never religious, never religious. Spiritual? You mean the power force? I suppose there's a bit of that, yes. Sense of our lives, yes, I suppose a bit of spiritual and a bit of philosophy.

"Well I'd like to believe it. I mean, a friend, he's got a stepmother who's into faith healing, and some of the things that he tells me, you know, and you hear stories. I'm a sceptic. ... I accept his views, you know, and what not. I've not had arguments, but discussions with him, you know. And I said, 'Well, the Ten Commandments are very good, I mean they hold. If you look at it over a whole spectrum, the Ten Commandments are very good for society, for the whole. You keep that kind of thing, yes, very good, but I don't hold with that life after death or ... there's another actual human being somewhere, you know.' I say to him, 'I uphold the law and, in myself, I treat everybody decently and what not. What's the difference between that and going to church you know, and all this praying?'"

He saw himself as someone who accepted life, accepted fate:

"A lot of things are meant to be, you know ... people that try to find the meaning of life. ... I wouldn't even bother to try. I just accept that's what it is."

But this was not a stable belief. By the time of the second interview, six months later, it had changed, and there was evidence of spiritual questioning:

"You say 'thank God', you know. Obviously something's out there, but what it is I don't know. I'm not deeply religious, not deeply religious, but something's got to be out there. I mean I live by the Ten Commandments, you don't really think about them. If you're a law-abiding citizen the Ten Commandments covers nearly everything doesn't it? Shan't steal, you don't, you shan't commit adultery, you don't, all the other things. I mean you accept them as a normal basis anyway ... if you accept there's nothing, then there's no meaning in life is there? Everybody got to have a hope that there's something after death don't they?"

Interviewer: "Do you ever hope there is something?"

NC: "Of course I do, a lot of people ... hopefully ... but at the back of my mind I can't see how. Religious people do, they think, they're absolutely convinced there's something don't they? ... Yes, like I say, you've got to hope that there's something or else you'd just go mad. You'd just go mad. You hope there's something there."

Interviewer: "You hope you might be wrong?"

NC: "Yes. Well, 99% sure that I'm not."

He mentioned fate again:

> "I'm a great believer in fate. I mean lucky, when I think how lucky I am … I didn't go on national service, I missed Korea. … And you know other blokes that I knew, my friends, I mean 'a couple of them got killed in Korea doing national service. You know, that's the way it is. I've never been beaten up. I've never tasted war. I've never been bombed, although I went through the war. I had a lovely childhood … good teenager … I had a good start working. I met a wonderful wife. I had a wonderful marriage for 38 years, you know, so I've been extremely lucky."

It is not uncommon amongst older people who have changed or challenged their previous beliefs, and are still unsure, to explain life events in terms of chance, fate or luck, both good and bad. However, Mr Creech saw himself as strongly questioning.

> "Well I've always had this, yes, asking questions … but it takes me a long time because I got all my opinions on what my life has been … and to realise how other people live."

He said he enjoyed discussing things with his daughter and having debates with his religious friends, even when their views were at sharp variance to his own. He particularly enjoyed the television programme *Question Time*. This echoes Bakhtin's view of the dialogic self in which thought consists in dialogue with significant interlocutors within the self, a process whereby the self is continually reconstructed. The thought–dialogue tests ideas with these 'selves' in a continual process as a way of deciding how to think and move forward with living (Hermans and Hermans-Jansen, 1995; Zappen, 2000). Certainly Mr Creech presented himself as in continual dialogue both within himself as well with others. The process of dialogue seemed if anything to be more significant than the conclusion. He found pleasure in debate, in asking questions, both of himself and others.

This account of Mr Creech indicates the difficulties inherent in exploring beliefs with older people who have a low/moderate belief system. He gave no sense of an integrated belief system, and it was hard to pinpoint his beliefs with any great clarity, underpinned as they were by the shifting foundations of an impersonal fate intertwined with a personal destiny, and an added element of fortuitous chance.

Mrs Ella Bright

The third case study is that of a participant who held strongly religious beliefs. Unlike participants with low or moderate beliefs, responses to searching questions were given with clarity and little hesitancy.

Mrs Bright was aged 72 years old at the time of the first interview. She was a sturdy, warmly welcoming woman, with an amazing zest for life. She lived alone in a well-cared-for bungalow, with her two small dogs, who liked visitors as much as their owner. She had supportive neighbours who helped her when necessary. They enjoyed helping her as she was appreciative of their assistance. She said she tried not to bother them too much. She had been married to her husband for nearly 50 years. They had no children, but she had several nephews and nieces. One niece lived in the same road and she had one sister who was still alive.

Her husband had died 14 months previously. He had dementia for the last eight years of his life. She looked after him for nearly seven years until he went into care:

> "So I kept him for six and half years and I looked after him myself, because that's my job wasn't it? But then in the Home I'd go in every day and see him. … Yes, in the last five months I went every day to feed him at lunchtime."

She brought him home at weekends. As he became worse, she spent most of her time by his bed. She was distressed that she had not been there the moment he died, but she thought she had coped well with her bereavement:

> "Yes I would say I've coped fairly well, but I must say I think the reason being with his illness. I would say 'God, don't let him stay here too long, getting steadily worse losing all his dignity.' So when he died I could not complain. I'd asked for it to happen and if people say to me, 'I'm so sorry', I said 'Don't be sorry, he's out of everything now'".

Mrs Bright was a strong believer, as assessed by the Royal Free measure of strength of belief (King et al, 1995). She had adapted well to her bereavement and she was not depressed. She led a busy life and was very involved with the community:

> "Mothers Union – I've been their Treasurer for many years now. I joined the Carers Association – I used to belong to the carers group at the hospital. The City Carers Association, they asked me if I would take on their treasury work, so I do their treasury work. The Old Farmers Association, I do three to four hours' voluntary work on a computer and then putting accounts on the computers, so I've had all sorts of things that's kept me going."

She also took people to church:

> "… I mean Wednesdays, I pick up three elderly people, take them to church with me because they're in their 80s and one has a steel rod, so she can't get about a lot. I pick her up Sundays as well. Tuesdays, I take three other old people out to bingo in the afternoon, because

they like to go, so I take them and I stop and play bingo. Wednesdays, I go to church and then I meet a friend or bring her back here. ... I mean in what I do and what I think, and what I think is part of your faith is helping other people isn't it? I'm sure it is."

Mrs Bright had a religious background and upbringing. Both sets of grandparents were lay readers. Her mother was very religious and attended an Anglican church. Her father, who was a semi invalid, was also religious. She associated religion with a sense of joyfulness and fun. Her beliefs and her relationship with God ran through all conversations. Her beliefs acted as a foundation for her entire life:

"Every fraction of every minute He's there for me, I never have a moment's doubt. He doesn't turn anyone of us away. He'll knock the door, but if you don't open it, He can't get in, can He? So that's not His fault. My mother always used to say, 'See, I don't think there are real atheists in the world, because when things go wrong, what do they say? "God, what am I going to do, or God, help me"'. So she said, 'If they were atheists they wouldn't mention the word God.' So, yes, I think He's there all the time, I do."

The church she attended was important to her:

"Well the church I go to is a very old one, it's about three hundred, going up towards four hundred years old now. I like the building, I like the services, I like the atmosphere. It's so easy. Everybody's so friendly. I – it's love. There's a lot of love in the church. Can't describe it any other way really, because you're all there as one. I mean you get the odd, you get strangers come in, but they're treated as if they've always been there. And yes, there is a lot of love in the church, and people have said to me to go in there, there is love comes out of that congregation. And also to see the little ones that go to Sunday school. And then when they come over before the end of service and bring over and show you what they've done, or they sing you a new little hymn or a little song they've heard. All those things to me are important, yes."

She also attended ecumenical services and enjoyed meeting fellow believers:

" ... July, in the Park. Must be about three or four thousand people there. It's a wonderful get together because it was all, all religions and nationalities obviously ... and I have been to the Salvation Army ... and they're all great get togethers. So you are as one with each other."

She had made new friends since her husband's death. Some of them, too, had husbands who had died of dementia:

> "I said to Eileen, 'That's the only good thing that's come out of this Alzheimer's'. She said, 'Yes it is, we've got each other, we've got a good friendship'".

She was asked if she thought these friendships were a gift from God:

> "It's got to be hasn't it? That's it, yes I think so. We had to meet didn't we? Sad circumstances, but we had to meet and it's the good that's come out of it."

Unlike Mr Creech, who believed in fate or predestination, she believed in a personal destiny planned by God:

> "So I can't understand when people say, 'Oh, you know, you go to church, but what about this, what about that, what's happening here, what's happening there?' And I say 'Well that has to happen, that is laid down. From the time we're born to the time we die our lives are mapped out.' … Well I think that our lives are laid down from the time we're conceived to the time we die, and the things that happen there have already been mapped out for us to go through. We have to go through them to come out the other side."

> Interviewer: "But you think we also have a choice about whether we, we follow it or not?"

> EB: "We have a choice, yes, we do have a choice, but in the end it's going to come back to what is laid down. That's what I believe anyway."

> Interviewer: "Who maps it out?"

> EB: "The One above."

> Interviewer: "So God maps it out?"

> EB: "Yes, yes. He got it all worked out."

Mrs Bright did not provide much evidence of internal dialogue concerning her beliefs, rather there was a steady acceptance of the 'truth' which underpinned her beliefs. She spoke about Nature:

> "Well, I think there's nothing better. Don't know, there's nothing better to me than if you're up early morning and you go out and you can see deer and a fox and all the glory that there is around, isn't there? I often look this time of the year at the trees, and I think it's true, it's

a picture no artist can paint, isn't it? But it's all there and yes, nature does mean a lot to me, you know animals and what's in the ground, yes, definitely. You look out there and you think man couldn't make this, doesn't matter where you drive, all the colours are green. It's a picture no artist can paint, isn't it? You can't get those colours. Yes I think so. It fascinates me when I put seeds in, day in and day out kind of thing and the seeds are growing and to watch them is absolutely marvellous, yes. Yes I think so. Look at life, new born babies, what better sound than the cry of a new born baby?"

She did not overly question her beliefs:

Interviewer: "It feels as if, do you, you don't question things very much, you accept them?"

EB: "Well, that's, that is the inevitable isn't it? That has to be accepted, you can't, you can't just walk away from it because you know at the end of the day, that's what's going to happen to each and every one of us, but I don't dwell on it."

She said she was happy with her life and found the world a beautiful place:

"It is to me, you know. I like it, yes. I'm quite happy with it. There's sad things in it, a lot of those are beyond my control, I can only voice my opinion about them. Doesn't mean to say it gets you anywhere, but whatever we do here, we do ourselves. You should know right from wrong, each and every one of us shouldn't we? … and this is part of the trouble in the world, people will not help one another as they should. People want something all the time, they won't do something for nothing and I don't think that's the way of life to be. I'm quite happy with my life, I'm happy with my lot."

Mrs Bright possessed a strong faith that enabled her to cope with her husband's illness and death. She had managed this by helping others at every opportunity. She acknowledged the influence of her early years on her beliefs, the joyfulness and humour that she associated with religion and the church. She felt called to service. However, she had no rosy view of life. She saw it as hard and difficult. But she firmly believed she would never be asked to bear too great a burden, one that she could not manage. She said that she would never change her beliefs. They were an essential part of her personality. She was at peace with them.

'Listening' to written expression of beliefs in later life

The brief mention of our initial bereavement study in *SAGA Magazine*, a specialist magazine for older people, led to many readers writing to us with their comments. Over a period of seven months more than a hundred letters were sent to the research team. Many of these letters were extremely long and detailed. Some used it as an opportunity to speak of past traumas, and help was given where possible. This consisted of a gentle and understanding reply outlining the statutory or voluntary help available in their area, and the offer to be of further help if necessary. A substantial number of letters were from bereaved older people. Some wrote about the importance of their belief systems, and their satisfaction or dissatisfaction with the support received from their local faith communities or the Church in general.

This led to our second study. Fortunately, the publishers of *SAGA Magazine* were interested in their role in generating interest in this topic and published a second article, *Does the Spirit Move You?*. This ended with an invitation to readers to comment on the supportive nature of their religious/non-religious beliefs in later life, and the impact on their beliefs by churches and/or other faith communities. Nearly 450 older people responded, and the mean age was 70.

They expressed their comments freely, negative as well as positive:

> I read somewhere that you are engaged in research about the Churches. Over the years I have taken an interest in the shenanigans of the C of E.

In some cases people felt abandoned by their childhood faith, with others expressing feelings of disillusionment. Many of the letters were anguished:

> I lost my wife five years ago and my daughter to cancer last July. The support I didn't get from the church I had attended and supported for over 30 years has led me to break off all association with it. If you feel I can help you with the research please contact me!

> In Germany I was confronted by the indescribable horrors of Belsen. My faith was shot down. … I value the moral teaching of the church, but spiritually it has become an outdated ritual that has little meaning for me.

> During the war my family became very involved in the local Church of England – there was such a need to unite and pray in those dangerous times. I continued with a very firm faith, and in my twenties became a full-time evangelist in the C of E. However, when I married in my thirties, and had to face the realities of normal life I began to question the faith. In my forties, as a result of teaching in inner ring Birmingham, I became very interested in the faiths and cultures of the children

in my care. I took a Multi-Cultural Education Degree, and became very involved teaching in that subject area. This all continued my questioning of the Christian faith, not only as the church interpreted it, but also in the tenets of belief. After retirement my husband became very ill, and I cared for him for five years, watching him suffer terribly. This resulted in the end of my faith for me. I could not get around the 'God of love' doctrine and the problem of pain. So I have become a Humanist – a philosophy of life which I now feel I held from the beginning.

I have been a church member since I joined a choir at the age of eight and am now in my seventieth year. For most of that time I have been a faithful and regular attender. I have held most of the offices open to lay persons and have been a member of numerous committees. I became Headmaster of a Church Primary School and was a governor, and for two years Chairman of Governors of a Church Secondary School. My week did not seem complete unless I had worshipped and worked for the faith I held. In 1992 I retired to another area ... I still attended, but some of the sparkle had gone, but I attributed this to the difference in attitude of the two churches and soldiered on. In May of last year I returned to live in my old area and anticipated a renewal of zeal when once again in my old haunts. It has not proved to be so. I can hardly believe how easily I can forgo Sunday worship and have determined not to get involved in any of the groups available. I try to convince myself that it is not a lack of faith, but is due to disillusionment with the practices of the church and the behaviour of some of the clergy. I am not sure that I have succeeded. I want to believe, or a great deal of my life has been futile, but I cannot pretend that the situation is other than as it is.

Some felt they had no need of a religious belief and were untroubled by this absence of belief. They appeared to be quite content:

I have had a long life sustained by the Arts – music and visual arts, which may have displaced any desire for a spiritual search or a need for a belief. I do believe that people are disillusioned (with their beliefs) in old age because they have had naïve beliefs in the beginning.

I think it is probably my stance as a Humanist paradoxically makes me interested in people's attitude to religion. I feel it is so peripheral to real life yet so many people seem unable to envisage being without what I consider to be 'fairy tales'. I wanted to make a contribution to counter those who would be sure to participate from a religious standpoint.

Many felt that their Christian faith had developed over time and was now stronger than earlier in life. Often this had been as a result of a variety of life events which had led to a re-examination of their beliefs. Sometimes this had led to abandoning their belief, but frequently it had led to reaffirmation:

> Beware the Slough of Despond! The ecumenical movement in this country is an encouraging advance, while world-wide steadfastness, even in places of persecution, is inspiring. The existence of God is incontrovertible because God is life.

> I now have more time to consider the Glory of God and wonder at His creation of the world.

> We are both in our 70s – full of life and enthusiasm for living. We are aware of many people's attitudes towards faith, belief, and raison d'être within our age-group, and in some instances this is very sad. Yes, we've had our share of bereavements, health problems and pains, and various family situations, but that does not influence our faith – only enhances it and strengthens our belief. Churches in general seem to try to please all the people all the time giving a watered-down interpretation of what Christianity is all about, and so many people who have never really 'got the message' tend to fall into this disillusioned group. I won't go on any more, but I just wanted you to know that we want to redress the balance in that there are many older folk about who have an enthusiastic attitude towards the meaning in our lives.

> We DO hope you will include us in your research.

Others, too, wanted it known that they were supported by their faith and that they very much enjoyed life and the communities in which they lived. They stressed the fact that they found life fun. They had a zest for living life to the full:

> From much of the Radio and TV one could think that the over 60s are depressed and whingeing. I want people to know that many of us love life. We have so much to give (school governors, trustees of charities etc) and we have a positive outlook. Older Christians find real fellowship and fun in their churches. I'd like others to know this.

> I consider we live in an Ageist society. I never felt the urge to burn my bra, but I might lash out with my walking stick sometime in the future if I find myself treated like some elderly people I have seen. The spiritual life is often disregarded these days and it means a lot to some elderly people. I suppose the afterlife or lack of it is uppermost in one's

thoughts in the wee small hours as one gets older, but surprisingly it doesn't give cause for concern.

All letters received an individual, friendly and personalised response, addressing any concerns that were expressed. One such example is given below:

Dear Mr ....,

Thank you for replying to my request for your help with our study, and I am most grateful to your wife for filling in the questionnaire also.

I well understand your antipathy towards quantifying beliefs, sharing your views somewhat myself, but I thought I should answer some of your queries as your views are valuable. 'The Royal Free Questionnaire' was developed by Dr Michael King and Revd. Peter Speck (now the senior chaplain at Southampton General Hospital) while they were based at the Royal Free Hospital in London. As you say, it is very difficult to measure beliefs, but this questionnaire has proved sound in a number of studies and does highlight the strength of belief (whatever that belief might be).

Having read your writings, you appear to me to be a very strong believer, however others are not. There does seem to be a correlation between strength of belief and well-being, but that is only one part of our study. We really want to find out what changes to churches and other faith communities might help support beliefs in later life. We also need to demonstrate to others that encouraging/ supporting belief will improve quality of life. This might seem self-evident to strong believers but not everyone in authority/government who could influence change is a believer. Studies into beliefs in later life are very sparse in this country (unlike America). We are really just beginning the task which was influenced by Professor Peter Coleman's finding in the Southampton longitudinal ageing study that beliefs in late life tended to decline. This was only a small number and it is not possible to say this is a trend but the findings were worrying (or as academics say, interesting!) enough to investigate this further.

For me this study certainly is fascinating but it is above all very worthwhile. Many people have written to me and shared many life experiences. Some painful, some joyous. All have wanted to try to help. I hope to encourage their voices to be heard by others.

With all good wishes and thank you once again for your letter

Marie

This second study found that older people had much to say about their beliefs, but also had suggestions for practical changes in faith communities. They felt these changes would be beneficial to all. Primarily they felt that buildings used for worship needed to change, to provide more comfortable amenities and to be used for other purposes besides services. They felt that the church as building was a valuable resource for the community. They felt that services should not be too long and many wanted them to be age appropriate. The more traditional services were often held too early for older worshippers, who, although they appreciated the need to have family-orientated services, were uncomfortable with the style of such services. One older person wrote:

> I went last week and the vicar tied all the pews up with string and I thought to myself 'What's this all about then?' It didn't suit me at all.

Many asked that sermons should be shorter and more interesting. They should not contain too much 'deep and dry theology'. Another participant wrote, 'They are not an opportunity for a lecture!' But, as later comments show, this did not mean that they were uninterested in learning and exploring more about their beliefs.

Fellowship was also seen as important. If people weren't at a service it was felt that someone should make it their business to enquire if all is well. Various activities were also proposed. One suggestion was for a monthly Sunday lunch for older parishioners, and for more social activities geared towards their needs. Yet they did not want to be mere recipients in these changes. They argued for 'challenge not chaplaincy'. Many wrote that older people want to be 'used' in the church, and want to be asked to do more. But there was a fear that offering to help might lead to rejection. Some wrote that they needed to be challenged to do more by the clergy and others. But there was a recognition that older people were not used to challenging authority. In addition, there was a definite interest in learning more about their faith. Suggestions to meet this need included forming discussion groups to discuss the sermon and points of common interest.

One of the most moving aspects of this research came from a 73-year-old male retired manual worker, Mr Robbie Belman. He described himself as a thinker with philosophical beliefs, and was deeply interested in the project. He wrote the following letter:

> *Dear Marie,*
>
> *I hope this letter finds you well. By the time you read this, you will have received my part two of the project, which I hope you will find interesting. (For my part it's been great!) I feel a bit silly writing this, but I am sure you will see what I am about when I explain. My family know I'm from the SE London backstreets. And all that goes with it. So I have been having a laugh with them with regard to my implication in our project, with me saying, 'Your Dad's a university student. How about that!' Anyway, this has led me to*

wonder if you could possibly issue me with a kind of mock diploma for having been part of the study, for which I feel proud. …

PS I understand if it's not possible.

A result of this letter was that all participants were offered a certificate of course completion. Half of the sample accepted. Mr Belman wrote to tell us that his certificate was now framed and hanging in pride of place in his sitting room. It meant a great deal to him. This finding will inform future work. Perhaps expressing gratitude to older participants who take part in research might not always require monetary reward.

Above all, this study revealed the untapped need for older people to demonstrate a lively interest in their beliefs and to express their joys, fears, doubts and anger to an interested 'other'. The participants used the questionnaires as an opportunity to express their views, often developing their comments to a particular question. One of the questions in the Royal Free Questionnaire on Beliefs and Experiences asks 'Have you ever had an intense experience (unrelated to drugs or alcohol) in which you felt some deep new meaning in life, felt at one with the world or universe or experienced God? It might have been for a few moments, hours or even days.' The majority of participants felt they had, and went into some detail, adding extra pages.

We received many letters of thanks for our work and warmly expressed gratitude for the opportunity to share their thoughts and feelings about something that was deeply personal. Some sent cards and continued to do so on important holidays. Many participants were sad that the project had ended and offered us further help. Some two years later, those who were able took part in further projects with other researchers who reported a warm response to their requests.

Perhaps some final words from several participants who took part in these studies will underline this. They are a mixture of thanks to the Southampton team who undertook the research, together with continued questioning of beliefs and values and testimonies:

> May I say how glad I am that I saw this in SAGA and responded. It has enabled me to express feeling lying dormant to someone highly professional and confidential. One's life is so important … but being able to acknowledge this to oneself and a comparative stranger is so helpful, thank you.

> I have found it very valuable to think things over and to try to express my feelings in words for the first time. Because, in a way, all my life has been a search for something, which may be God. I have assiduously thought about it. The only way we can come to understanding is through our own experiences.

I see the practice of my faith as a time of quiet each day, making all the difference to my outlook, relationships and work.

As I have grown older (and been left alone) I have become increasingly reliant on worship and prayer, both private and collective, to confirm that life still has purpose and meaning, and to help one cope with problems, anxieties and decision making. They have become an essential discipline to control self-centredness, and help one reach out to others.

I was created by a God who loves me, and who has a special role for me on earth. My life is a journey of pilgrimage. True happiness is found in trying to follow His will for my life.

The final quotation comes from a longer testimony that was kindly offered to us. It is a very interesting description of losing a faith that had once meant much to the person in question. Such testimonies are of great value in trying to understand the dynamics of belief throughout life:

Up to the age of 10 my brother and I occasionally went to Sunday School.... There is a clear date of conversion – during a Remembrance Sunday Service I felt a huge response of love for Jesus who had died for my sins. I went to see the Baptist Minister afterwards and he emphasised the importance of remembering this date when I 'gave my heart to Jesus'.

At school I became President of the Student Christian Movement … enrolled for a 2 year Diploma Course in an evangelical college and subsequently remained to take the University of London BD (Bachelor of Divinity).... During this time I ... became an Anglican. I was aware that as a person I needed some beauty and 'spirit' and less 'word' and I found it … also found other books on spirituality which resonated for me in a way that evangelical thought didn't. All the guilt I'd been carrying around for years – I found that I wasn't alone in struggling with 'wrong' feeling, doubt etc etc. … For some time the intellectual questions – Does God exist? Is it true? etc were not in any way the ones I was addressing. Over time I recognised that I had turned to the church amidst big changes at home and uncertainty about my parents' marriage (which had broken).

Here I found a safe haven, people 'who cared' and, above all, a Father who would hold me whatever happened. But … I found rules and Christian peer pressure. Now, many years later I felt angry about an institution that stifles and sometimes extinguishes individuality within its system. It was hard to stop going but harder to go to services and when I went occasionally I found it increasingly difficult to connect with any of it. ... The other side of the coin was anxiety and a great sense of grief at losing what had been a major part of my life for most of my life. For some time I hoped that my experience was 'a dark night of the soul' one but after all this time I really do not think it is.

I think it is probably impossible for anyone who hasn't been this way to understand that you do not choose to cease to be able to resonate with a dear, deep and long-held faith. In many ways, I long to 'step back inside'. There have been times of terrible fear, grief, yearning – almost unbearable occasionally. My particular journey seems to be deeply emotional in that I cannot find any connection or resonance with any idea of God and all that once connected me with him and the intellectual questions seem irrelevant.

I hope in time to move into some sense of an 'Other beyond' but that is not a part of me at the moment. The anger against the church has long gone but there is a certainty that I never want to be part of it again.

Conclusion

As this chapter shows, encouraging older people to speak about their beliefs and values is not always an easy task. These difficulties are due to a number of reasons. Personal beliefs are perceived as private and are not generally discussed in everyday life. Moreover, following centuries of religious conflict in the UK, there is a wide emphasis on tolerance of beliefs. It may well be that older people are unsure if their beliefs are acceptable to the listener, or even if the listener wishes to discuss them. As a result people are not used to speaking publicly about such matters. It must be remembered that it was not until the 2001 census took place that people were asked to define their beliefs. This remains true even in religious contexts. Our research indicated that a significant number of older people who regularly attended a church did not fully ascribe to the teachings of their particular faith, and that their beliefs were not necessarily discussed with other worshippers.

Reflexive testimony, as in the last example given, is rare. Many older people may have imperfectly formed views and struggle with finding words to express their beliefs and values. They may find it embarrassing unless the listener is patently interested in their search for meaning. However, beliefs and values can be conveyed in other ways through the use of metaphors, or description of a meaningful event accompanied by photographs and other related objects.

Further, there is a need for instruments more sensitively suited to a British population to aid this work. As some participants have pointed out, the wording of questionnaires designed for a North American population are not always suitable and were sometimes seen as an irritant.

We hope that this chapter has emphasised the great importance that we place on the initial invitation offered to older people to take part in research of an intrusive nature, together with the giving of time and patience to older people so that they can convey their narratives. Also, the interest, gentleness and respect with which we have heard their many stories, however they have been 'told' to us. In the 'telling', we have also considered and described in detail the interviewing skills required to undertake such work. The rich stories that have emerged during our research show how important it is to create the personal space to allow these stories and testimonies to be told, and also to be heard.

A final aspect of our research worth stressing is the evident need for consultation expressed by the many older people who contacted us in order to comment on the religious and spiritual services they received from ministers in their Christian churches. Now that 'service user involvement' has become standard practice in the monitoring of quality of health and social services, it is not too much to expect that religious organisations will also seek more to obtain critical as well as appreciative comments from their members. Older people in particular may have had a long experience of religious communities and much to offer from this experience in helping negotiate the inevitable changes and adjustments in styles of worship and religious practice that occur with cultural and social development.

FOUR

Ageing and faith: trajectories across the lifespan

Peter G. Coleman, Marie A. Mills and John H. Spreadbury

Stability and change of spiritual belief in later life

Traditionally older people are expected to be more religious than younger people, and there are good social and psychological reasons for this. Religious leadership is seen as an appropriate role for an older person, and advancing years are associated with increasing spirituality rather than materiality of goals. Discussion of this subject within the social science literature dates back at least as far as William James (1902) and most commentators since then have attributed the association between religion and age to the way religion answers questions about the meaning of life which become more salient as people age (Marcoen, 2005; McFadden, 2005).

Of course it is not only in later life that religion provides a sense of significance, belonging and rootedness to both individuals and societies. But increasing life experience and the growing closeness of death encourage greater reflection on the meaning of life and death. Thus it seems natural that traditional cultures have typically required older people to be the guardians of the community's spiritual values and beliefs that sustain its life, especially in times of crisis. Religion can thus provide older people with an important social function, and this role in turn promotes their sense of generativity and consequently benefits also their mental health (Gutmann, 1997; Coleman and O'Hanlon, 2004).

At the more personal level religious beliefs help to address concerns arising from increasing awareness of limitation and finitude as well as questions about loss and suffering. For example, religion provides resources in responding to questions about survival in states of growing dependency. Early work conducted by Duke University in North Carolina demonstrated the salience of religion, including the use of religious forms of coping, for older people (Blazer and Palmore 1976; Koenig et al, 1988a, b). Subsequent studies have also strongly supported the mental health benefits of religion among ill older people (for example Dillon and Wink, 2007). In fact the empirical evidence suggests that the health associations of religion, from quicker recovery from physical and mental illness to lowered mortality rates, are stronger in older age groups, suggesting an age-related benefit to continued belief (McFadden and Levin, 1996). Also in the UK stronger beneficial associations of strength of spiritual belief with well-being have been found in older people of greater degrees of frailty compared with those less frail but also living in supported housing (Kirby et al, 2004.)

A number of psychological and sociological theorists have developed models and frameworks to explain what may be the processes involved in developing greater religious/spiritual sensitivity with age. These include some of the early pioneers in systematic thinking about lifespan development, such as Carl Jung and Erik Erikson, as well as contemporary theorists, such as James Fowler, Harry Moody and Lars Tornstam (Marcoen, 2005). Often these models involve successive stages of change, which Robert Atchley refers to as awakening interest, inquiry, endeavour, integration and intention (Atchley, 2009). For some the process of spiritual development may involve considerable spiritual struggle but the end result is a new or renewed sense of harmony and direction. More recently there has been an interest in linking this area of research to more mainstream theory in psychology and the social sciences, in regard to motivation for self-enhancement and for control within an uncertain world (Kay et al, 2010; Sedikides and Gebauer, 2010). Attachment theory has also been employed to predict for later life a return to the faith of childhood and the associated memories of parental security (Kirkpatrick, 2004).

There is, therefore, a considerable theoretical background for analysing the content of religious and/or spiritual development that occurs in later life. But at the same time it has to be admitted that a good part of the theories have been developed in relatively stable religious societies (among which the US can be counted) rather than decreasingly religious societies like the UK. There is little evidence as yet that these theories apply to ageing within contemporary Britain and Western Europe. Indeed, not only has it to be taken into consideration that there has been a change in the character and extent of religious education in Europe over the last 50 years (and in diverse ways in Western and Eastern Europe), but that the religiosity of the population has been affected by a rise in numbers of immigrants from more religious societies. As a result one cannot generalise about age differences in religious attachments in the UK. Any existing greater religiosity in the older members of the original population may appear enhanced as a result of declining religious education, whereas many of the newcomers to the country are more likely to be both young and religious.

Most of the evidence to answer questions about religious change and age is limited in explanatory scope because it is cross-sectional. Data from North America and Europe on religious affiliation, belief, prayer and attendance at communal worship demonstrate higher levels of religiosity in older age groups. The latest figures from the US (Population Reference Bureau, 2010) show, for example, that whereas only 53% of those born in 1981 or later believe in the existence of God and 41% pray daily, the corresponding figures for those born in 1945 or before are 70% and more. In the US, these age differences have been found consistently over the last half century during a period of considerable secular change. David

Moberg (2001b) has argued that this suggests the need for a genuine developmental rather than only a historical explanation of these differences.

In most Western European countries there is, compared with the US, an even larger difference between older and younger people in church attendance, and the age at which the change occurs is rising. For example, Anglican censuses in the UK show a large over-representation of the over 55s and a large under-representation of the under 45s at Sunday worship. But this tends to be interpreted more in terms of secular change than human development, with the younger British generations being both less socialised and less well inclined to attend church services than their American peers.

The only exception to rising levels of attendance with ageing is among the very old, which is explainable in terms of their reduced health and mobility, but this is often compensated by increased rates of other forms of religious and spiritual activity. Important evidence from US longitudinal studies of the dying process confirms that older people's religious beliefs and practices such as prayer hold up in the face of death, despite declines in religious participation (Idler et al, 2001).

Longitudinal studies are indeed the only way of demonstrating true change in this area, and there are few such studies over the requisite length of time. By far the most substantial and longest lasting are two Californian studies. The first examined a large number (1,151) of survivors of an original sample of children of high ability recruited throughout California in the pre-war years (McCullough et al, 2005). Data collected at six observation points during their adult years from 1940 to 1991 were analysed to produce measures of religiousness for each occasion. The results demonstrated considerable stability in religious behaviour, with people of high, medium and low religiousness maintaining the same relative position over their lifetimes. At no stage did the three groups overlap. Those of high religiosity tended to become even more religious in their later years, whereas those of medium religiosity increased their religious activities in their middle years and thereafter declined to original levels. The authors interpret the latter finding in terms of the utility benefits of religious membership in the child rearing years.

The second study by Dillon and Wink (2007) has investigated people in Northern California over 60 years and was originally designed as a growth and parenting study. Their analysis of 200 people, now all over the age of 60 years, makes a distinction between religiousness and spirituality, using the terms 'religious dwelling' and 'spiritual seeking' suggested by Wuthnow (1998). Their presentation of findings illustrates a group of older people more prepared to break the norms of conventional religiosity and to embrace the new language of 'spirituality'. They demonstrate an increase in spiritual seeking but at the same time also show great stability of religiousness (although they note that much religious behaviour continues for social reasons). Dillon and Wink are careful to avoid strong conclusions as to whether the relatively small changes they observe are age or period effects. Certainly there seems to have been an influence of the 1960s at work in the greater emphasis on personal choice in religious matters, but this does not rule out developmental effects as well. Nevertheless, the overriding conclusion from their work is also of stability of religious involvement over the course of individual lives and indeed over generations of the same family.

However it is important to place these studies in context. As the US is not representative of the western world, so California is not representative of the US. McCullough et al (2005: 80) note that their 'sample of bright young Californians grew up to be considerably less religious, on average, than the general American public'. Moreover, new spiritual movements are longer established and stronger in California than elsewhere. An earlier study presented findings that showed that less than half of persons aged 85 years and older living in San Francisco stated that religion was important in their lives (cited in McFadden, 1996). Such figures would be expected to be much higher elsewhere in the US. Nevertheless, one of the most useful points that Dillon and Wink make is that it is quite possible for religion and spirituality, also in the new sense of 'spiritual quest', to coexist.

As regards the UK, the little longitudinal evidence that exists suggests greater losses than gains. The Southampton Ageing Project demonstrated a significant decline in religious affiliation among older people in the decade of the 1980s with no recovery occurring in the subsequent decade (Coleman et al, 2004). In addition, Sadler's (2009) analysis of data from the British Household Panel Survey indicated a small decline in importance of spiritual belief in the sample aged over 60 years who were followed over a six-year period from 1991 to 1997. However, even if the Southampton findings could be generalised more widely within the UK, they also need placing in the context of its time, one of major social change in the UK following the economic decline of the 1970s and the opening up of private markets in the Thatcherite period. As Dillon and Wink themselves point out (2007: 209-10) one can make distorting inferences when the focus is only on historical periods as short as 10 or even 20 years.

However the Southampton data also draw attention to a relatively new perspective within social science research on religion and ageing, one that examines the processes of doubting as well as believing. The subject of religious/ spiritual conflict/questioning is a significant growth area in the study of religion (Exline and Rose, 2005). One of the limitations of previous analyses using religious or spiritual indices is that they tend to be based on the assumption that being 'religious' or 'spiritual', once developed in youth, is a relatively fixed and stable characteristic, similar to race, gender and social class. But just as the processes of becoming religious or spiritual when young are interesting in themselves, so also are the possible changes in character or intensity of faith during adulthood. There is a growing realisation that later life, particularly in modern fast-changing societies, far from being a period of stability or consolidation, can be a time of questioning and spiritual turmoil in regard to personal beliefs and values.

A number of studies in the US and the UK suggest a curvilinear relationship between strength of religious involvement and measures of well-being and adjustment, including feelings of self-worth, and death anxiety, with those of uncertain belief doing worse (Kalish and Reynolds, 1976; Krause, 1995; Wink and Scott, 2005; Krause, 2006; Coleman et al, 2007). However, questioning and doubt may be inherent to the ageing process. Indeed, the findings of one study (Krause et al, 1999) supported an Eriksonian view that older people would be more able to tolerate religious doubt with less loss of well-being than younger people because they were actively involved in questioning many aspects of their lives. UK studies, on the other hand, suggest that these findings might not be repeated in a less religious society. Rising rates of uncertain, unsupported and troubled belief have been observed among older people, related to disappointment in ministry offered by clergy, particularly in situations of loss and frailty (Coleman et al, 2004).

The small amount of evidence available both from the US and UK therefore suggests a rise in spiritual questioning with age, and it is the different contexts of the US and the UK that produce the different results. Older Americans already have a well-established language for talking about individual choice and autonomy in religious and spiritual matters. This allows them to refer to new spiritual directions while retaining links to a local church. This is still unusual in Europe, especially for older people, who are more tied to concepts of loyalty to a particular tradition of belief and worship. Conflict with that tradition can more likely lead to isolation.

In the following sections we will explore these issues further at the individual level with samples of British older people drawn from two qualitative longitudinal studies on coping with ageing: successive interviews over 10 years with 70 survivors of the Southampton Ageing Project (already mentioned), and a smaller study of 12 bereaved spouses interviewed one and seven years after their bereavement. We examine the contexts and consequences of changing belief with age. What provokes change and how do such changes affect other areas of the older person's life?

Increasing belief in later life: context and consequences

The Southampton Ageing Project demonstrated a variety of trajectories of belief from a lifelong strong Christian faith to a long-established atheistic worldview, with many variants in between. Numbers appeared evenly balanced between those who had maintained a religious faith and those who had rejected the predominantly Christian culture of their upbringing (Coleman et al, 2004).

Most of those who had maintained their Christian beliefs attributed their faith to the example of their parents. But there were at least two examples of narratives of conversion in young adulthood. Mrs Monroe shared the experience of developing a strong commitment to evangelical Christianity with her husband. They had deliberately chosen when young to live on a poor council estate so that they would be in a better position to help others. Subsequently they had worked together as missionaries abroad. After his death and until her own death in her mid-90s she continued to remain socially very active, and also in the Christian-based residential home where she lived in her last years. Even more striking as an example of sudden change was Mr McGregor's story of being converted by an American Baptist missionary while he was working in India in his early 20s. He referred to this as the most meaningful incident of his long life. Readily accessible in his living room were books of spiritual guidance, including meditations on the Christian scriptures, clearly well used. There were particular passages to which he said he regularly returned.

Of the other 68 participants who were interviewed in greater depth about belief in the later stages of the Southampton Ageing Project, by which time they were all aged over 77 years, none indicated as strong levels of commitment to their faith as these two individuals. But there were some interesting cases of persons who showed an increasing firmness and clarity of faith in late adulthood that could be objectively evidenced over successive interviews in the course of the study. All of these participants were men, which is consistent with the view that men, although generally less demonstrative of religious faith than women, are more likely than women to discover in later life that religious belief is a valuable asset and to become less inhibited in expressing it. Taken together with observations of women's greater inclination towards growing scepticism, a hypothesis has been suggested of a gender cross-over effect with age in religious feelings (Gutmann, 1987; Henry, 1988; Coleman et al, 2004). For most of the men concerned in this study the change in feelings was demonstrated in growing identification with a particular faith throughout later adulthood.

Harry Parker

The best documented example of this type of trajectory was Mr Parker, who had first been interviewed in 1978 at the age of 69 years, and was interviewed on a further nine occasions over the following 22 years. In his youth he had been an active member of a political party, but had then become disillusioned with political work. Although baptised a member of the Church of England, he had converted to Roman Catholicism, his wife's religion, in his 40s. Regular attendance with her at the celebration of Mass had been the key influence. Over time he had gradually taken on increasing responsibilities at his local church. Following the new opportunities for lay people's service after the reforms of the Second Vatican Council, he had become a special Eucharistic minister, serving alongside the priest in administering the sacred host and wine to fellow parishioners at the time of communion. He was also licensed to give communion to sick and disabled members who were unable to attend Mass. He said on a number of occasions that he greatly enjoyed his life in the church, and saw it as a continuation of his vocation to help other people. References to the church featured strongly among the examples he gave to illustrate statements relating to his generally positive sense of self (Coleman et al, 1993). But it was clear that his beliefs were more than sources of self-esteem. They also provided demanding goals that allowed for the possibility of failure. In 1990 his described his main fear as being unable "to live up to my ideals" and his goal as "to really earn my eternal reward".

Mr. Parker's wife died after a short illness in 1993. Interviews conducted during the same year showed that he regarded his strong religious beliefs as essential in coming to terms with her suffering and his bereavement. In fact he was not unduly distressed by her death:

> "I knew she was where she wanted to go, she wasn't afraid to die, she was quite prepared for the life which had been prepared for her, she was no longer suffering and it was really a great relief and happiness that she was happy and there was no sense of being morbid and worrying about it."

He was also prepared to witness to his beliefs in the face of his wife's death. He provided testimony within the church itself to strengthen other people's faith in the life beyond death:

> "I did put a little bit in the [church] newsletter that we mustn't be sorry for ourselves but happy for her, and people remarked at the Requiem [Mass] that I did seem quite happy, not too distressed at all, which was strange enough what I was feeling. ... I was only lonely when I was here on my own, which I was sometimes."

Later the same year Mr Parker married a lifelong friend whom he and his wife had shared. She was a Methodist, and they continued to lead an active social life centred on both their churches. When interviewed in 1995 he read our written account of his life and strongly agreed with us that religious faith constituted his principal source of identity. The second Mrs Parker developed dementia and suffered a series of falls before her death in March 2000, which again Mr Parker bore with a strong expression of faith.

When interviewed explicitly on the subject of his beliefs in September 2000 at the age of 90 years, he said that his conversion to Roman Catholicism had been the "right" decision for him. The feeling of God's presence in his life had got stronger as he had got older. He expressed a very high level of strength of belief to the items on the new questionnaire that we administered to him (Royal Free Questionnaire on Spiritual Beliefs, King et al, 2001). He also described a strong belief in "destiny", that his life had been mapped out by God, a view he had already expressed 20 years before, and also at the time of his first wife's death. The concept of destiny, as noted in Chapter Two, has similarities with belief in 'fate' but also crucial differences. Mr Parker experienced God as "looking after us" and "giving us nudges in the right direction". Therefore it was so important to listen to God throughout life. Mr Parker talked to God in prayer every day asking for advice, and "usually [got] a reply". God had certainly bolstered him after the death of his first wife. Without Him he said he "would be nothing".

He had no idea of the form life after death would take, but expected that it would be a "pleasant surprise". He believed that we were on trial in this life and that our behaviour would determine the nature of life in the hereafter. In support of this view he mentioned Christ's reference to 'His Father's many mansions'.

Mr Parker interpreted this as meaning life in varying degrees. Both after his first and second wife's deaths, he had felt their presence. In fact he had "seen" his second wife come into the living room. This had been a positive experience, but interestingly he said he was also "mystified" by it, because he wondered what the point of the experience had been. He did not need proof of life after death.

A short time after this interview Mr Parker moved into sheltered accommodation in the North of England near where his son lived. He wrote to the research team in Southampton saying that he had settled in well, and that his new parish priest had called on him the day after he arrived. He died a year later in October 2001, two days before what would have been his 92nd birthday.

Other examples of strengthening belief included Mr Rowan and Mr Thwaites. At the beginning of the study in 1978 Mr Rowan indicated that he and his wife sometimes attended church services in his local Church of England parish, but gave no indication that it was a very important element in his life, which revolved very much around his wife. They had not been able to have children but had become inseparable as result. Her death in 1996 was a devastating experience for Mr Rowan as he had never imagined life without his wife. However, after a period of prolonged grieving he did make a surprisingly good recovery, which he attributed in large part to his religious faith. Although he had always believed in the "Good Lord" he said that religion had come to mean much to him after his loss. He confirmed the same again three and six years later. He said he felt "very close" to God on a personal level, thanked Him for a happy married life, and also for being with his wife when she died. However, he received much less help from his church than did Mr Parker. Indeed, when he ceased to be able to walk up the hilly road towards it, and therefore stopped attending services, he said that he received no enquiries from his church community. Nevertheless, Mr Rowan did not complain but relied on the strong relationship that he had built up with God through prayer. He also appreciated the regular visits he received from Salvation Army visitors. But in the last interview we held with him at the age of 99 years he specifically asked us to make contact with his local Anglican minister on his behalf.

Mr Thwaites was also one half of a devoted couple. In the early stages of the project, when he was in his late 60s, he gave ambivalent answers to the question whether religion meant much to him and did not accompany his wife to church. However, 10 years later he expressed more positive attitudes and by his mid-80s was regularly attending church with his wife. Although agreeing that his own faith was not as strong as his wife's, he said that he had now become a "believer" and tried to live accordingly. He also referred to "faith" as becoming an important theme in his life.

Even more dramatic was the case of Mr Rank. A man of great self-confidence, both physically and socially (he had built his own house and successfully raised five children from two marriages, his first wife having died of meningitis during the Second World War), he was shaken at the age of 70 by the rapidly developing dementia of his second wife and signs of his own incipient physical disability.

Ten years later his sense both of failure in coping with his wife's condition (she had died in a residential care home) and of his own decline had led him almost to the point of despair:

> "I haven't coped you see, that's the point, I haven't coped, not without help, and I object to having help."

His recovery from low mood took a further eight years and encompassed a change of attitude to life from extreme active mastery to greater acceptance of help and of his own limitations. Although he had attributed no significance to religion in his early interviews, religious belief seemed to play an important role in this late-life development. He referred to praying every evening, something he had not mentioned before. But he said that he had started praying again after his second wife died. His initial comments on prayer were hesitant because he imagined his sons would laugh if they heard. He reminisced about attending Sunday school in the local parish church, singing in the choir, and being confirmed. He had recently contacted the vicar asking for his cremated remains to be buried in the churchyard. It was, he said, important to teach religion to children. Even if they did not take up a religious life when they were young, it was always something to which they could go back.

By the end of his life (he died just beyond the age of 90) he had achieved a considerable measure of resolution, and could describe his life in positive terms, although he remained concerned and worried about the decline of values in the society around him. He said his only remaining aims were "to live until I am 90" and then "to join my two wives".

Margaret Jennings

Although there were examples of continuing strong belief on the part of many women in this longitudinal study, the best example of strengthening of belief came from a female participant in our second study, which followed bereaved older spouses over the course of seven years. Although both her parents had been religious and she had often attended services when young, Mrs Jennings' attendance at church declined as she became adult, and it was only in later life that her faith has become very strong. She attributed this to the friendliness and atmosphere of the Salvation Army, whose services she began to attend regularly in her early 60s, when a close friend who had been a member of the Army died. In fact it had been Mrs Jennings' husband who had suggested taking this step, and she quoted him as saying, "'I thought they were ever so good, can we go there next time, dear?'"

At the time she had been a little taken aback:

"I felt a little bit 'Oh, well you wouldn't come to congregational church where I was married and had been brought up more or less, but you want to go there!'"

However, they had been made to feel so welcome that they soon asked to become 'adherents', a stage before becoming a 'soldier'. She quoted from the testimony that she gave when she joined the Salvation Army:

"It is almost a year ago that we started worshipping with you all here, and as most of you know it came about through the sad loss of our very dear friend Edith. It is said that God works in mysterious ways and how true that is. How strange that from losing one soldier from your midst you should gain two new people who have now become adherents. I don't know whether 'gained' is the right word for the Salvation Army, I know it is certainly the right word for us, we've certainly gained a lot. From the first Sunday morning that we came along, we've been made so very welcome and we've come to know what friendliness and fellowship mean. Whereas once we looked on Sunday as a day we didn't have to go to work, we now look forward to being with you all, and with the Lord, and we have discovered so much more meaning to our lives. Thank you Edith. I am sure you're happy that, through you, we have found our place here and thank you Lord for leading our lives in the right direction. One of Edith's friends said to me recently, 'Now that you go to Salvation Army does that mean you've come to love the Lord?' My reply was that we'd always loved the Lord but never until now found the right place to express our feelings. I know that here we have found the right place."

Practical help was the feature that struck her about the Salvation Army. Significantly, when she remembered the church of her childhood she focused on a vicar from her early years. She said he was "a real family man, interested in young people. He was lovely. He didn't preach at us, it was his actions."

Members of The Army had supported her after her own husband's death, accompanying her as she searched for a suitable place to bury his ashes and actually digging the hole near a tree where they placed them, and praying together after the ashes were buried. Like Mr Parker she believed in a personal destiny, and trusted God was with her at times of need:

"I know there are tragedies and people say, 'Well, why could God let that happen?', but I just feel that there must be a reason, I just feel God is there in time, not just all the time, but particularly in times of need. I mean I felt very close to God when I lost my husband. There are times when I really feel, you feel you can talk to Him. I mean nobody knows for sure, but you just feel that there is another Presence, you know, and that you can talk to Him."

When interviewed six years later she had successfully overcome an operation for cancer, still missed her husband greatly, but was generally coping well. Her religious attitudes had remained constant. In fact her scores on the strength of belief scale had increased. Elsewhere in the interview she described her beliefs as "very strong, 90%, 95%". She referred to the role of the Salvation Army in their strengthening:

> "I've always believed in some other being, something greater than we are ... but now I have the feeling that God is there in the background all the time. He's watching over you and you feel you could turn to Him in prayer when you need Him."

She spoke in detail about her practice of prayer and also about her love of music, and how the two connected together. She played the piano when the Salvation Army visited a local block of council flats once a week, and had been invited back to accompany other church services. She had adopted one particular melody, *Jesus You Are Changing Me*, as a "signature" tune:

> "I'll sit and play that before I close the piano up, you know, it's a lovely one that one, and I find that one is on my mind quite a lot – *Jesus You Are Changing Me*."

Decreasing belief in later life: context and consequences

The evidence from these two longitudinal studies would suggest a growing security of religious faith and of importance attributed to it with increasing age in those who had already attained some measure of faith commitment to Christianity. But it does not necessarily follow that increasing religiosity is a feature of ageing. This may well be so in a highly religious society such as the US, but in an increasingly secularising society like the UK, which has become more open to questioning of religious faith, it seems that older people themselves can also be subject to doubt.

As mentioned earlier, the evidence from the Southampton Ageing Project is consistent with a hypothesis of a gender cross-over effect in regard to ageing and religious faith, with women, in contrast to men, appearing to show increased questioning of faith as they aged. This may, at least in part, reflect an increased questioning of many previously accepted features of life among older contemporary women. Most women of their generations had accepted socialisation into religion along with other social institutions when they were young, perhaps to a greater degree than men of the same generations.

In fact it is quite rare to find older British women who already indicated lack of religious faith prior to the Second World War, and these provide interesting case studies in themselves. One such case in the Southampton Ageing Project was Mrs Shields. She had been brought up in Scotland within the Episcopalian church. By the age of 13 years she had actually wanted to become a nun, and she still attended church sometimes on her visits back to Scotland. But her mind she said "had broadened" when, together with friends, she began attending philosophical debates organised by the local Unitarian church at the age of 19 in 1922. She had subsequently studied all the world religions and found them interesting, but also the cause of conflict. Her eventual husband was a Protestant from Northern Ireland, and a dedicated "Orangeman" who went back every year for the 12th July parades commemorating victory over the Catholic army of James II at the Battle of the Boyne. She described vividly her own experience of the drumming and its "jungle like" effects. Sectarianism was so ingrained there, she said, that it would take a very long time to eradicate.

She was confident in her own views. In fact she had "taken aback" the local Anglican minister when she asked him not to pray with her after her husband died as she "would feel uncomfortable, also for him". Nonetheless, she remained open to other people's faith. Like her father, who also did not believe, she had brought up her own children to go to the local Anglican church and make their own decision, and her younger son in fact had become a regular worshipper. She felt strongly that ministers should visit their parishioners more, especially those who no longer went to church. She thought there had been more pastoral care provided by the churches in the past.

Mrs Shields was unusual in her views. Most of those interviewed as part of the Southampton Ageing Project who had distanced themselves from their churches of origin had done so at a later stage of life. Some expressed discomfort with this. Mrs Willis, for example, was nostalgic about the past and did not like the ways in which society had changed. She remembered how as a child she had gone to church three times a day on a Sunday, both to morning and evening service, and to Sunday school in the afternoon. It had meant a lot of walking. She still felt shame about not attending church much as an adult. As she commented: "we all pray when we are in trouble; God must think 'They only come to me then!'" But her husband's death of cancer at the age of 63 in 1966 had led her into a prolonged period of depression. It had also made her start questioning things that she had previously taken for granted, such as the truth of the Bible and its accounts of creation. She remembered once asking "and who made God?" and being disturbed by her own question. Yet she marvelled at the detail and perfection of created organisms, and argued often with one of her sons about the theory of evolution, which he had come to embrace with enthusiasm.

The length of the Southampton Ageing Project allowed us to witness loss of church allegiance in a number of women in the study. In the initial three interviews with Mrs Chester, in 1978–80, she reported regularly attending Mass at her local Roman Catholic church and that religion had actually come to mean more to her than when she was younger. She was then aged in her later 60s. But 10 years later, and following her husband's death, she expressed the completely opposite view and also a declining allegiance to the Roman Catholic church. Dissatisfaction with her church eventually led her to cease to be a practising member and to join a Pentecostal group in her neighbourhood where she felt included in activities and not discriminated against on the basis of age. She particularly appreciated having younger people in the church as friends:

> "It compensates for me not having had a family. I take interest in their progress in life. … It gives me a new interest to follow daily life. … They have babies, they have studies and exams."

She felt that "born again Christians" really cared for one another. This was very important to her because as a child she said she had not known "the love of a true mother". But at the same time she kept in contact with a previous Catholic parish priest who had become her friend.

In the ensuing years Mrs Chester appeared to move towards a sense of belief in God less rooted in particular church membership. By the time she was 80 years old she described a feeling that God was looking after her, helping her to go in the right direction and that she was thankful for what she had received in life from Him. She stressed her interest in "beautiful things, beautiful flowers and beautiful furniture". In her later 80s she again said that religion itself did not mean as much to her as when she was younger, but repeated that God was looking after her. She appeared to have come to see her relationship with God as separate from the practice of a particular religion. But at the age of 90 years, when she could not live alone any more, it was her old friend the priest who found her a place in a care home which was run by an Irish Catholic family.

Mrs Willis, another previously very active church member, also came to express huge disappointment with her church, but for different reasons. In the first part of the study she said that she regularly attended services in the local cathedral, and also on weekdays, but 10 years later, at the age of 76 years, she had separated from High Church Anglicanism. She later commented that she had come to disapprove of church hierarchy and the "traditional side" of religion. But she did not join another Christian denomination and instead moved to a practical belief in learning from one's own mistakes and "never giving up". She had received hard knocks in life, being deserted by her husband soon after the birth of her second son and losing one of her sons some years before our first interview. Although she said she no longer subscribed to religious beliefs she made ready references to God. Like Mrs Chester she felt she could obtain guidance from God without the mediation of a church. A strong example of her faith attributions was her statement in our last interview with her that she had come to accept her son's death as God's will.

The influence of bereavement

Bereavement appeared to be a source of decline as well as of increase of faith. In fact decline was especially marked among widows (Coleman et al, 2004). This may seem surprising considering the benefits of belief in an afterlife that is an essential part of orthodox Christianity and that will be discussed in more detail in the following chapter. But some women as well as men seemed shaken in their faith after the loss of a spouse. One woman commented after her husband's death that she no longer knew what to believe in. Some at least of the loss of faith seemed related to the church's failure to meet expectations. Since it was precisely at the time of bereavement that religion was expected to provide its benefits, disappointment with what the church actually provided could be devastating. One man expressed this view in very explicit terms. He had once been an active church member but experienced a sudden distancing after his first wife died suddenly four years before the beginning of the study:

> "I felt very let down with religion, because I was always brought up in the Church of England. ... After the funeral the parson just said 'Cheerio, I'm off', and nobody even bothered whether I was alright or not. ... I've nothing against the church, put it that way ... but it doesn't bother me that I don't go to church. ... I try to do the best I can for everybody ... well, if that's not enough, it's just too bad."

This observation of bereavement as a crisis point for religious allegiance was one of the reasons that led us to want to study older bereaved spouses longitudinally. This confirmed a relationship between duration of pronounced grief and strength of belief, in that those who expressed strong belief whether of a religious or even atheistic humanistic nature seemed to avoid depression more successfully than those whose religious faith was of a weak to moderate nature (Coleman et al, 2007).

Mrs Girton was the most striking example of unease with her level of belief. She expressed moderately high beliefs throughout the study, but tinged with many doubts. She described her father as a believer who attended church regularly, whereas her mother was not a believer. When growing up, she had felt closer to her mother and "distanced" from her father (a man who had been severely traumatised at the sinking of the *Lancastria* in the early stages of the Second World War and to whom she found it hard to become emotionally close). She had been confirmed as a Christian at 15 years of age, and had positive memories of the church to which she belonged during her young adulthood. But her life experiences, including divorce from her first husband, led to loss of faith.

This meant that she had ceased to feel confident in prayer. When asked what prayer meant to her initially she said:

> "It means that I hope someone's listening but I am not sure whether they are or not. I feel hopeful that they are."

She regularly attended church in the hope of regaining her faith, to which she attributed great importance:

> "I hear the church bells ringing … and I think, if you don't go today you're never going to believe in any of it again, so you'd better go and see. … I'm hoping that He might give me some kind of a sign but I don't know what it is. … Life is so easy when you believe in it all and you feel that you're shielded from everything."

She envied others their belief, but nonetheless began to articulate doubts about an omnipotent and all-loving God:

> "I think, well, there He is, wherever He is, and all these people who've died … they can't all be up in the sky somewhere … and He's looking after them. And in actual fact, I don't think I can believe that could possibly be true."

She seemed to have taken on her mother's beliefs and was more inclined to believe in a cold and uncaring fate. Her 'personal meaning' score was very low, and she admitted in our final interview that she was not at peace with her beliefs. She had become less sure about belief in life after death. Mrs Girton seemed an obvious example of a person who could have benefited from spiritual counselling, yet appeared to be receiving no individual pastoral care from her own church. As a result the doubts she expressed were not shared with other members of the community.

Some of the participants in the study were followed up over seven years, and our observations support a gradual bifurcation of religious attitudes, with those whose faith was already stronger becoming even stronger with age and those who faith was weaker becoming weaker still. For example, Mrs Matthew was one of the few in the sample who expressed her faith initially as spiritual rather than religious. Her upbringing was Roman Catholic, and she described her childhood church as a happy and friendly place. She remembered that her grandparents were devout but not her parents. She gave up practising her faith when at university. Despite being an only child, she described her parents as cold and distant (her father, like Mrs Girton's, had also been a victim of the Second World War, returning in a very poor state from a prisoner-of-war camp). She had few memories of her mother's nurture, and her father was very strict and forbidding. One could appreciate how her second husband had given her the protection and love that she had not received as a child, and how great was the loss that she experienced when he died. She believed in a spiritual power that influences our lives, but not to any great extent:

> "I think there is a power … outside ourselves, but I really am not always sure that it does influence our lives. I suppose it influences our

lives from our point of view, because in moments of distress, you sort of think about God, but I don't think that anything comes directly from above to influence our lives."

She did, however, admit the continuing influence of a Catholic upbringing, saying:

"It is too much in one's self that even if in your teenage years or earlier you rebelled against it and you stopped going to church, it is part of yourself, and when I think of something above I think of the Virgin."

But she found this help insufficient:

"I don't think I believe enough to find it soothing or comforting. …
I probably think there is something there, but not something which could relate to me."

Mrs Matthew went to church a few times after her husband died but it did not help. As she explained:

"It upset me more because I couldn't bear all the talk about the departure … allusions to the other world … I didn't want to think of it precisely as that."

She said she found more help from a rabbi who had known her husband than she did from local clergy. Still, by the end of the second year after her bereavement, she indicated that she had started praying again. When asked what it meant to her, she said:

"It means a quiet time. I pray to the Virgin because she takes the place of my mother [she cried]. I also pray to God sometimes."

Clearly Mrs Matthew's bereavement had triggered old sorrows and she was much in need of support, not only to recover from the devastating loss of her husband but also the deep-seated sadness in her life. Her faith, weak as it was, offered only limited help.

Five years later her depression had lifted to some extent but she was still grieving a great deal. Her best friend now seemed to be her husband's rabbi friend, and she indicated that she had come to identify more with the Jewish faith than with Christianity. She had also found solace in Jewish prayer:

"There's a lovely Jewish prayer which I say every night, I've got the book in there, and it says 'We light the candle for the soul of Jonathan, who has left this world, and we are grateful for the love that he has given', or you can include your parents, 'the understanding they have given you and what they have taught you'. And I think that's very important, what they have taught you, you know, because obviously Jonathan's life has had an enormous impact on my life and he is living in me now, you now. So, sort of my attitude's changed."

But any strength of belief in a spiritual power acting in her life had almost completely disappeared. She had lost faith both in God and in "human nature". She remained unsure about an afterlife, which she said she tried not to think about. Like many of the weakly religious older people already referred to in Chapter Two she was more inclined to believe in an impersonal fate operating in matters of both life and death. Fate had brought her and her husband together and had also separated them.

Conclusion

The evidence from both the Southampton studies provides insufficient basis for suggesting major developmental changes in religious and spiritual belief among older adults in the UK. But what they do indicate is a growing clarification of views about belief among older people, either towards or away from religious faith. The changes tend to be subtle, but appear to be towards greater sureness of perspective, perhaps because of the closer awareness of life's end. The data also show that strengthening of religious faith is not an inevitable consequence of the ageing process. Loss of faith is the more striking feature in some biographies. Among such cases in these studies disillusionment appeared to be focused more on the institutional church than on the idea of God itself. Indeed, some have argued (Fowler, 1981) that later life development brings with it a greater universalising of faith, and perhaps therefore a move away from a particular religious identification towards a more general spiritual perspective on life. But there is also little evidence to support such a change of attitude in the current generations of British older people, who understand both religion and spirituality in terms of institutional allegiance. Only a few — Mrs Willis is an example — indicated something akin to what would now be classified as a non-church based form of spiritual belief.

Of the factors involved in maintaining faith into late life, there is striking illustration from the case studies reported in this chapter, as well as in the previous chapters, of the continuing importance of early and especially parental influence. Where believing parents did not provide strong attachment memories, as in the case of Mrs Girton's father, they lacked significant influence, but where they had been a strong source of encouragement, as in the case of Mrs Bright's mother (see Chapter Three), they remained resources with continuing messages. Mrs Bright referred often to her mother, for example as she commented on adjusting both to her husband's dementia and his subsequent death:

"My mother always used to say to us, 'He never gives you a cross without He knows you can carry it.' I never worry on that score. That was always her view. He will never give you a cross unless He knows you can carry it. And I think that's quite true too. And He carried His and we've got to learn to do the same haven't we?"

David Voas and Alasdair Crockett have provided strong quantitative evidence from their analysis of British survey data that by far the main source of religious transmission comes via parents, and that in Britain this influence has been steadily weakening over the last half century and more and is now only effective in about half of cases. Absence of religion on the part of parents, however, is almost always passed on to their children (Voas and Crockett, 2005).

Although religious faith can be transmitted in other ways during adult life, it clearly makes a difference if an element of religious faith has been instilled in childhood. As Mr Rank commented, it was something persons could go back to and build on in later life. His memories of church life when young had been sufficiently positive to encourage him to make contact again as a very old man. At the other extreme are persons who have experienced abuse at the hand of religious educators and who could be left with lifelong anti-religious attitudes but not necessarily with any resolution of their feelings of hurt. Such cases have also been observed in our longitudinal studies (Coleman et al, 2007). It is only in recent years that this important issue of offences against children by religious authorities has received publicity and consideration, also in terms of the effects on their victims' beliefs (Kennedy, 2000). The failure of churches to confront such crimes adequately has greatly exacerbated the harm done.

However, not all cases of development of strong religious or irreligious attitudes can be attributed to early experience. Mrs Monroe and Mr McGregor were interesting examples of adult conversion in our Southampton longitudinal study (see also Coleman et al, 2004). Mr Parker provides an intriguing example of movement from political to religious commitment in the course of adult life. Mrs Shields' case, by contrast, shows that disbelief can also be the result of a process of adult searching.

Bereavement appears to be a key time for testing faith. This was a consistent finding of both the studies from which the illustrative cases in this chapter are taken (Coleman et al, 2004; 2007). As Mrs Jennings commented:

"It is your beliefs that help you to keep going and to cope with everything. As I say, friends and family are very important, but I think you also need something more than that. You need to feel there is something greater than you."

Indeed, the evidence in general, not only from the US, but also the UK, indicates that religion is a significant, although neglected, resource in coping with bereavement (Walsh et al, 2002; Coleman et al, 2007). The following chapter will explore further the means by which religious faith provides sustenance at times of grief over death of a spouse or partner. But, as some of the cases we have cited suggest, there can also be an influence in the opposite direction, where the experiences associated with bereavement lead to questioning of previously held beliefs. Our first study of bereaved older spouses highlighted in particular the problems associated with weak belief. In a sample of bereaved spouses drawn from GPs and funeral directors, those of weak to moderate belief displayed more depressive symptoms and poorer sense of existential meaning over a period of years (Coleman et al, 2007). However it is important to note that the few strong atheist non-believers in the sample also did well, which suggests that level of security in beliefs may be more important than the nature of the belief (an issue we will return to in Chapter Six).

FIVE

Religious responses in coping with spousal bereavement

John H. Spreadbury and Peter G. Coleman

Religion and bereavement

Up until recently the use of religion as a coping resource in circumstances of bereavement has been relatively ignored in both psychology and sociology. Indeed, as Holloway notes in her review of 'negotiating death in contemporary health and social care', little 'intellectually rigorous' attempt has been made to integrate theological (and philosophical) reflection with psychosocial approaches to dying and bereavement (Holloway, 2007: 91). This is particularly surprising when one considers that up to 85% of the world's population is thought to have some kind of religious belief (Sedikides, 2010) and that most if not all religions have specific teaching about the meaning of death. Even more surprising is the fact that neglect of the relationships between religion, death and bereavement also apply within gerontology. Not only are older adults (as we have seen in Chapter Two) the most religiously active members of society in both the US and the UK, but also the rises in life expectancy have led death and bereavement to be increasingly concentrated in the later stages of life.

Religion may be a unique resource with distinct potential benefits or therapeutic properties for helping older adults cope with bereavement. Whereas other factors or resources such as social support, the circumstances of the bereavement, or even counselling may all be involved in coming to terms with a loss, in gradual readjustment, and in preventing social loneliness, these factors may be less helpful in addressing the existential issues or concerns that can be evoked by a significant bereavement and that may also become more important in later life. In this respect religion can provide sources of meaning or ways of understanding bereavement, loss, and death that can be experienced as more personal, profound or philosophical than reliance on rational details about the loss itself and may in different ways be experienced as helpful or beneficial. Indeed, there is much anecdotal evidence to testify to the usefulness of religion in circumstances of bereavement.

For most British older adults, religion, or more specifically the Christianity with which they were brought up, may at some residual level still be an important influence, particularly at times of death. As discussed in Chapter Two, the majority of contemporary British older adults were socialised during a much more religious time when attendance at Sunday school was a frequent occurrence. As such, Christianity is still a part of the identity of most British older adults even if religion is not now a central part of their life. They may have made at some point in their lives a conscious decision to reject the Christianity of their upbringing, but the ideas that they were presented in childhood are still likely to provide a link which allows them to return to religion at times of crisis such as bereavement. Unlike other potential resources that can decline in later life or may be more difficult to acquire (for example, social support from friends or family, financial resources, health), religion is a potentially accessible resource available to all regardless of socioeconomic status, education, gender or living circumstances.

With regard to the empirical literature on religion and bereavement, a recent systematic literature review by Becker et al (2007) has highlighted that as few as 32 studies met their strict theoretical, methodological and statistical criteria for inclusion. These studies were published between 1990 and 2005, involved participants ranging in age from 14 to 93 years, and covered a time since bereavement from 1 month to 41 years. Becker et al found that in 94% of the studies religious or spiritual beliefs had a positive influence on bereavement outcome.

Of the few studies that have been conducted specifically with older age groups, again mainly positive results have been identified. For example, in a Canadian sample of older adults (aged 65 to 87 years) who had experienced recent spousal bereavement, Fry (2001) found that the importance of religion, spiritual beliefs and practices, and accessibility to religious support were all predictors of increased psychological well-being. In addition, in a longitudinal study of British adults (mean age 53 years) who had experienced a range of recent bereavements, Walsh et al (2002) found that those with a strong spiritual belief showed faster resolution of their grief over the first 14 months following bereavement compared with those for whom spiritual belief was less important. Furthermore, in a separate study of British older adults (aged 61 to 89 years), Coleman et al (2007) found that those with a strong religious belief reported lower depression and increased personal meaning during the second year following spousal bereavement compared with those for whom religious belief was less important.

However, the review of the literature by Becker et al (2007) highlights a number of limitations and omissions in the research examining religion's influence in bereavement that deserve consideration. For example, very few studies have focused exclusively on older adults or have investigated responses specifically to the loss of a spouse. Also, only a small number of studies have been conducted outside of North America, with Becker et al (2007) highlighting as few as two studies conducted in Britain. Other limitations that can be discerned include the fact that religious findings have seldom been linked to existing bereavement theories, while only a limited range of religious responses and religious content have been identified.

With some of these limitations in mind it was the aim of a study conducted by Spreadbury (2010) to investigate the religious responses to spousal bereavement in older adults with a strong religious belief and to attempt to identify the actual content of Christian belief and the religious practice that are experienced as most helpful or beneficial in coping. As part of this process the study also aimed to identify whether religious belief and practice are used in meaning reconstruction: that is, the processes of making sense of one's bereavement, identifying some benefit from the loss, and experiencing a change in identity that are considered to be central to grieving (Gillies and Neimeyer, 2006). Semi-structured interviews were conducted with 26 older widowed adults and analysis of transcripts was conducted using Interpretative Phenomenological Analysis (IPA). IPA is a qualitative method of analysis that attempts to understand how people make sense and interpret some aspect of their personal world. Using this approach four main themes were identified – benevolent religious cognition, Biblical assurances, religious ritual, and spiritual capital – that accounted for the main ways that this sample of participants used their religious belief and practice in coping with spousal bereavement. The following sections provide a brief description of each theme and offer a brief case study account to illustrate the role played by each theme in the overall coping experience for that particular case. A much fuller account of the interview material and the analysis is presented in Spreadbury (2010).

Benevolent religious cognition

The first theme, labelled benevolent religious cognition, attempted to represent and capture the primary religious cognition and beliefs that were expressed as most salient to coping and meaning making. The beliefs that were central to benevolent religious cognition included belief in a God, who was characterised as benevolent, omnipresent, and omniscient; belief in a life after death; belief in a life after death reunion with one's spouse (and other loved ones); feeling a sense of providence (that is, the protective care of God); and having confidence in prayer as a method of appealing to God and deceased loved ones for support, protection, or guidance. These benevolent beliefs were then used in the meaning-making processes of sense making and benefit finding. For example, benevolent religious beliefs about the bereavement being part of a plan or purpose known to God for either the deceased or the bereaved, or the bereavement occurring in accordance with God's will, and belief that present suffering is ultimately linked with future compensation in heaven, were used in sense making. Also, benevolent religious cognition involving belief about the deceased being in a better, safer place (that is, heaven) and no longer suffering (a consolation of course also for those without religious beliefs), and belief about the deceased spouse achieving their spiritual goal of ascending to or entering heaven, were used in benefit finding. These benevolent beliefs and meaning-making processes formed the basis for positive interpretations that could be used in the theorised rebuilding or reconstruction of less threatening or more benign understandings about the loss, about oneself, and about the world.

Harold Stevens

One participant who was a good example of being able to draw on his religious belief in order to make benevolent religious interpretations about death and bereavement was Mr Harold Stevens. Mr Stevens was 65 years old and had been bereaved for 13 months. Mr Stevens described himself and his wife as "cradle Catholics" and commented that he had a strong belief in a life after death and described God as "merciful" and "gentle", whose love was "unconditional", and who was "recklessly generous" in giving people the "grace" and "strength" to cope.

Mr Stevens had been married to his wife for 34 years and described their relationship as follows:

> "We had a very strong, a very strong marriage and ... the spiritual content, the spiritual aspect of our lives was very important, I think that's probably what actually brought us together because we, we realised we shared, we needed if we were going to get married, we each needed to be married to somebody who shared our, you know, our deep core values, and we found that in one another."

Mr Stevens also added: "we were a gift to one another by His design". Indeed, for Mr Stevens, his belief in God's guiding influence being involved in life events was an important way of understanding life and his bereavement.

For Mr Stevens, his strong religious belief had been helpful to him during coping in several ways. For example, he described finding it helpful to give thanks to God for the beauty of each new day and for his loving family, which often improved his mood, gave him motivation to cope, and helped him to focus on the positive. Also, he found great understanding through the meaning and symbolism of the crucifixion, relating this to his own experience as coping with one's cross being a necessary process in order to reach heaven. Using a quote from Paul's Epistle to the Corinthians, Mr Stevens remarked:

> "God, He never puts us in a situation which we can't actually overcome [I Cor 10:12-14; 14:33], we may not be able to do it on our own but we need to do it with His help, we need to recognise that, that it is His help that actually enables us to overcome our trials, and to cope with whatever cross ... again now this is the other aspect of it, you know, there is no salvation without the cross, there's no way to heaven without the cross."

In addition, Mr Stevens was able to find some solace and comfort in the belief that his wife was now in heaven and also from the belief that due to his wife's chronic illness, God had given them some time to prepare and to say their goodbyes.

However, perhaps one of the most important aspects of his belief that was involved in supporting a benevolent religious interpretation was the religious significance related to the date his wife was diagnosed with her terminal medical condition, which linked him and his wife's suffering with the suffering experienced by the Virgin Mary in accepting her role as the mother of Jesus. Mr Stevens described his thoughts on this as follows:

> "She was diagnosed with [disease] on the [date], which actually set the whole pattern for the way we were going to handle this, because it was the feast of Our Lady of Sorrows, and we both had a strong devotion to Our Lady, to Mary, uhm. ... And so, if you like, that set the scene of how we were to go about this ... in other words we were going to have to accept it as part of God's plan for us ... and that feast of Our Lady of Sorrows is really, it celebrates the difficulties that she went through, which obviously she came through afterwards but, you know, where Simeon tells her that, you know, a sword will pierce her, her heart [Luke 2 : 34–35], where she has already accepted and has conceived Jesus, and she's accepted that, so in other words although she knew not where she was going and how this was going to turn out she knew that she was doing the will of God and therefore had implicit trust that He would be there to support her providing she kept tuned in to Him, you know through prayer and all sorts of things like that. So, so that, if you like, set the pattern for us, we didn't know where this was going to end, we knew it was terminal, we didn't know how it was going to shape out but we just, we just knew, that was almost a sign, it helped us to say, well, we've just got to trust ... we've just got to accept that this is what the Lord wants from us, it's part of His plan for her and for me."

In addition, Mr Stevens had carefully monitored the thoughts and feelings elicited by his bereavement and, although these new thoughts and feelings were not always pleasant, he described his experience of coping, saying: "it's up and down but it's always progressing". Moreover, during a period in his life where his adult children were "flying the nest" and starting careers and families of their own he commented on his bereavement and the role of his religious belief as follows:

> "I don't actually feel abandoned, I do sometimes, humanly I do, but spiritually I don't and that's what I have to keep focused on, on that ... you know. I like to think that I can, by not feeling spiritually abandoned I can. That, that helps me to cope with feelings of human abandonment."

Poignantly, perhaps, for Mr Stevens one way of focusing on not being spiritually abandoned was by regularly reflecting back to his early catechetical teaching that rooted him back in his personal relationship with God.

Biblical assurances

The theme of Biblical assurances represents the use of Biblical material, for example passages, verses, stories, themes, metaphors, or identification with biblical characters, in meaning making and coping. The use of the word 'assurances' comes from participant descriptions in which selective Biblical scripture that provided assurances about the central tenets of the Christian faith were used to facilitate benevolent, non-fatalistic interpretations about death and bereavement.

Amongst the different types of passages that were mentioned included those emphasising life after death and resurrection; those about God, specifically God as a supportive, omniscient, omnipresent companion during times of suffering; passages containing themes about light overcoming darkness or good versus evil; and passages that allowed participants to draw inspiration from Biblical characters of suffering. This diversity of biblical material was used by participants to reaffirm and reinforce the content of their benevolent religious cognition and to support meaning-making processes including sense making and benefit finding. In the case of sense making, one way Biblical passages were used was in reaffirming beliefs that events in life, including bereavement, unfold according to God's plan or will or for a reason known to God. With regard to benefit finding, one of the most innovative ways Biblical passages were used involved participants comparing their grief-related suffering or experience with the suffering, or the significance of the suffering, of important Biblical characters, which changed how participants perceived their own loss as something that was less negative or manageable.

Biblical assurances also had the potential to contribute to coping via several other pathways, including: by helping the bereaved to understand in a more manageable way the complex set of thoughts and emotions aroused by grief; by encouraging positive thoughts and emotions such as hope and optimism to be experienced; by inspiring determination and motivation to cope; and by providing techniques such as repetition of Biblical phrases/verses that could be used to regulate emotions.

Florence Knight

One participant for whom Biblical assurances were central to coping was Mrs Florence Knight. Mrs Knight was 69 years old and had been bereaved a number of years earlier. She had been married to her husband, who was several years younger than her, for approximately 30 years when he died prematurely in his mid-50s. Mrs Knight had been an Anglican all her adult life and was always very involved in church life. She described herself as having a strong belief in God and life after death, although, like many of the participants, she highlighted having difficultly in visualising what an afterlife might be like.

Following her bereavement, Mrs Knight described experiencing a very difficult initial 12 months marked by loneliness and prolonged sad mood. Furthermore, in the absence of close family, Mrs Knight had moved to a different county following her bereavement to be nearer to a friend. However, after dealing with the stress of finding a house and moving to a new area, Mrs Knight described significant difficulty in meeting new people and, importantly for her, difficulty in finding a new church in which to be a member. In addition to coping with the early death of her husband these experiences had posed perhaps the biggest challenge to her faith. In deciding to move to the new area she had been partly influenced by what she had felt as a calling to be a member of a large well-known church. However, she had been very disappointed by the unwelcoming and unfriendly response she had received when attending and trying to integrate. This experience, combined with the early death of her husband, had put a severe strain on her perceived relationship with God:

> "As I say, terribly miserable because I just, you know, couldn't get to know anybody and nobody wanted to know me, and obviously I was – I didn't know anybody much here – I really was very, very, lonely in that first 12 months, and … one still prayed, one still had faith, but my faith, I wouldn't say it was shaky but I wasn't in a, I didn't feel I wanted to be much in a relationship with God at the time because … I wasn't angry, some people say they're angry with God if somebody dies and things, I wasn't angry, but I was disappointed and sad that He had let it happen that way and therefore I did find it very difficult to pray."

However, Mrs Knight did eventually find a small village church that she described as "super-friendly" and she had been there ever since and had become well integrated. Indeed, there was a sense that this smaller church had given her far more than she had anticipated the larger church would have. Throughout all these difficulties and during the course of her coping, Mrs Knight remarked that the Bible had arguably been the most important religious resource to her. Indeed, at the time of the interview Mrs Knight was reading the Bible on a daily basis. For Mrs Knight the Bible had been helpful primarily because it provided "assurances" of there being a life after death but also because it provided a sense of certainty of an omniscient God who is in control of events:

> "Yes, it was the Bible mainly, with the assurances. I mean, right from the Old Testament and through there's this, this, uhm, comments on there being something more, I mean for instance in Job. I read Job practically [every day], funnily enough, while my husband was ill and found it very helpful, but he's saying 'I know my redeemer lives, and I will, though this body dies yet in my flesh I will see God' [Job 19 : 25-26]. Job is from Old Testament times, and certainly when you get to the New Testament with Corinthians, with Paul saying, you know,

absolutely, very surely that we will, there will be a resurrection, uhm … so Bible more than anything I think, that is the helpful thing on that line."

Mrs Knight followed this up further, highlighting the logic that she derived from Biblical accounts of the resurrection, that if Jesus can be resurrected then so can other people, including one's spouse:

"I mean in Christ saying 'I am the resurrection and the life', and John, 'Who believes in me though he be dead yet he will live' [John 11:25-26], you know, I mean there's loads and loads in the Bible on that kind of line you know … that you think about, you think about these things. I mean, there would be no point in Christian faith at all if Christ hadn't risen, and if Christ can be raised, you know, so can other people, obviously".

Mrs Knight also felt it important to mention the Biblical reading she had for her husband's funeral and again repeated the word 'assurance' to describe the Biblical life after death content:

"You see, yes, and it was all parts of this that I had, 'and this is what Christ Himself has promised to give us eternal life' [The First Epistle General of John 2:25], you see. I mean the whole thing is on that kind of line … but there's 'eternal life in Christ'. … Yes, that there's an assurance of some kind of a resurrection and that we will be with Christ. I mean, that's … the thing that makes Christianity as, well, different from, obviously different from other religions as, well, is Christ … that's partly why I like the First John's Epistle. It's full of, it's God's love personified as it were … you know, love is one of the, as you know, a very strong emotion and … if one doesn't think that God loves us, you know, you, why would He do all sorts of things and certainly that is one of the very big whys. Nobody would go through all that like Christ did without love being involved in it."

Mrs Knight reported that through having to cope with her bereavement and after what she considered as adjusting to the "physical" aspect, the actual physical absence and loss of her husband, she felt her faith had become stronger. Furthermore, she was able to look back over her experience and interpret events, even those that had been particularly difficult, in a benevolent way:

"He does still hold you, and He did, He must have. I'm sure He knows what you need more than we know what we need, and I perhaps needed this patch to go through before I found [my] church. … I do think that He has got His hand on things and it's just that we don't often, we can't see it until afterwards and we look back, but He can see it before, as it were, that's the thing."

Religious ritual

Religious ritual refers to the specific activities and behaviours involved in the practice of one's faith. In the present study, participants reported several ritual practices as helpful to coping, including prayer, engagement in the Communion/ Eucharist service, reading religious scripture, lighting candles, using the rosary, and meditation. Although individual rituals were used in different ways, overall engagement in religious ritual served multiple purposes during coping, including: facilitating a psychological and emotional closeness to the deceased; encouraging emotion regulation and catharsis; maintaining a familiar routine during a time of discord; providing a sense of being proactive; and stimulating positive remembrance. However, the most frequent way religious ritual was described in relation to coping and adjustment was in providing a way of maintaining or continuing the perceived cognitive and emotional relationship with the deceased spouse. During these processes, participants described using particular religious rituals in adaptive ways depending on the cognitive or emotional needs of the participant at their individual point during the grief process.

Andrew Fields

One participant who found engagement in religious ritual particularly helpful in coping with his bereavement was Mr Andrew Fields. Mr Fields was 81 years old and had recently lost his wife unexpectedly after 53 years of marriage following a short illness. Although now a Catholic, Mr Fields had originally been an Anglican but had converted to Catholicism after meeting his wife. Mr Fields described his relationship with his wife and his conversion as follows:

> "We had a very common foundation in our faith, myself as an Anglican, and my wife as a Catholic, and I became a Catholic before we were married because I couldn't see the, I couldn't possibly agree to children of the marriage becoming Catholics if I couldn't accept the Catholic teaching myself, so I had a course of instruction and became a Catholic."

Mr Fields had a strong belief in God and in a life after death and reported that his faith had been essential in helping him cope. He commented on the expectation that his adult children had and how his belief had been helpful:

> "They [his children] expected to see me distraught and, you know, completely shattered but I, through the gift of my faith, I was able to

cope with that almost in a miraculous way, the strength was there. ....
I mean they [beliefs] have been very important, I think I would have
been absolutely shattered and devastated if I thought that this life was all
there was, that would be a loss which would be very hard to get over."

Indeed, Mr Fields was able to highlight that it was his belief in a life after death
reunion with his wife that was most essential for him:

"That was it really ... 53 years of happy marriage and the prospects of
eternity in each other's company, that was the key to it all, you know,
that gives me great hope and optimism."

Furthermore, Mr Fields' religious belief had also enabled him to make several
benevolent interpretations about his bereavement that had helped him to cope.
Mr Fields summed up his benevolent thoughts as follows:

"Life in the faith prepares us for death, but with the conviction that
in death our souls return to their source. Sadness at the loss of a
companion is softened by the belief in a reunion when the survivor
dies. Confidence that God's will for us is being carried out throughout
our lives. Everything experienced is as required by God – trials, joys,
sorrows, temptations, tests, to ascertain our integrity and sincerity.
... Learning to adapt to a new way of life and accepting the loss of
a loved one as God's plan is drawing us closer to Him ready for our
own death."

Related to Mr Fields' benevolent interpretation that his bereavement was a "test"
of his faith, sincerity, and "trust in the Almighty", part of the process in order for
him to reach heaven, he also expressed certainty that through his bereavement
he felt closer to God. Mr Fields commented:

"Through the loss of Rita I am closer to God, He took her away
and I've drawn closer to Him as a result, no doubt about it, no doubt
about it. You know it's a great blessing and I, you know, I sort of feel
that this is part of the purpose. ... I say, 'for goodness sake keep me,
keep me clear of sin so I can come and join you', that's important."

In addition to being able to use his belief to make benevolent religious
interpretations, Mr Fields was also able to enhance his ability to cope and adjust
through engagement in the religious rituals that guided and shaped his religious
practice. In the present study the religious ritual that nearly every participant found
particularly helpful was prayer. Indeed, most participants also reported that their
religious practice, especially prayer, had increased following their bereavement.
Mr Fields described his religious practice, including his use of prayer, as follows:

"Yes, I pray morning and evening and during the course of the day. I go to Mass everyday, and so I participate in the Mass, but also I say the rosary and pray for people and events as I pass, as I pass perhaps other people's houses or see a sad sight, you know … prayers come readily to mind throughout the day."

Interestingly, with regard to prayer and bereavement, Mr Fields described the advice that he had received from a friend of his who had also lost his wife and which he had found useful:

"I knew this man, lost his wife. When I lost mine he said, 'Prayers'. He said, 'Pray a lot, that will be helpful,' and I've taken his advice and done that and found it helpful, so that would be my advice to somebody else, you know, pray, pray, pray. Pray for strength, pray for consolation, and pray for support, and you will get the help you want."

As with several other participants, Mr Fields highlighted that it was important to pray for and on behalf of his spouse in order to help his wife in whatever her afterlife fate or progress may be. In addition, it was also important to feel that the deceased were in some way able to help or influence the living. As such, prayer offered the bereaved a useful activity to express their need to be proactive, to channel their need to act or do something perceived as positive, and to express emotions felt toward the deceased:

"We in the Catholic Church are convinced that our prayers are valuable in helping them *to get* to heaven, and conversely we believe that the prayers of the souls of the departed are beneficial for our benefit here, I think it's a two-way thing … you're purely attempting to assist them in whatever process they're going through."

Religious ritual such as attending church also served a useful purpose in providing structure to daily living during a period of discord, whereby the bereavement may have disrupted or ended daily routines, traditions, and habitual ways of thinking and behaving built up over a long marriage. Mr Fields described how Mass provided him with the motivation to begin each day in a positive way and how he could continue his role of caring for his wife through his use of prayer:

"It is very important to me to get out of bed at a reasonable hour and think, well, I've got to be there [at Mass], because this is an opportunity to pray for her … and it's the best thing, it's the most useful thing I can do for her, you know. I still feel I'm caring for her."

Mr Fields also described a number of ways in which engaging in religious rituals as part of his daily religious practice also helped him to feel a cognitive and emotional link, bond, or relationship with his wife. For example, Mr Fields described the bond that he felt through attendance at Mass:

> "We have this bond on a daily basis, that … I sit in the same seat we always sat in, and, you know, we're reunited on a daily basis in anticipation of the great reunion."

Mr Fields also described feeling a similar connection with his wife through his use of the rosary:

> "We used to say it together. My wife and I used to say our rosary together for some good reason, so we were joined in that, and … there you go, you know, I still feel united with her in saying the rosary on my own."

Indeed, these descriptions provide examples of religious rituals being used as methods of feeling a continuing bond with a deceased loved one (see Klass et al, 1996). Although continuing bonds processes have been theorised as helpful in bereavement and non-religious examples have been frequently observed, there has been little theorising and few examples of religion's role in promoting continuing bonds processes that can be experienced as helpful. Furthermore, in the present study, other participants identified theological support for the validity of religious rituals in continuing bonds by referring to the belief known as 'Communion of Saints'. According to this belief – reaffirmed in The Creed – 'faithful Christians who have died still enjoy a relationship with believers on earth' (Browning, 2004: 75). Thus, for those with a strong belief and for whom religious practice is important, there is the potential for believers to experience a personal closeness or a continuing of the relationship specifically through religious rituals.

Mr Fields, by drawing on the certainty of his belief and through having ways of expressing his thoughts and feelings, was able to accept his present circumstances and attribute responsibility for the cause of his bereavement in a way that was personally meaningful and poignant. He described his thoughts on how he viewed his present circumstances as follows:

> "I'm not seeking any union with any other person male or female because I think that marriage was unique and this is what God has chosen for me, to be alone and to be content with what I have."

Furthermore, instead of causing him to doubt or question his belief, Mr Fields' bereavement, although difficult, had contributed to reinforcing his belief:

> "No, all my old beliefs have been sustained and I've never had, I've never had any doubt … my beliefs from early days have been sustained and confirmed by these events."

Spiritual capital

A very different religious activity to one based on belief, Biblical scripture, or religious ritual was labelled spiritual capital. This theme referred to how participants' engagement in roles, jobs, or activities on behalf of or related to their church helped them to gradually reconstruct a new, purposeful and meaningful post-bereavement identity. The term 'spiritual capital' is used because it represents how the church, from a certain perspective, can be viewed as a source of community wealth or capital that all church members can part own through investment of personal time in performing jobs, roles, or activities on behalf of or related to the church. For example, in the present study, many participants, following the bereavement of their spouse, took up unpaid jobs or roles, or increased the number of roles they performed in relation to the functioning of their church. Such roles included being a welcomer, sacristan, reader, lay pastor, catechist, Eucharistic minister, church warden, member of the parochial parish council, or member of a church group, to name but a few. Importantly, engagement in these roles and jobs had gradually come to be integrated within the participant's post-bereavement identity, through which they could be identified by others and could come to identify themselves.

Amongst the benefits gained for bereaved older adults of invested time in these activities included finding new meaning and purpose in life, and developing an increased sense of confidence and autonomy. Other useful benefits included increasing participants' social involvement, which in turn buffered against negative aspects of grief such as feelings of loneliness, hopelessness, or boredom. Furthermore, through church-related activities involving interacting with the sick, frail, and less fortunate, participants were more likely to perceive their own circumstances in a less negative way.

Angela Lloyd

One participant for whom spiritual capital had been useful in coping and adjusting to spousal bereavement was Mrs Angela Lloyd. Mrs Lloyd was 76 years old and had been married to her husband for 43 years. Her husband had died of a chronic medical condition and she had been bereaved for several years.

Mrs Lloyd had been an Anglican most of her adult life and reflected on her experience of coping by saying:

> "God gives you the strength to go on. It's through His strength that you go on, really. I think without my Christian faith it would have been much more difficult."

Amongst her benevolent religious beliefs, Mrs Lloyd had a strong belief in a life after death that she felt would be free of pain and problems. She believed that one would ascend to heaven immediately on death, and believed that she would experience in some way a life after death reunion with her spouse. Furthermore,

Mrs Lloyd had a strong belief in God and felt that God was involved in guiding events in one's life and that, although not always easily understandable at the time, significant events in one's life such as bereavements and the meeting of one's partner could be understood and put into place, like the pieces of a jigsaw puzzle, with hindsight. Prayer was also important to Mrs Lloyd and she commented on one use of prayer as a way of seeking guidance to act in life in accordance with God's will:

> "I think if you believe that God has a plan for your life then you pray, 'help me to do the right thing', whether it's in your own life or in your interaction with others."

Furthermore, Mrs Lloyd also felt she could hand over responsibility for coping to God, could seek refuge in God, and that God would provide her with all she needed to cope.

Mrs Lloyd's belief in God was also important in managing feelings of loneliness aroused by her bereavement. Through religious rituals such as prayer and church attendance, and through her reading and reciting of Biblical scripture, Mrs Lloyd was able to enhance feelings of the presence or companionship of God in her day-to-day life. Indeed, she was able to draw on her knowledge and use of the Bible to regulate and manage her grief. Mrs Lloyd described her use of Biblical scripture during coping, and importantly the role of repetition of Biblical verses as a regulatory mechanism in managing her grief-related feelings as follows:

> "In the early days, when, you know, you really, really do feel alone, you just used to say 'Oh God, please get me through this day', you know, and perhaps keep saying to yourself 'I am with you, you are not alone' [Deuteronomy 31 : 6; Isaiah 41 : 10; Matthew 28 : 20], you know, 'my presence will go with you' [Exodus 33 : 14], phrases from the Bible that I know because I was brought up with lots of Bible phrases, which has been beneficial of course, and by saying it it sort of gets into you, if you know what I mean, you just repeat it in times of need."

Although Mrs Lloyd's religious belief and practice had been important following her bereavement she was also keen to point out that the coping and adjustment period had not been easy. As reported by many of the participants, in addition to loneliness being a problem, the physical absence of a loved one was difficult. For Mrs Lloyd the absence of "touch" was most significant:

> "Touch is so important … and that's what you miss again very much is … that shoulder, you know, if you have a problem, and that arm that goes round you."

The loss of day-to-day companionship was also difficult:

"Coming back home I didn't find it easy. I was alright while I was in the study. My computer, my mind was on it, practically doing things. It's when you sit down to relax, reading the paper, you know. If you're there with somebody you say, 'Oh listen to this', share a bit of news, but there's nobody to do that with, when you come in there's nobody to say, 'Oh I met so and so', that's when it really strikes home."

In addition, Mrs Lloyd also found it difficult adjusting to what were once shared traditions and routines that she enjoyed with her husband:

"Even now I hate Sunday lunch time, because it was a special time. We'd come in from church, talk about it, have a coffee, have a nice lunch. So I have people in for Sunday lunch if I can, that does that. And, or if I come in and I do something, *then* sit and have my coffee, but to walk in and just sit down and have a cup of coffee, that is still difficult even now, after nearly 9 years."

However, Mrs Lloyd had also recognised that following her bereavement it was necessary to rebuild her life:

"I have a friend whose husband died and she'll say, 'I wish I was dead', you know, 'I don't want to go on'. You can't do that … yes, you have to build a new life, different, completely different, in so many ways, and it's a lonelier life, it's not the same life of sharing at all. Harder … but you learn to cope in different ways."

For Mrs Lloyd, part of this process of rebuilding had involved developing a new identity or sense of self through engaging in church-related activities that provided an ongoing sense of meaning and purpose. Following her bereavement, Mrs Lloyd had become very involved in the running of several church activities. She described some of her current activities as follows:

"I do all sorts of jobs in the church. I'm a deputy warden, I arrange readers and intercessors, welcome newcomers, [and] help in the church office."

Mrs Lloyd further added:

"I think, because of my beliefs, I do a lot in the church, church work, and that gives me a focus and a purpose."

Indeed, Mrs Lloyd followed this up by describing how she had become involved in performing jobs on behalf of the church and emphasised the purpose and focus to life these activities provided. Mrs Lloyd also highlighted how performing these jobs and activities provided a remedy to her loneliness by encouraging social involvement and providing the access to human contact that she needed to feel following her bereavement:

"I remember on one occasion saying [to the vicar] can you come up – it was the previous vicar – I'd like to have a chat, and he'd come up, you know, and you chat, and then I remember on this occasion I said, well … that I would like a job, as it were, to focus on, and I remember him asking what, and I said, 'Oh something to do with people, not sitting at my computer doing something on my own.' I needed people, and I was given the job of welcoming newcomers to the church, which I still do [laughs], which I find very, very useful. It's things that give you a focus and a purpose in going on with life, because you can think 'What's the point of going on', you know, 'I lost the one I love so life is meaningless'. You need something to replace that."

Furthermore, Mrs Lloyd also commented on the importance of her role as a lay pastor. This type of role, which involves helping those who may be less fortunate or who may be in poor health, was helpful in part because it allowed Mrs Lloyd to take a different perspective on her bereavement and current circumstances:

"What we have started recently is lay pastors, which we've gone through a training for, visiting people, uhm, whatever the different circumstances. You know, they may be new, they may be bereaved, they may be in a nursing home. … I strongly believe that in helping others you help yourself, very much so, you gain a lot from it, partly because you sometimes see somebody that is in more need than you are, and it gives you a different perspective doesn't it? You know, 'What am I worrying about?' You know, 'Look at them'".

After several years of being involved in performing jobs and activities related to the running of her church, Mrs Lloyd was able to reflect back on the time since her bereavement and when she was still married and see how her identity had changed. Mrs Lloyd considered herself a "stronger person" and more independent, and commented, "Whereas I was probably his wife, I am now my own person". Furthermore, Mrs Lloyd was able to recognise the contributions she had made within her local church community, and although these contributions were no substitute for the loss of her husband they did provide some benefit.

Conclusion

For those with a strong religious belief, religion is likely to be experienced as beneficial in coping with bereavement, in part because religion can provide responses, some of which may be proactive, that address certain aspects of the grief experience. For example, bereavement often elicits an urge in the bereaved to search for some kind of meaning or explanation for their loss, beyond the meaning and explanation derived from rational facts or details related to the cause of death, which in themselves may be unsatisfying or even distressful. Religious belief tends to address issues of the meaning of existence, of death, and about what may come after death. Indeed, these characteristics may contribute toward defining what religion is, beyond being defined by ideas of a God or other transcendent supreme being. Benevolent religious beliefs that address issues of existence and death can be drawn upon in the search for meaning and can facilitate the development of explanations or understandings of bereavement that bring some level of cognitive acceptance, and that can engender or support overall benevolent religious interpretations of bereavement that have personal significance.

In addition, benevolent religious beliefs, meanings found and interpretations can all be supported or reinforced by Biblical assurances. Indeed, the Bible itself can be used as a coping resource in circumstances of bereavement in several different ways, for example in helping the bereaved person to regulate or manage grief-related emotions, in normalising or providing understanding about one's feelings or experience, and in giving motivation or inspiration to cope. As one participant in the present study reported, the great conviction in the language itself can transfer to the reader. Also, certain books of the Bible, such as the Book of Psalms, which were frequently mentioned as useful both in coping with bereavement and in day-to-day living, capture a wealth of complex human emotion with which the bereaved may identify or from which they may gain understanding.

Perhaps one of the least theorised helpful aspects of religion in the context of coping with bereavement concerned the role played by religious ritual. One characteristic of grief is of physical agitation or restlessness, with the bereaved person often feeling an urge to act, move, or do something physical that may be perceived as useful or positive. It is in these circumstances that religious ritual may be particularly helpful by providing physical outlets for grief and specific activities in which to express emotions or thoughts aroused by grief. Furthermore, religious rituals may reduce the religious, existential, or death-related uncertainties that the experience of bereavement may elicit. Indeed, the perceived antiquity of religious rituals, with in some cases rituals being passed down over centuries, may make religious rituals appear more valid, legitimate, or useful in relation to grief than newly created rituals or other activities, thus enhancing their perceived effectiveness or importance. In addition, religious rituals may also be experienced as useful by providing familiar and reassuring patterns of post-bereavement behaviour as well as providing brief respite from thinking about the loss during the performance of rituals.

In contrast to the loss-easing benefits of religious belief and practice, performing jobs, activities, or roles on behalf of the church may contribute toward developing a new sense of self or identity following bereavement. Indeed, engaging in roles or jobs on behalf of the church may encourage social involvement and provide new sources of meaning and purpose in life.

In thinking about the role of religion in coping for future generations predictions are difficult to make, because of the failure of religious transmission remarked on at the end of the previous chapter. Despite the fact that Britain has seen a continuing decline in church attendance and religious affiliation since the end of the Second World War, there has not necessarily been a corresponding embracing of agnostic, atheistic, or humanistic perspectives (although these attitudes have no doubt become more acceptable to express). Indeed, one interpretation of the state of religion in contemporary Britain is that there has been an increase in religious uncertainty. With the perceived gradual erosion of different forms of social and moral authority, and especially the authority of the Christian churches, many British people may have become increasingly uncertain in what they believe and uncertain in how to express their belief.

In parallel with these trends Holloway (2007) has noted that within the western world the religious content of Christian funerals has declined (for example the practice of commending the deceased person to God's care). Rather they have come to reflect the increasing individualising and memorialising trend common to secular funerals. Nevertheless, because the UK population still has the potential to be influenced at some level by its religious heritage, secular observers may be disappointed by the amount of continuing request for religious services, especially in circumstances of bereavement. It should also be taken into account that Britain is increasingly a multi-cultural and multi-faith society and that for many of these new immigrant cultures a more religious way of life goes hand in hand with a more conscious preparation for death and clarity about the need for religious rituals following death (Firth, 1999).

SIX

Coping without religious faith: ageing among British Humanists

Peter J. Wilkinson and Peter G. Coleman

Atheistic and agnostic positions on life

In the previous chapter we examined the benefits of a religious faith in providing meaning at times of loss in later life, in the context perhaps most favourable to religion – following a major bereavement. But meaningful lives can also be constructed both in and out of difficult times without recourse to religious faith (Andrews, 1991). It has been a major deficiency in much of the literature on religion, coping and well-being to compare people of different levels of religiosity without considering other strong belief systems that they may hold. Although it may be demonstrable that persons of strong religious faith cope better than those with a weak religious faith, it does not follow that other systems of meaning do not provide equally good resources in dealing with life's difficulties. In particular the failure to study atheistic and agnostic positions on life alongside religious viewpoints has been a serious failure. This fundamental paradigmatic error has led authors to conclude much about the psychological benefits of religious or spiritual belief without reference to, or comparison with, the opposing belief – atheism. Moreover, even debates on the subject of religion and atheism have tended to focus on the rationality of the respective positions rather than their functions and capacities when stretched or tested. Advocates of an atheistic world view have arguably more often resorted to critiquing the faith and motivation of religious believers rather than laying out the cogent basis of living life well without reference to God or other supernatural entities.

In this chapter we intend to attempt to begin to remedy these gaps in the literature by reporting case studies conducted on older British Humanists. They come from a larger study examining matched cases of committed religious believers and Humanists confronting particular challenges in late life such as bereavement, frailty and facing death. Analyses suggested that both coped remarkably well with the challenges they faced (Wilkinson and Coleman, 2010). In this chapter we examine and give voice to the neglected Humanist perspective in old age, whether it is based on an atheistic or agnostic position. These people constitute a significant proportion of older populations in western societies today, and these case illustrations provide a much needed counterpoint to the claims made about the benefits of religious belief made in the North American literature in particular (Coleman, 2010). The interviews conducted show various facets of atheism and agnosticism and their interactions with coping in old age, and enable an appreciation of what it is that sustains those with a humanistic belief system.

To begin with, though, it is necessary to address a possible objection to including a chapter on atheists and agnostics in a book about belief. Surely, one might ask, atheists and agnostics do not have any beliefs? Indeed, many of the case subjects featured in this chapter resented the use of the term 'beliefs' to characterise their position, because they felt very strongly that they had none, that they were in fact 'non-believers'. This is largely a linguistic issue. If belief implies religious or supernatural belief, then clearly the Humanists interviewed do not have beliefs. But in the sense in which we use the word 'belief' in this book, as that which one values and puts one's trust or hope or 'belief in', Humanists do have beliefs. They do not put their belief in a god or gods but in other faculties, such as humankind's power to reason, or, more abstractly, in the progress of civilization or the advance of science. These are humanistic beliefs because they are beliefs centred in the power and capacity of human beings rather than in a Judaeo-Christian/Islamic God or other supernatural entities.

Whether one is atheistic or agnostic does not have major implications for this fundamental belief or reliance in humankind. The dictionary definition of atheism is simply 'the theory or belief that God does not exist' (Allen, 1990). Agnosticism, on the other hand, is a position characterised by the belief that God's existence – or the existence of any spiritual or non-material phenomena – cannot be known presently and/or can never ultimately be known. Agnosticism does not therefore pertain to 'sitting on the fence' about the big questions in life: an agnostic is someone who has pondered life and has reached the conclusion that humanity cannot know whether or not a transcendental reality exists. For an agnostic, as Kenny (2006) explains, both atheism and theism make too strong and unjustified knowledge claims about the existence of God. But what is important for practical humanistic belief is that both agnosticism and atheism dismiss any value to religious faith, and maintain their reliance on human capacities alone.

In this chapter most of the atheists and agnostics we will describe are members of a Humanist group affiliated to the British Humanist Association (BHA). The BHA's website (www.humanism.org.uk) describes Humanism as essentially derived from atheism and agnosticism but as being a positive concept over and above these two constructs – more an ethical life philosophy aimed towards improving the common good. Humanists reject religious and superstitious beliefs and believe that leading a good life can be founded on reason, experience and innate human sensibility, as opposed to religious dogma and instruction. As one Humanist interviewee Natasha Wilson put it, the defining creed of Humanism is essentially "morality without God".

It will be argued that the Humanist interviewees we will hear from in this chapter are independently minded individuals with advanced and total world views based on a purely material conceptualisation of the universe that can be a workable alternative to a religious world view. Atheist writer Richard Dawkins has already suggested that an atheistic set of beliefs can give rise to a world view that fulfils the same four basic functions in people's lives that religions traditionally fulfil – 'explanation, exhortation, consolation and inspiration' (Dawkins, 2006: 347). Humanists are rationalists who value the evidence-based approach of scientific endeavour and who therefore see current scientific understanding as the latest and best way of explaining the universe and humanity's place in it. Suffice it to say that Humanists, where informed, are Darwinists. The Humanist stance on moral guidance is that knowing what is right and wrong is within us as a product of both our genetic makeup and our experience of living in society as individuals, and that our altruistic nature has evolutionary origins that are becoming better understood in modern times (Kirkpatrick, 2004; Dawkins, 2006). Because the Humanist view is that life is finite, it is admitted that deriving consolation from this belief is hard, and the special consolation that religion offers may well be the greatest trump card of the religious outlook (Dawkins, 2006). The Humanist response, though, is to indulge in life with gusto and without fear of judgement and damnation beyond the grave, believing as they do that life and the joy of living it has an extra potency and significance once one believes it is all there is. Humanists also argue that focusing on shared human interests and experience through ethics and the arts is enough to provide inspiration in one's life without needing to invoke the divine (see www.humanism.org.uk). This depiction of Humanism may seem quite elaborate, but it is still apparent that Humanism is a far less diverse, more homogeneous belief set than the world's religions in all their colourful splendour.

Despite the emotionally seductive messages of religions and the polished words of some Humanist thinkers, it is still not known whether or not a humanistic world view can compare in practice with a religious belief system in supporting individuals and helping them to cope with ageing (Dein and Stygall, 1997). While it is known that psychological religious coping methods are seldom used alone without practical secular coping means such as obtaining social support (Pargament, 1997), it is not known whether atheistic and Humanist belief-based coping is an equivalent resource. The main function of this chapter is to present case material on this subject as evidence for the role that Humanist beliefs can have in coping with ageing.

Exemplar material from the interviewees' testimonies has been organised into categories based upon Dawkins' four basic functions of a belief system – explanation, exhortation, consolation and inspiration – in order to paint a descriptive picture of coping with ageing among British Humanists. For each belief function, material is presented that shows how that particular facet of belief has helped people to cope with a variety of the challenges of ageing. In reality the functions of a belief system are interrelated and do in fact overlap when helping the individual cope, and belief-based coping is rarely the only way a person copes with a problem, if it is indeed relevant to coping at all. Here, however, we are looking at the point of interaction between atheistic or agnostic belief and coping, not a person's overall coping approach. In addition, hardly any consideration is given to why these persons hold these beliefs. Generally speaking, reason is the principal force that moves someone to adopt an atheistic or agnostic belief and, although it was covered extensively in the interviews, the rationale behind the interviewees' beliefs was fairly similar for all of them, but it is unimportant here and therefore not discussed further.

Explanation

It can be argued, at least for educated people across the world, that science has now superseded the simplistic attempts of the world's religions to explain the world in which we find ourselves (Dawkins, 2006). Understanding life and what happens to us when we age from a scientific perspective is the basis of the humanistic standpoint on ageing. Here we hear from a few people whose naturalistic conceptualisations of the universe have helped them understand events in their old age better and have therefore helped them to cope.

Malcolm Lockyer is a man in his late 70s whose wife Avril died in 2004 from a rare liver duct cancer, which she had endured for a two-year period. Although Mr Lockyer coped with his great loss principally by just carrying on with the day-to-day and making sure he had meaning in his life and relationships, his Humanist beliefs were relevant to how he coped and has been coping, firstly by helping him perceive what had happened as a non-determined chance event:

> "If I had been a believer, I'd have said, 'What's really unfair is that we lived very healthy lives.' … We didn't have salt in our meals, and we had no sugar, and she was very conscious of eating the right things and trying to keep a balanced diet. … And it didn't seem to make much difference, you know. … And that's another thing that I suppose makes me angry about, you know, this sort of creationism, this scientific creationism that is intelligent design. And you think, 'Well, what intelligent design produces something that has the potential for a cancerous cell, you know, for a cell going wrong?' … In fact one of the [atheistic internet] blogs said, 'If God did design it, he ought to be sued.' … It's just … the way the cookie crumbles … I mean …a split second can alter your life."

It would seem that Mr Lockyer's grasp of probability and of cancer as a disease process of cumulative risk has helped him come to terms more easily with why his wife Avril became ill and died. Rationalising the process naturalistically has meant that he has not had to address any conflicting issues surrounding why a loving, all-powerful God would have directly caused – or even passively allowed – her untimely death when she had led a good life and had been so health-conscious for much of her life. Mr Lockyer accepts the theory of evolution by natural selection as the best explanation of how people have arisen on this planet, and accepting the human body's vulnerable DNA and its potential to mutate and cause cancer is just a part of this comprehension of nature and physiology.

Jan Frew is a Humanist who considers himself to be technically an agnostic because he is not absolutely certain of what life is really about. However, he is in little doubt about what it is not about, and he feels that the Christian view of life is undoubtedly false; he can only believe in things for which there is positive evidence. Mr Frew's first wife died of cancer in 1985. Although he coped with her death "with sadness and difficulty", his humanistic understanding of the human being as a temporary – albeit tangibly successful – animal species on a tiny planet in a vast and indifferent universe, as well as his understanding of the insignificance of his suffering in the scheme of humanity's history across the world and time, helped him transcend his own loss somewhat:

> "I know that people are suffering and dying all over the world, so I have tended not to make too much of my own suffering, my own problems, just to put up with them. … Whenever you have a misfortune and you meet others who've had a similar misfortune, there's an immediate bond …, and it lessens the suffering of both people. … I believe that the human condition is universal and that I do not regard myself as being outside or more important than my fellow man. I mean, a lot of people find that difficult, that concept difficult. They think, 'Well, I'm a person and I'm important to God; you know, I'm a very important person.' I have never been able to accept that, so I don't regard my own experiences as being of great importance. … In a way I suppose some people would say I've coped exceedingly well. … In fact too well, perhaps you might say."

Natasha Wilson is a 69-year-old Humanist who is approaching old age with many memories of varied experiences to look back upon. Having never had a personal religious faith, her essentially humanistic world view has been with her most of her life, but it has been augmented since retirement by her undertaking of counselling training under Jung's psychoanalytical model. Mrs Wilson concurs with the Freudian view of religious belief as an infantile regression and she believes it is a crutch that she has no need for in her life. By using her understanding of psychology, Mrs Wilson can aim to age in the most mentally healthy way in which she can. When her brother died from lung cancer in late 2006, Mrs Wilson was aware of the psychology behind the grieving process she was going through, but she did not force herself to follow any particular grieving protocol:

> "The usual grieving process of being very caught up with, very tearful initially, and allowing myself to express my tears, getting together with other family members to talk about his life, reminisce, crying together. And then, gradually, that becomes less and less. And they don't go out of your life – you still have all the memories about them. But normal

life picks up and resumes. ... And, because I'm a trained psychoanalytic counsellor, I understand how the mechanisms of the grieving process work psychologically, so I allowed myself to go through all the stages that one needs to go through ... It just happens and ... I wanted to be open to allowing my emotions to come through. I didn't try through any sort of manic activity or denial to pretend that it wasn't going to happen. ... And I knew that I'd done the best I could for him, so I had no guilt about it, which is, I'm sure, a huge relief. It must be dreadful to have to deal with grief when you're carrying a lot of guilt and it's too late to do anything. ... I'm okay. I'm over it now. I've totally accepted that life has to end. I think I've dealt as much as I can with the fact that my own life is in its latter years."

Mrs Wilson's conceptual combination of Jungian psychoanalytical theory and Humanism is also involved in her emotional preparation for her physical decline in old age and eventual death:

"Who'd want to have one's powers diminishing and know that one was approaching the end of life, because this is what it's about – we can't escape it. It's like having a very enjoyable holiday. ... If you're having something that is wholly enjoyable, you don't want it to come to an end. So that is basically it in a sort of, as a meta-narrative. ... I'll just do the best I can when it comes. ... I haven't started doing preparatory dying work yet, psychologically, because I'm still immersed in life. ... I think that's how I will approach my own death: that I will allow my emotions, whatever they are, to surface, and to deal with them, because I'm not into escapism. ... If you consciously try to deny them, they'll come out psychosomatically or in other ways. ... I shall deal with what's happening inside in an honest way. ...

"I don't fear death at all. I think there's nothing to be frightened of, really, because it's just a state of non-being. ... I don't feel as if I've missed out on anything by being an atheist. ... Going to the Humanist group, they are as a group the most un-neurotic group of people together that I have ever met. ... I think because people are more grounded who have questioned all of these deeper issues in life, have come to terms with the reality in which we live, and have accepted that and adjusted their lives, they've made a good adjustment to life as it really is, and I think a lot of that is because they haven't tried to call on supernatural props in any form to help them. ... The Humanists, they're not like people who just claim non-belief if asked but haven't really thought about it. ... Humanists have really wrestled with the deep issues and come through, and have reached a position that is wholly satisfactory for themselves – that ... we are on our own basically on this planet. And I think that is a huge maturational position, psychologically, to come to, and therefore you are more grounded to deal with what life throws at you I think. ... This is the life we've got. Deal with it. ... Be happy and do good. It's as simple as that."

So taking on board the scientific view that we are purely material beings who cease to exist once we die can be a self-empowering step to make. And Mrs Wilson's concluding words bring us onto the next topic for discussion: the drive to act ethically and how this can be based on one's beliefs.

Exhortation

The philosophical question of why atheists should act morally if they do not believe in a supernatural judge and jury is beyond the remit of this chapter. However, from the Humanists' point of view the issue is moot, as they believe that our moral compass is something unchangeable and irremovable from ourselves, as an inevitable product of both our evolved human nature and our experience of social cohesion, and not something that can be obtained only through religious belief and scriptural study. The Humanist view is simply that we do not need any beliefs in order to act morally, that we just do, and that there are cases where altruism and working towards bettering mankind are founded on a humanistic imperative and can, as a by-product, help the Humanist individual cope with aspects of ageing.

Mrs Ella Hamilton is a widow in her 80s whose moral intuition was moulded in the first half of her life by a communist husband and also by her father, who taught her that we owe something to those less fortunate than ourselves. She holds the view that one's upbringing has a huge influence on one's eventual basic morality and she believes that a world where everyone created their own value systems based on reason and experience would be a better place. Her husband Gregory, also a Humanist, feels very strongly that Humanism is not about beliefs, and also that it does not have a place in instructing him how to live: "it is not like a guiding religion". However, Ella thinks that the humanistic view of life as a finite period makes life that more precious, and she therefore thinks that acting morally is extremely important:

> "We believe that human life is the only thing there is and that you create your own morality, if you like, by realising you're here for a short time and, in whatever way you like…, you make your own rules for life. … Humanists tend to have … a sense of responsibility for their own lives, because we haven't any excuses. … I mean, there's no-one to tell us what to do and nobody who is going to punish us if we don't do. … And so we've got to have a sense of responsibility about our own behaviour."

This humanistic sense of responsibility is sometimes translated into charitable endeavour, which can also serve to provide meaning in the lives of older people and help them to cope. In coping with the death of his first wife and in approaching the end of his life ponderingly and philosophically, Jan Frew has been able to deal with his problems by focusing on working for the good of others and, in turn, his own mental health has been nurtured. He links morality to acting socially and again believes that rationally formed morals are superior to those handed down by authority figures or religions:

> "To my way of thinking, social really means global, and thinking in terms of humanity per se and not any particular nation or race or whatever. But, thinking of humanity, you could say that my aim would be to try and help towards the continuing survival and, if you like, refinement of humanity, the human species. So that's what I see as really the overriding morality. Actions should be based on that to try and improve the lot of humanity. ...
>
> "I think people love to follow gurus. People love anybody who's absolutely sure they know exactly what is right and what is wrong. Like Tony Blair – he's a good example. ... And he's devoted to doing the right thing. The problem is we can't agree on what right is. I mean Hitler was convinced that, you know, he was right. ... There are so many people who need somebody to tell them what is right and what isn't, and they're willing to follow anybody. ... It would be far better if we could persuade people to take responsibility for their actions rather than saying, 'Well, I'm doing this because so and so said it', regardless of whether so and so is a politician, or a mass murderer like Hitler, or God or whatever. I think people should be trained to make up their own minds on what the world is about, and to that end I think it's probably desirable that we should give the best possible education we can to as many people as we can. ...
>
> "[When my first wife died] I felt it was important to continue with my social obligations as they stood, and not to abandon them just because of my own misfortune. So I tried to maintain my lifestyle ... and cope with my ongoing responsibilities – you know, the children and so on. And just dealing with the everyday problems does take your mind off ... your own problems. ...
>
> "I've always had more things to do than I've had time for. ... As I say, all my activities are geared towards trying to improve the human lot – and I'm not talking about my lot. As long as I have the physical ability and energy to do that, that's fine, you know. Perhaps there will come a time when I am no longer able to promote that."

Mr Frew's main retirement activities include running a small charity which funds research into pain management – a project that was inspired by his first wife's suffering and death from cancer. Mr Frew also has two books he is working on and he occasionally contributes to the local and Humanist press. He feels that bettering humanity by promoting rich aesthetic experiences – such as good art and good music and good literature – is a worthy aim. Like Mr Frew, some of the other Humanists who had been bereaved were also able to find meaning and purpose in their lives through charity work, and in general many of the group who were interviewed do some sort of voluntary work as a way of giving something to the community in their old age.

Consolation

What, if any, consolation can be taken from a belief system that does not promise life after death and the reuniting of loved ones; a belief system that asserts that the universe is totally indifferent to human suffering? For a start, finding positive aspects to a situation one is coping with is a useful process but one that is often unrelated to one's beliefs about the divine. For example, Ella and Gregory Hamilton described drawing a lot of comfort from the fact that they are experiencing the frustrations and aches and pains of ageing together as a couple, but a religious couple could experience this consolation in the same way, and so it would be unjust to claim Humanist ownership over such a feeling of satisfaction. Moreover, a number of the religious participants who were interviewed for the project into strong beliefs and coping with ageing expressed an awareness of how lucky they were to be fairly healthy compared with associates of theirs or people they would notice at their local doctors' surgery. However, there are nevertheless some unique consolations pertaining to atheism that Humanists can claim as their own.

Laurence Robson is a research professor at a local university who is in his early 70s but still working. Although not a signed up Humanist, he has been an atheist since losing his Methodist faith in his early 20s and has subsequently grown into a stern critic of religion and religiousness in all its inter-individual and politicised forms. Five years ago Professor Robson underwent emergency surgery for a tardily diagnosed bowel cancer and had to face very seriously the possibility that he might die. At the time he was able to find a lot of comfort in listening to "great music" and rereading some of his "old friends" – selections of classic literature that he loved such as works by C S Forrester and William Shakespeare. But, again, marvelling at human consciousness through art in this way and finding consolation in this would be equally possible for a person with a religious belief system. However, Professor Robson came out of his ordeal with what he calls "a confirmed atheistic position", and he was able to draw some consolations from what his scientific knowledge and atheistic belief system both uniquely tell him about his insignificance and finiteness:

> "In the week I was ill *The Guardian* published a photograph of ... a galaxy at the ... edge of space. And this was just remarkable, truly mind-blowing. And I found great comfort in that, because, you know,

I myself will someday, as you will be, with yesterday's seven thousand years. So what is interesting about religion – no doubt in my mind – is it's one way we humans (a) try to explain an incomprehensible world and (b) try to … palliate the … almost unimaginable thought of our own deaths. … When one really faces, as one did in a real way, the possibility of one's death, this is a time to think very hard. I would find nothing in formal religion any comfort whatsoever. I would say … as an evolving notion of thought – I don't mean to say this unkindly or condescendingly or patronisingly – I see most formal religions … as a kind of childish, early effort to understand the world. My science tells me more about my finiteness. It's enormously sad. …

"So, in a sense, religion was an early scientific way to explain the world. It was also a very frightening world and they wanted to placate the powers. … So there's this massive vested interest, in all sorts of ways, of keeping these cultural things going. … And because we're told these stories as children, we believe them. I'm sure people believe in ghosts and things that go bump in the night etcetera. You know, people listen to some kind of frightening music and it goes back to the … childhood days of being afraid of the dark etcetera. … And then you get all sorts of … interesting coincidences and so forth. And of course we are so – as my lecture is showing you – so incredibly egotistical … Every human being sees themselves as the centre of the universe, because we actually project God in to ourselves and out of us; that's just who we are. …

"You climb a mountain: wow – you're nothing, are you? You're flotsam and jetsam. And it doesn't worry us. It shouldn't worry us."

The consolation Professor Robson has been able to take from his atheistic world view during his time on the abyss has been two-fold: first, there is the consolation derived from putting things into perspective and realising his incredible insignificance in the scheme of things more potently than any religious believer ever could; second, there is the special kind of comfort or intellectual satisfaction that he was able to take from being able to truly accept the totality of his own personal finitude and keep a hold on to his atheism – not giving in to any emotional desire for a religious belief. Ella Hamilton did muse about whether there might be a certain pride here associated with accepting what is a reality of the adult world – that we all die, forever – and she wondered whether holding the rationale high ground might prepare one better for facing up to various other realities when coping with ageing. She also felt that the atheistic stance on life after death and its non-existence was certainly not an emotionally compelling view but just simply a mature position that some people are able to reach more easily than others. Indeed, most of the Humanists did concede that the emotional appeal of the major religions is a potent force and a few of the Humanists thought that Humanism was not consoling in any way.

Mrs Eileen Hodges, a retired speech therapist, was uncertain as to whether Humanism can provide one with any special comfort or consolation:

"It is difficult to face that you will die, and in a sense you can never quite face it until it happens and you have to, I suppose. But one does things like try to be healthy and eat the right things. Why are you doing that? Because you want to prolong life I suppose, particularly to try to preserve being independent ... and feeling some sort of sense of well-being, which I mostly do. ...

"Everything – every plant and tree – is either growing or declining ... And really, when you think of the universe, you are just such a microcosm that ... in the space-time thing, it's nothing. ... That's one you've got to tell yourself. I don't get much comfort from that really, because the here and now is the major thing, isn't it. ... You cope mostly with the immediate future, and the immediate future is going to happen. ... You look in your diary and expect to be there. ... Humanism just makes you a bit more realistic about it."

Mrs Hodges' partner Reginald Williams is equally neutral on the subject and just takes a pragmatic view on death and coping with the challenges of ageing:

"When you're dead, you're dead. That's it. I can't ... reconcile myself to any belief that there's anything else. ... Before you're born, where are you? You don't exist. After you die, you still don't exist. That's it. ...

"I've no illusions about God helping me, or that anyone's going to help me in that way. There's no sort of magic lamp to rub and a genie appears. There's no God going to solve my problems. I've got to solve them myself or elicit the help of, say, social services and various other organisations to help me."

When Professor Robson compared his own near-death experience with that of a late friend of his, Werner, who converted from atheism to Catholicism on his deathbed, he felt very strongly that he would never want to accept the "insurance policy" of Christianity because he felt it would be a false consolation that would undermine the man of science and reason he has become, and that really there is no disadvantage in accepting that there is only one life:

"The priest was a good guy and a friend, a pal, and [he] offered him [Werner] the consolation. And Werner shook me rigid by telling me he was praying for me and that he'd now got hope. My response to Werner – 'cause we wanted to climb our mountain together, which we'd only climbed a year ago – was to say: 'I too have hope. We will climb the mountain together, at another time, another place, without effort. And we will dance in the wind, we'll laugh in the rain and bask in the sun without the effort, because … we … belong to the whole world, and the world belongs to us.' And that, to me, is a reasonable position, because we understand that matter doesn't change, or it simply just changes its form."

Of course Professor Robson stood by his atheistic belief at his friend's deathbed, because the gross insincerity of embracing religion with him would have been a betrayal of the bond they had shared throughout their lives together as friends.

It can be argued that there is another consolation that atheists can take from their belief system: that they can die with ease knowing that they will not be judged by any God after they have died, that they will simply cease to exist in any form. The same goes for contemplating the loss of a loved one and whether they might be punished after death or not. As Malcolm Lockyer put it:

"Sleep is death's counterfeit. That's, to me, what death is like: it's sleep from which you don't wake up. …

"I don't believe she [Avril] exists anywhere. I don't believe she's sitting somewhere and waiting for me, or anything like this. But she does exist in my memory and my children's memories … I mean, I've only got to … not to do something here and I think, 'I'll do this thing afterwards', and then I think, 'No, Avril wouldn't want that', which is silly. Avril exists within me, almost within everything I do. She's been so much a part of my life for 40 years – well almost 40 years – that you just don't say, 'Well, I'll move on.' That, to me, is what immortality is: the continuing of that person … as long as our family lasts.…

"The loss of somebody is really a self-pitying thing. … Like they say, 'Oh, poor person', you know, 'Poor chap's died.' Well he's not feeling anything any more. But the people who are left are feeling. And I think that's the point. So I don't think it's of any consequence to think, 'I wish I believed, then I'd have something to hang on to', you know … I don't find that."

Inspiration

Professor Robson's encounter with *The Guardian* article that revealed a distant galaxy gave him some comfort by revealing his ultimate insignificance, but it was also an inspirational moment for him. His trust in the scientific process and his awed fascination for the secrets of the natural world perhaps should not be likened to religious fervour, but the inspirational power of a total atheistic belief system is a force to be reckoned with nonetheless. Again, it would be naïve and blatantly incorrect to claim that only the non-religious can find science inspiring. Clearly it is true that many religious persons could interpret scientific revelation as a process of unravelling God's intricate and wondrous handiwork. However, for those who see religion as a primitive precursor to science and something that simply cannot be embraced alongside scientific thinking, the inspiration to be found in a materialistic conceptualisation of the universe can be stimulating and energising. And this inspiration and wonder is something which Professor Robson believes should be nurtured:

> "The Buddhists have this sense of loss of self, which we find sometimes in music. … For example, I used to sing in a choir. … What I love about the music, or playing in an orchestra, is getting totally lost and being part of this incredible sound, so I literally can't hear my own voice or the part of the music I'm playing, and that's wonderful. I call it aesthetic, call it spiritual. There's no question about it; that's a dimension of human lives. And that aesthetic needs to be developed. … So it's that ability for humans, that potential for humans, to go on enhancing not only their physical and their emotional, but also that intellectual aesthetic, spiritual side. But it doesn't mean there's something out there. No, it's human beings whose reach will always be shorter than their grasp."

Mrs Ruth Collyer, who was born in 1930, is another Humanist who finds science inspiring:

> "I think the world is fantastic, and the more I find out about, or hear about, exploration. … Our grandson, who's been at [name] University actually, he's just qualified, and he's an astrophysicist. And when he talks about the things that he's investigating, I mean, I find it quite mind-boggling and amazing and … awe-inspiring I suppose. I think it's incredible. And how people are discovering more and more and getting, so they think, closer and closer to the … Big Bang … I can't understand it, but I'm fascinated to hear about it and just think it's extraordinary and wonderful."

One other source of inspiration from the whole of the atheist's world view palate is the belief that life is finite. Malcolm Lockyer feels that this belief brings with it an extra pressure to use time well and to live life more fully and morally. To him this is largely an inspirational view – encouraging him for his own sake to have a busy and rich experience of life while it lasts – but it also makes him feel as if he ought to live well and correctly, believing as he does that his legacy will be all that he leaves behind after he dies. So his retired life involves some voluntary charity work but also an indulgence in things he finds interesting and enjoyable, and this helps him to cope as a bereaved person and as an ageing individual.

Conclusion

In this chapter we have heard from a small number of Humanist interviewees who have been enabled to speak about their beliefs and coping with ageing through volunteering and helping with a research project. The approach of this chapter has been simply one of content analysis with clustered quotations. It has been important to make a start at researching and documenting atheism and agnosticism in old age since these belief structures have been largely ignored in the literature on belief and coping with ageing. It has also been important to look at this under-researched subject with a certain degree of depth. By immersion in the worlds of the atheistic older person we have tried, through this intimate experience, to comprehend sincerely their way of viewing life and death and to represent their thoughts straightforwardly and with empathetic understanding. Producing this chapter has been an exercise in giving voice to these Humanist individuals and it is intended to be no more than this. While the chapter has been a forum for presenting case evidence for when and how atheism can help the individual cope with aspects of ageing, it is worth restating what this chapter has not aimed to achieve.

This chapter does not oppose or deny the value of religious beliefs in helping individuals to cope. As previous chapters have documented, strong religious beliefs can help people enormously in times of adversity (Dein and Stygall, 1997; Pargament, 1997; Gall and Cornblat, 2002; Nelson et al, 2002; McClain-Jacobson et al, 2004). It is also known that people's beliefs are rarely used exclusively as a lone coping tool (Pargament, 1997; Wilkinson and Coleman, 2010). A case-by-case selection of individual stories about atheists coping with ageing could fill a book unto itself but would be mainly made up of examples of coping strategies that are focused on the day-to-day and that are somewhat removed from people's existential or philosophical beliefs. This chapter has merely attempted to look at the interface between humanistic beliefs and coping with ageing.

It is intended that this chapter be thought of as a descriptive sketch and guided snapshot of what atheistic belief can bring people in times of hardship in old age through atheism's capacity to inform, guide, console and inspire the individual. Provided one accepts Richard Dawkins' assertion that religions mainly serve to provide explanation, exhortation, consolation and inspiration for people (Dawkins, 2006), the similarities between having a strong atheistic world view and a strongly religious take on life are hopefully now obvious. On the basis of the interview material presented in this chapter, it is therefore suggested that a strong atheistic belief system can be a genuinely workable alternative to a religious world view and can indeed fulfil the same role(s) in people's lives as a strong religious belief system. To what extent this is true for the wider population of atheists is another question.

While this chapter has been a small beginning in this arena of study, many more testimonies could be extracted from willing individuals without much difficulty and the weight of case evidence could well build up. Exploratory and descriptive work is useful in the early stages of research and understanding (Coleman, 2002), but atheism and coping in old age can become better and more critically understood if more directed and methodical work is begun in this area. Questions remain as to whether the model of strong atheism as an analogue to strong religious belief would stand up to empirical scrutiny, but the question also remains as to what it is about beliefs that most affects how well individuals cope when mobilising and utilising their beliefs. In other words, what would affect the outcome of coping with ageing more: belief content or belief strength? Perhaps the more an individual has challenged their own assumptions and beliefs about the universe, the more their eventual conclusions are better refined and of a higher calibre. On the basis of the exploratory work that has been conducted for this chapter and for the study into strong beliefs and coping with ageing (Wilkinson and Coleman, 2010), it would seem that the old adage that the examined life is worth living is certainly true: it appears that individuals who have questioned life's mysteries and have found answers that appeal to them on many levels demonstrate an ability to cope well with the challenges of ageing, and this includes atheists and agnostics.

SEVEN

Religious memory and age: European diversity in historical experience of Christianity

Peter G. Coleman, Marie Gianelli, Marie A. Mills and Ignat Petrov

European religious diversity

Although this book's focus has been on the beliefs expressed by British older people it is no longer possible to draw strong boundaries around the beliefs of a particular nation, society or culture. We live in an increasingly globalised world, of regular tourist travel as well as of migration in search of better work opportunities, and also, increasingly in mature adulthood, of hopes for an improved quality of life. Religious influences from neighbouring and more distant cultures impact on our lives in ways that can be illuminating but also unsettling. This is particularly so if the new culture exemplifies a more vibrant form of faith, which raises questions about the depth of our own commitments. The arrival of Pentecostal peoples from Africa and the Caribbean has not only broadened the spectrum of Christian worship in the UK but has also provided an unaccustomed degree of witness to the action of the Holy Spirit in people's lives. The recent influx of Catholics from Asia, as well as from Eastern European countries such as Poland, is changing the culture of the Roman Catholic Church in the UK, just as Irish immigration did in the 19th century. The new religious practices which the immigrants bring with them can provide attractive invigorating new models for the host population.

In this and the following chapter we shall consider what can be learned from better acquaintance with the experience of ageing within different religious cultures. Religious attitudes tend to be shaped early in life, but their influence lasts a lifetime, and the cultural and communal memories associated with the practice of a particular religious faith often achieve maximum impact in late life. The historical and cultural experiences intimately connected with one's religion are therefore important factors to consider when attempting to understand and assess older persons' spiritual needs. This experience is far from homogeneous. In this chapter we will examine three examples of older people's memories of Christian faith in Eastern and Southern Europe that vary considerably from that of their counterparts in the predominantly Protestant societies of north-west Europe. The following chapter will consider the other great faiths in Britain, particularly

Islam, but also Hinduism and Buddhism, as well as Judaism, which for centuries was the only other major religion with a noticeable presence in the country.

It is important to realise just how narrow this book's cultural focus has been so far. Most of the British data considered has been drawn from studies in England, and, as far as our European neighbours are concerned, we have only given attention to data from the Netherlands because of the high quality of the research studies conducted there on religion and society. Moreover, Dutch evidence has been consistent with British in highlighting trends towards individual eclectic spirituality and away from respect for church teaching and authority. However, Britain and the Netherlands do not necessarily provide a representative picture of the state of Christianity in Europe. They both present a picture of religious decline over the last 50 years, a distancing from churches and an increasing interest in private spirituality. But data from other countries could be cited to exemplify increasing religious belief and practice (Eastern Europe), relative stability of significantly higher levels of religiosity (the Mediterranean region), as well as stability at lower levels of religious attendance combined with a continuing public approval (including financing) for religious organisations (Scandinavia and the Nordic countries) over the same period of time. Even within the boundaries of the 27 countries currently belonging to the European Union, there is a wide diversity of Christian cultures (Scheepers and Schilderman, 2010).

Historical and other reasons can be cited for the quite dramatic differences in religiosity to be found across Europe. Moreover, the kinds of geographical generalisations given above only have a very rough validity. Europe presents a kaleidoscope of different types and intensity of belief (Eurobarometer, 2005). For example, some of the lowest levels of belief in God and church allegiance are found in the relatively small area of the Czech Republic, where only 19% express a belief in a god. The origins of antipathy to church authority in matters of belief have been traced to the religious wars in central Europe of the 17th century, and even further back to the particular event of the dishonest execution of the Czech church reformer Jan Hus in the early 15th century. Similarly Greeley (2003, 2004) has attributed the decline of the Anglican Church in England to its lack of creditable origins in the enforced replacement of popular Catholic culture and monastic institutions with an established state church by Henry VIII and his successors in the 16th century. Whatever the truth behind such undoubtedly over-simplistic associations in time, it is clear that historical experience of Christianity has varied across Europe and needs close examination to explain why, for example, a prosperous and harmonious country such as the Netherlands should have become markedly less religious, while an equally if not more prosperous and harmonious country such as Switzerland has not.

Welfare provision is one area of European life where the religious dimension is being included in research studies, and this of course has major implications for ageing. Of particular importance in this regard are the project on 'Welfare and Religion in 21st century Europe' (WREP), and its successor project 'Welfare and Values in Europe' (WaVE), organised by the Religion and Society Research

Centre at the University of Uppsala in Sweden. These studies examine the current place of religion in Europe, and its role in the wider society, by examining case studies taken from eight countries, all from the western part of Europe, with the exception of Greece. They include Orthodox Christian as well as Protestant and Catholic Christian cultures, and the second study expands the consideration to include also minority religious cultures within these countries.

The first report of this group (Bäckström et al, 2010) demonstrates the different patterns of expectations of welfare and the role played by state, family and church in the separate parts of Europe. The societal context in which older people encounter churches in their role in providing welfare differs greatly from country to country. In some, the churches play an open and, particularly in Germany, a major role in welfare provision, whereas in France, as a result of the principle of *laïcité* that banishes religion from the public sphere, the role of religiously motivated individuals in welfare provision is more hidden. In the south of Europe, where expectations of the family are greater and of the state much less, the role of the churches has come under increased scrutiny, with the greater pressures on families as women work more outside the home. To what extent should the church take on or expand its role in welfare provision, especially if this should weaken its religious role? How should it balance its obligations on both material and spiritual fronts?

In this chapter we shall give illustrations of older people's experience of Christianity in different parts of Europe that provide particularly striking contrasts with the British situation. The first two examples are drawn from Orthodox Christianity in Eastern Europe, which has only in the last 20 years emerged from a long period of persecution by secular authorities. Most older Christians in these societies have spent the greater part of their lives resisting the power of state atheism (Froese, 2008), and their models of religious life are provided by their parents and grandparents, who maintained their faith sometimes at great risks to their careers and even their lives. Our interviews also illustrate the varied experience of church life during and after the communist period. We cite memories of the earliest severe persecutions in Russia before the Second World War as well as the somewhat contrasting post-war experiences of Bulgaria and Romania. The final illustrations in this chapter are taken from Southern Europe, from the heartland of the Roman Catholic Church in Italy. The Church has remained a very important social, political and cultural power throughout current older people's lives. Not all older people will have supported the Church but they will not have been able to ignore its very visible presence in their local communities, especially at key religious festivals during the year. Particularly in rural areas, in which many of our interviews have taken place, religious practice lay at the heart of family and communal life and continues to sustain a now ageing community's sense of itself in the face of social change.

Older people's memories of religious life under atheistic persecution in the USSR

Besides the vicious record of destruction, murder and imprisonment, what is strikingly apparent from oral history investigation of religious life in the former Soviet Union is the stubborn faith of many older people (Ware, 1997). Older women in particular, who were less subject than men to surveillance, persisted in religious practices that they had learned from their parents and grandparents, and continued to transmit them within their families. They seized opportunities to take their children and grandchildren to church for services of initiation and gave them basic instruction, often protecting the adult men by keeping these activities secret from them. Continuity across the generations was therefore preserved to some extent. The present generation of older people who attend church in Russia mostly did not do so when they were younger adults because it was actively discouraged, but they often have the memory of the example of their mothers and especially their grandmothers, and therefore once the restrictions were lifted they were able to continue in the pattern of their elders. As a result, religious practice has survived relatively intact through more than 70 years of persecution and has grown back strongly in the post-communist era.

In retrospect it appears that the Russian Orthodox Church's survival as a major institution was rescued almost at the last possible moment. Persecution, which had reached a crescendo of death and destruction in the late 1930s, was suspended during the struggle against Nazism because Stalin calculated that he needed to employ the Church's moral authority to bolster the population's motivation to resist the Nazi invasion. Although this led to some recovery of religious practice, including monastic life, persecution was renewed again under Krushchev. Nor was the Church an immediate beneficiary of Gorbachev's policy of glasnost and perestroika. Religious practice continued to be discouraged, although in 1988 the Russian Orthodox Church was allowed to celebrate the thousand year anniversary of the conversion of the Russian people. Therefore, by the time Soviet Union was dismantled in 1991, the older generation who had remained faithful throughout the persecutions was fast disappearing to be replaced apparently by only a small number of new converts. In the 1980s young people constituted no more than about 10% of the congregation at Sunday services.

With the sudden fall of communism in 1991 the situation changed. People were free to explore religious belief without constraints or punishments. There were no longer the informants at the back of churches noting down the names of those in the congregation who should not be there. The result was a mass curiosity about what the Church offered and also an evident wish to recover old habits and reconnect with pre-revolutionary Russia. Although now the older generation of continuous practitioners has died out, older people, particularly older women, still maintain their traditionally strong presence in churches throughout the working day. However, their religious behaviours, although based on strong remembrance of older family members, are relatively new for them.

We conducted a small study in 2002–03, thus just over 10 years since the lifting of restrictions, in which we interviewed 20 people over the age of 50 years known via contacts both at one central Moscow church and at Moscow State University (Coleman and Mills, 2004). All participants had some memories to recount of church and religious life in their early years, but none had received any formal education at the hands of the Orthodox Church. Those who had learned some religious faith and practice had done so from mothers, nannies and grandparents. It had been impossible for their family to have done more. As a woman of 67 years stressed, her mother would have been "fired" from her work if she had let her daughter attend a lesson at church.

However, 12 of the 20 had been taken to church when they were young, even if only to put up a candle. Some remembered their mothers asking the priest to pray for a sick or dead relative. Three of them stressed that these visits had been made before they reached the age of going to school and not afterwards (in the Soviet period children were encouraged to denounce parental behaviour of this kind to schoolteachers). Most tellingly, to the crucial question whether their parents had been religious, not one of the 20 participants knew for certain whether their fathers believed. Some commented that their father had been a member of the (Communist) Party and therefore forbidden to have any religious allegiance. They were more likely to be sure of their mothers' beliefs. Four knew that their mothers believed, although they did not necessarily go to church. Others were more or less unsure. One commented that "mother believed in her soul". Another commented of both her parents that "even if they believed they tried not to show it". Evidence of belief was stronger in the behaviour of their grandparents, and some of the most vivid accounts of early religious memories, examples of which we now describe, were associated with grandparents.

Not all of the people in our sample were currently strong believers, and there was an evident association in our sample between current strength of belief and the affective quality of the earliest memories of religion. A woman aged 75 years, while recognising the calming influence of church attendance on others, did not attend and saw "almost no meaning" in it for herself. She remembered the beautiful foliage and flower decorations of the churches at Pascha (Easter) and Pentecost (Whitsun), and even now enjoyed watching the Paschal services on television. But the predominant memories of church services were mostly unattractive, of "old women kissing priests' hands", conveying an impression of the people there as "a mass of something old and mossy".

The vast majority, however, had very positive memories of church activities: of the internal beauty of the churches; the religious processions with crosses and banners; the bells ringing; the ceremonies of baptism, marriage and funerals. Above all there were the Paschal festivities:

> "Early morning light, a white wall, dark wooden tables with a lot of Paschal cakes on them ... the priest going around those tables blessing

the cakes and the people … it's just a visual image, but it's very bright
… striking beauty … when I was about five or six."

Church services were remembered above all for their beauty and the good feelings
they engendered.

Even potentially frightening memories could be interpreted positively. A woman
aged 67 years commented how when she was small she went with friends to a
church wedding in the country, and fell asleep:

> "I don't know how long I was in the church, but I remember that
> I regained consciousness when I was already alone in the church. I
> looked above me and saw a big icon of Christ who was wagging His
> finger at me. I was very scared. I was trying to find an exit and couldn't
> find it. I couldn't understand why I was alone there. When I came
> to my friends and asked them why they had left me, they told me
> that they had lost me. So, I consider even this positive, because now I
> understand that it was something like a warning to me."

More memorable still were the witnesses to faith within the family. A woman
aged 64 years told us of her earliest memory of going to church:

> "Secretly, so my father, who was in the Communist Party, didn't know
> and didn't have any problems at work and wasn't arrested, my mother
> took me to the church. It was in early childhood. I just remember its
> darkness, the lighted candles and beautiful singing and it was good. I
> was seven or eight at the time, maybe even smaller."

Others remembered family discussions. Another woman aged 67 years remembered
her aunt saying to her mother:

> "Vera will soon go to school, let us take her to the church so she
> receives communion, because soon it will be time for her to start
> confessing by herself. … Then I was taken to the local church, confessed
> and received communion."

Most striking of all were the memories of grandparents. They had not all
abandoned their icons and prayer books, which they often kept in hidden places.
Their grandchildren remembered them going to the icons in difficult times.
Priests held funeral services for their grandparents and small icons were placed
on their graves. A number of the sample said that grandparents had taught them
how to pray. General discussions on the subject of religion were also remembered:

> "My grandmother on my mother's side was very religious. Very often I talked to her about God. I still remember those talks. I saw her burial service and it impressed me a lot."

Particular episodes associated with grandparents could leave a lasting impression. A woman aged 64 years remembered visiting her grandmother in Leningrad at the age of 12 or 13:

> "I was lying in my bed in the room where she had icons, but I couldn't fall asleep. She came to my room and started praying and for the first time in my life I saw a blue light – nimbus – over the head of the praying person. … I wasn't surprised or scared."

Thus the home itself, particularly in the circumstances of the Soviet persecution, could take the place of the local church as the centre of prayer and worship.

Experiences of conversion following the ending of persecution

The statistics from our sample – none knew whether their fathers believed, none felt able to lead a religious life as young adults – are compelling evidence of the depth and success of the persecution. School indoctrination had a decisive influence on religious practice:

> "After I started studying in school, I was dissuaded of the existence of God and never went to the church again."

Another commented:

> "When I was younger religion didn't mean anything to me. I was absolutely sure that there's nothing except the world that I can see and feel."

At most they had visited churches as tourists, admiring and learning of its architecture. One woman, whose family had possessed many icons, worked in the Ministry of Culture for many years, treating icons only as works of art. Her religious education had begun again in recent years.

Most had entered or come back to the Church during middle or later adulthood, but relatively few in the period before the fall of communism. One of the men in the sample, a university professor, explained how he had begun to take an interest in religious reading in the 1970s in the period of growing dissidence, although he did not become a member of the Church until the fall of the USSR. The pressure that people still felt, until late in the communist period, was expressed by one woman. Her mother had been a believer, had seen that her daughter was baptised but otherwise did not visit the church. When her daughter joined the

Church and made her first confession in 1983 she admitted she was afraid lest it be reported to the place where she was working. A number of others attributed their reluctance to the "warlike atheism" that characterised the USSR. Another commented:

> "All of my life until 1988 the Soviet agitation told me that I had to be against the Church. It was only because I did not like the pressure put on me that I did not become an enemy of the Church, but I had a strong fear of it."

Family relationships remained an important element in people's final conversion. The woman referred to earlier, who had ceased believing after attending school, attributed her second conversion also to her mother:

> "I think I came to the church after the death of my mother. I started seeing her in my dreams. Then I noticed that she came to me in my dreams after the Saturday for the commemoration of the dead, when I didn't go to the church to write a note to a priest asking him to pray for my dead relatives. When my mother was alive, she wrote those notes by herself and just asked me to go to the church to give them to a priest. When she died I didn't remember about the Commemoration Saturday and didn't write notes asking for prayers for my dead relatives, and my mother came to me in my dreams. When I started attending a church and no longer missed religious holidays and always wrote the notes to priests, she stopped coming to me in my dreams. Also my mother always wanted me to go to church with her and when she died I wanted to do something that would please her and so I started to go to church. First just to please her, and then I began to listen to what the priest was saying. When the Soviet Union collapsed, I lost the sense of my life and the Church helped me to find it."

The woman aged 64, who remembered being taken "secretly" to church by her mother as a small child, explained how it had been "impossible" for her to attend in the time of communism. All the churches had been closed. She recounted a key experience when they started restoring the churches:

> "I was going somewhere for work and suddenly found myself near a church which was open. I couldn't just pass it. I went inside. It was something apart from my own will. I was coming from my work and then suddenly I found myself standing in the church. … My legs brought me to the church and I felt I couldn't leave it. I was told [later, when she attended church instruction] that it was because the place was steeped in prayer, and evidently, I felt the presence of God there, so how could I leave it?"

A number of the priests and older members of the central Moscow parish we studied had been influenced by Father Alexander Men, a charismatic pastor and writer, who had worked for the renewal of the Russian Orthodox Church (Roberts and Shukman, 1996). He was also active in making links with Christians in other countries and was a major influence on people from all walks of life in the 1970s and 1980s from his parish just outside Moscow. He had successfully outwitted the KGB for many years, but was murdered outside his home in 1990, shortly before the fall of the communist regime. No one has ever been charged with his murder.

At least five of our sample mentioned Father Alexander Men as a major influence on their conversion to Christianity: meeting him, hearing his sermons, reading his writings and also witnessing the episode of his death. He provided the intellectual and moral backbone for belief in those who floundered because of their lack of religious education. As one of those with no family religious background who had been brought to the Church by Father Alexander Men commented:

> "I still feel on the 'way to Church'. We were atheists for too long.
> There is such a desire for belief."

Generally our sample showed an extremely good awareness of the problems that the contemporary Russian Orthodox Church faced, particularly in regard to the training of priests. There was understanding for the effects of the years of persecution, which had eliminated the most talented and bold priests, encouraged formalism, and inhibited social challenge. At the same time they provided a more favourable context for judging the actions of those who sought to preserve the life of the Russian Orthodox Church in its darkest period. Dostoyevsky's comment that 'beauty will save the world' certainly seems to apply here. The childhood encounters with church life, although fleeting, had been sufficient to convey to many of our sample a sense of something divine beyond the power of this world. Although Soviet schooling had sought the most effective psychological means to destroy such cognitions, they had readily been revived after the liberation. Those without an early grounding in faith had much more difficulty in understanding religious faith, although they too could be reached by pastors such as Father Alexander Men.

Nevertheless, the relationship between faith and age seems to be a very important one. Older people's religious authority within the family in the past were acknowledged. An example of this comes from recent interviews with war veterans across the former Soviet Union about adaptation to social change (Coleman and Poldolskij, 2007). A veteran from Karelia in Northern Russia near the Finnish border referred consistently to his mother and to her faith in his accounts of the various trials he endured during the war:

> "[On returning] I bowed to my mother first of all. It's probably because of her prayers that I have survived. The old ones, they were the religious people of the country. They taught the children all of that."

But perhaps even more importantly the examples older people had given in the past were seen as valid models for present older people's transmission of the faith to younger people for the future. As one of our sample stressed, central to conversion and to the survival of a faith community is the "continuing experience of communication with people who believe in God".

Belief in a 'wounded' church: contrasts between Bulgaria and Romania

All communist states established in Eastern Europe after the Second World War followed the example of the USSR in attempting to impose secular alternatives to religion. However, the results achieved varied from country to country. The Bulgarian government was one of the most successful in gradually limiting the influence of religion to that of a cultural and historical relic. Religion by contrast fared much better in the adjacent country of Romania, where, although all church activity was kept under strict government supervision, the population remained largely religious in attitude. The difference is still very evident today, with 82% of Romanians stating religion to be an important aspect of their lives, compared with 42% of Bulgarians (the UK figure was 45% and the EU25 average 52%) (Eurobarometer, 2005). A comparison between the two countries may throw light on the contribution religion makes to a society, including the welfare of older people.

Bulgaria and Romania have many similarities. They are of roughly equivalent socioeconomic status and have both recently (1 January 2007) been admitted to membership of the European Union. Both are characterised historically by a similar Orthodox Christian culture, four to five centuries of Ottoman rule until national liberation was achieved in the later 19th century, periods of war and turmoil in the first half of the 20th century, and communist dictatorship in the wake of the Second World War up to the revolutions of 1989. Both countries developed their Christian faith from Constantinople and maintained Orthodoxy as their principal Christian denomination. Both countries also have significant levels of religious heterogeneity, Bulgaria possessing long-established Muslim populations, and Romania possessing Catholic and Lutheran and other Protestant Christians as well as Orthodox. There have also been long-standing ties between religion and politics in Bulgaria and Romania (as in most other Orthodox societies). This tradition goes back to the Byzantine Empire's close links between Patriarch and Emperor, was continued albeit in subservient ways in the Ottoman period, and emerged again strongly in the 19th century as part of the nation-building processes and the struggles for independence in south-east Europe.

Despite the shared dominance of Orthodox Christianity, Bulgaria today displays a curiously paradoxical form of religiosity in comparison with Romania (Kanev, 2002). Large numbers of Bulgarians indicate attachment to Orthodoxy but religious practice is low. The Bulgarian Orthodox Church has again been given an important symbolic role in the post-communist Bulgarian state but its social and intellectual influence remains weak. This is in striking contrast not only to neighbouring Orthodox countries, but also to Russia – a traditional ally, where churches and monasteries endured a much longer period of persecution and degradation, but are now in large part splendidly restored, often at great expense.

Explanations for the Bulgarian 'exceptional case' include the successful subversion by the Bulgarian communist authorities of the previous religious meanings of the annual calendar of feasts and festivals by reconceptualising their meaning (Koleva, 2007). The effect has been to weaken Christian connotations in favour of folklorist and older pagan meanings. Thus religion was successfully integrated into 'cultural heritage', a success largely pre-conditioned by the proximity between religion and nation. A certain degree of tolerance was (tacitly) granted to funeral rites and commemorations, where religion more or less retained its symbolic dominance. As Lambert argues, this can be seen as evidence of the 'intrinsic limit to a ritual system created by a dogma that does not … entertain any destiny after death' (Lambert, 2005: 28).

It is probably over-simplistic to attribute the success of communist propaganda to the post-war communist government's policy alone. Exploration is needed of other factors that may have made the Bulgarian church more vulnerable to subversion into 'museum pieces' of Bulgarian history and culture. These include the long Greek dominance over the Bulgarian church from the time of its inclusion in the Ottoman Empire until it was allowed its own clergy and language later in the 19th century, and the resulting strong association of the Bulgarian clergy with nationalistic aspirations rather than spiritual leadership.

The oft-cited intrinsic 'realistic' or 'pragmatic' character of the Bulgarian people may be a shorthand expression for an underlying awareness that religion has often functioned more as a communal source of identity – Easter night celebrations of the Risen Christ are again well attended – than as a personal source of coping or devotion. In a situation of 'militant atheism' (reaching the point of open repression between 1947 and 1953), these attitudes paved the way for the rationalistic arguments of a 'scientific' world view concordant with communist modernisation. However, it is also true that the communist period and its aftermath witnessed a proliferation of forms of 'popular' (informal) religiosity. These were mostly local cults performed by women in rural regions and centred round a 'sacred' place, icon or other marker and relying on ritual practices rather than on knowledge of the Orthodox canon. Such popular spirituality continues to attract attention to the detriment of religious practice.

A further complicating problem in the Bulgarian situation is the split within its Bulgarian Orthodox Church, which occurred after the ending of communist rule in 1989. The Church split in two, with a sizeable number demanding (unsuccessfully) the Patriarch's abdication because of his failure to oppose the communist regime effectively and then setting up a rival synod in opposition. The same patriarch is still alive at the point of writing, and the split remains a painful aspect of Bulgarian church life, and has certainly hampered the church in ministering effectively to the nation.

The Romanian Orthodox Church, by contrast, has shown a much stronger continued development throughout the whole period since the Second World War. A strong spiritual renewal movement took place in the late 1950s, and there has been a stream of strong spiritual figures both before and after communism. The Romanian church has produced one of the most distinguished of modern Orthodox theologians (Dumitru Staniloae). Again historical factors may be at play. The Romanian Church had a greater degree of independence than the Bulgarian under Ottoman rule (church bells, forbidden in Bulgaria, could be rung in Romania). There was also a lack of consistent communist suppression of the Romanian Church by communist authorities (in contrast to the Greek Catholic Church with links to Rome and the west). A large number of Orthodox churches were left open, and there were many monasteries continuing to function. The differences can also be attributed to the inherent religious character of the people. But this attribution is itself only a description of an underlying reality, which needs historical and cultural as well as social and psychological explanation.

In recent years we have conducted survey interviews in both Bulgaria and Romania among the older population who experienced the communist attempts to repress religion. These interviews confirm the huge difference in religiosity between the two countries (Coleman et al, 2011). Whereas as many of 61% of the Romanian participants express a strong level of spiritual belief in a transcendent power operating in their lives, the Bulgarian figure is very much lower at 24%. The same large difference applies to prayer, with 86% of older Romanians in the sample claiming to pray daily compared with only 29% of the older Bulgarians. Interestingly a similar contrast does not apply to church services. Attendance averaged near monthly in both countries. This is consistent with the view that in Bulgaria attendance at church is often seen as a traditional communal activity that does not imply a high strength of belief.

We explored older people's experiences of and attitudes to religion in subsequent interviews with a selected sample of participants from our Bulgarian survey. We interviewed 14 persons we knew to be members of the Bulgarian Orthodox Church. All had attended church services, although some no longer went because of physical limitations. There was an overall consistency in their views of the persecution of the church and of the effects this had had on people's religious behaviour, but not all condemned the previous communist government. Some considered they had lived better then. Those with longer memories also idealised the period before the communist coup of 1944, when, for example, everyone owned their own land. Some had joined the Communist Party and accepted its collectivist policies; others had not. One participant told how his father had refused to join a cooperative farm agreement and was forced eventually to sign with a gun to his head. His son, like his father, had remained religious and did not join the party.

However, not all experienced a conflict between religion and communism. One widow of 75 years told us that her mother had been religious and her father communist but there had been no difficulties in the home. She had been brought up religiously and the family celebrated religious holidays together. She herself had joined the Communist Party, but remained a religious practitioner, and her husband had developed a successful building business. She was proud of the help she and her husband had been able to give other people, but appeared to feel the need to justify herself:

> "My conscience is clear. I have done no wrong. ... I believe. When I see a person walking with two sacks, I ask, 'Can I help you?' When I go to sleep, I know that I have done no wrong. I say, 'Thank you God'. In the morning I cross myself. I read the Bible. ... [I believe] there is some force which is in charge. ... I had a church marriage."

Others, by contrast, clearly felt that they had to curtail their religious activities during the communist period. Another widow aged 63 years had also followed her father in joining the communist party and had been successfully discouraged from going to church:

> "It was difficult. I was a party member. I wanted to go to church, especially at Easter. But there were party meetings and there they told us not to go to church. There were persons on duty at the church to observe. But there were people who visited the church despite everything."

Others too remembered the checks on religious attendance and the sanctions taken as a result. One woman commented on the sense of "shame" that became ingrained with entering a church, not only the fear of losing one's job. A 71-year-old widower who came from a very religious family had continued going into the church despite joining the communist party, but took care, he said, not to "cross" himself (presumably so as not to be identified as a definite believer).

As we observed in our other studies, participants' religious attitudes appeared to be strongly associated with memories of their parents. Those whose parents had been very religious, tended also to have strong religious feelings. In most cases mothers were remembered as being more religious than fathers. Mothers also persisted in religious behaviours, taking their children sometimes a great distance to church, and persisting in the face of discouragement. Another widow we interviewed, aged 75 years, recounted how others had tried to persuade her mother from visiting the church but without success. A widow aged 71 years described how her parents remained religious parents throughout the communist period, and this had had a strong and continuing influence on her:

"I believe. My parents educated me in this way. They were believers. They always had an icon present, even during socialism. They always respected the [Church] days of fasting and feasting. ... I was free to baptise both my daughters in the church, in 1960 and in 1968. Nobody reproached me. Perhaps there were others who did receive criticism. Probably they were members of the party? ... In the evenings before sleeping I say, 'God, forgive me!', and when I start out to go somewhere I say, 'God be before me!', and I make the sign of the cross. I learned this from my parents."

Not all participants, however, reported very religious parents. A married man aged 75 years told us that his mother had been the daughter of a priest, yet she did not attend church services. "Perhaps", he said, "she knew better what priests were like." Such attitudes were reflected in his own critical approach to clergy.

In considering the beliefs of these older people, it is important to bear in mind that we did not set out to interview persons of varying levels of strength of belief, but rather to appreciate the characteristic beliefs of older members of a 'wounded' church that had undergone many trials over the preceding 65 years. Although there was much criticism of the Orthodox Church, Christian belief and practice seemed to have emerged unscathed, at least among those we interviewed. Besides church attendance, it was striking how many referred to a regular prayer life, centred on morning and evening prayers, and devotional Orthodox practice such as fasting, prayer before icons, crossing oneself at the beginning and end of each day, and lighting candles for special intentions. These activities derived from instructions from parents rather than priests. As the second widow aged 75 years said, describing her religious response to a recent health problem:

"It was my own decision to begin fasting. When I was a child, my mother took me to church. Then I imagined God was very far. But now I realise that He is in the heart of every one of us."

The widower aged 71 years had preserved the strong religious sensitivity of his parents. He spoke of his local church, which he had helped build, as a "sacred place", and that it was important to respect all religious places, objects and institutions. Although he had lost his wife 30 years previously, and was still very depressed following the sudden death of his son in the previous year, going to church and lighting a candle to pray gave him moral support and relief from his distress. Despite the pain of his loss he did not blame God. It was not right to question God's purposes. "Spiritual" aspirations, he said, were more important than "material" ones.

However, most participants spoke of prayer in the context of personal need and especially health requests. For example, the married man aged 75 years gave us his reasons for being religious in the following terms:

"Religious practice gives me hope, belief. It helps me in difficulties. ... Sometimes, when I have been in hospital for an operation, the confidence it gave me was a help to me. Also, when I was in hospital, my wife would visit a church and light a candle. Even now, whenever our grandson has exams, she goes to the church of St Petka, lights a candle and says prayers. And always our grandson gains excellent marks!"

Others, such as the widow aged 63 years, referred to help in battling illness – breast cancer in her case – and the hope that she could engage with "some force". Another married man aged 76 years spoke of the help he had received through prayer when he had been involved in a serious accident at his work, dealing with the transport of dangerous loads.

Many shared the widower's sense of reassurance that belief in God brought them and some made the comment that "belief [was] necessary". The oldest person interviewed, a married woman aged 84 years, showed signs of physical and mental frailty. In addition, she had sorrows related to the recent death of her first child, and worries concerning both her sick husband, who had recently returned from hospital, as well as the upkeep of her house. But she was still able to say at the end of our interview that "when you believe in God, all is well". Another woman, aged 83 years, was still recovering from a severe depression following the recent deaths of both her husband and son. For her, God was of help "sometimes, but not every day". Even those in the sample who described themselves as less religious could appreciate how religious practice helped others to lessen their anxiety and fears.

One striking feature of these interviews from a UK perspective was the frequent reference to visits to monasteries. Within Western Europe monasteries have lost much of their previous aura as sites of pilgrimage, where one could go in search of healing and other blessings, or in thanks for blessings received, or often simply for inspiration in meeting life's challenges. The long historical decline in the significance of monasteries is not the case in Eastern Europe. Monasteries continue to exist in large numbers and have retained their power of attraction for the general population, and not only for those of strong religious belief. In Bulgaria monasteries also have a major historical and cultural value since they were the principal means by which the Bulgarian people retained a sense of itself through more than 500 years of Turkish domination. Bulgaria as a nation had ceased to exist for that period of time and became known as European Turkey, being situated in very close proximity to Istanbul, the capital of the Ottoman Empire. In their often rural and isolated situation, the monasteries preserved the memory of an earlier history, when Bulgaria was a major Christian nation vying also with Constantinople for leadership of south-east Europe. Monasteries also became the natural rallying points of rebellion as that earlier sense of nationhood reasserted itself in the 19th century.

The special aura monasteries preserved even through the communist period is shown by existing reports that even communist officials took their children to monasteries – usually distant from the capital so as to avoid scrutiny – for baptism.

A large proportion of our sample referred to journeys taken to monasteries as individuals and as families. Regular outings were organised for older people's groups to the various monasteries that could be reached on day trips. Both the more and less religious joined in these excursions and they clearly meant a lot to the participants.

The recent conflicts and scandals in the Bulgarian Orthodox Church greatly disturbed many of our informants. The much-loved previous parish priest in one of the areas where we interviewed had been dismissed by the Office of the Patriarch following complaints from local business men over his refusal to cooperate with them. All the people we spoke to in the area regarded the accusations made against the priest as unfair. Some were very distressed by what they experienced as a personal as well as communal loss. In another area a married man aged 75 years, with experience of working for a bank, commented on the financial dealings of the Bulgarian Orthodox Church and was particularly critical:

> "After 1989 I tried several times to go to church, but I was greatly disappointed with the Bulgarian priests. They became 'politicians'. ... The two synods quarrelled. They even went before the European Court of Justice in The Hague. They appeared as [rival] business interests. ... Perhaps because of my childhood experiences I expected spirituality in the church. Now what I saw were 'merchants' struggling for power and business. That is why I now prefer to turn to God on my own. I have one corner in my home with icons. Every morning I spend some minutes there in prayer. I go to the church very rarely, at Christmas and at Easter time."

Although his financial work had also led him to see examples of corruption even in monasteries, he still retained more respect for monks and nuns, in particular for the Bulgarian monastery which he had visited on Mount Athos in Greece:

> "I was impressed by the conduct of the monks, their devotion and purity. Perhaps these people in their detachment from society have preserved better their morals and their faith in God."

Moreover, criticism of the church in Bulgaria has to be seen in the context of the considerable disquiet older people felt about the quality of people in public life and particularly their inability to deal with corruption at high levels. The loss of the securities provided by the previous socialist regime had been a major source of social unease for the older generations (Petrov, 1996). The same man commented on how it was hard to separate the church's situation from the political one:

> "There is complete demoralisation in Bulgaria. It's a serious situation. Two or three generations are needed to restore morale."

A number of other participants expressed scepticism about how former members of the Communist Party who had previously persecuted the church could so easily have switched to being "friends" of the church, wanting to introduce religious education in schools and performing so easily religious behaviours such as "crossing" themselves. How genuine could their conversion be?

Clearly there were many issues from the past that had to be dealt with before older Bulgarians could feel at ease in a society that they had seen change so dramatically in recent years. For the oldest among them it was the second major social upheaval they had experienced in their lifetime.

Religious life and community in an ageing Catholic society: Liguria, Italy

Liguria, the Riviera coastal region of north-western Italy has the largest proportion of older people of any region in Europe (25% over the age of 65 years). It has a mild climate even in winter time, and many of the other qualities that attract people wanting a pleasant and peaceful retirement. It also contains well-known holiday resorts. Many workers from the industrial cities of northern Italy have been used to spending their summer holidays there, and some had already acquired second homes before retiring permanently in the region. But not all older people's lives are easy. Liguria has a rugged hinterland, which like many rural areas in Europe suffers from depopulation and the loss of younger people to work in the towns and cities. The mountain villages can have very large proportions of older people, with sometimes up to a third of the population over 65 years. For them the church is a major source of social support.

Our interviews with older villagers in the mountains in the east of the region have highlighted the vivid memories of Catholic religious life in the past and also nostalgia for what has been lost. The role of the parish priest has always been particularly important in these communities. Partly as a consequence of the anticlericalism of state institutions following the founding of united Italy in 1860 and the accompanying dismantling of papal power within Italy, the Catholic Church and State remained in opposition for the better part of the following century. Education of priests suffered as theology was suppressed in State universities, and Church-based educational institutions took time to develop appropriate curricula. But this had the beneficial consequence that priests remained closer to the ordinary people. This applied most strongly to rural areas, where priests were usually of rural origins themselves.

Difficult access to these areas, particularly in winter, often led parish priests to identify more strongly with their parishioners and even to join in their agricultural work. They developed a strictly disciplined interpretation of Christian values and practices, which they applied both to themselves and to their flock. The bonds between priest and parishioners could become very strong because they shared the same fatiguing life, as the following quotations from some of our interviewees show:

Maria: "I remember my Dad telling me that when he was a little boy, they had to get up very, very early to attend the Novenas [prayers on nine successive days] for All Souls, or for Christmas. Don Podestà really set them TOO early – at five o'clock in the morning! My father's family lived quite far from the Church, down by the river. But the children were supposed to go to the Novenas – otherwise they would be given nothing to eat! Just think! And then on All Souls' Day three Masses were said, besides a visit by the whole parish to the cemetery."

Marida: "Yes, we used to go to the Novenas. It was a good, long walk – but we used to go just the same. I remember we had to walk four or five kilometres up a steep road – we couldn't make it in half an hour – and yet in those days we could really walk fast! If I were to do it now, it would take more than three quarters of an hour. But when we got to the top, there, waiting for us, was a priest who loved his parishioners – and they loved him."

Giovanni: "Yes, at Christmas Don Vittorio held the Novena at half past five to six o'clock. Because, you know, afterwards he had to go working on the land like everybody else in the parish. Yes, he was just like any other farmer – and he was not the only one: the parish priest in [the next village] cultivated the land as well. Poor man, he slaved away, digging the Church land like mad!"

Sometimes, however, a stress on the more exacting aspects of religious practice could cause pain in a people already bowed down by a life of fatigue, poverty and lack of physical satisfaction:

Carla: "I still remember one episode that hurt deep down for years, when it came to my mind. … After our first Holy Communion we were supposed to 'do' nine first Fridays of the month. At that time fasting started rigorously from the previous midnight. I must have got to my fourth or fifth Friday and I was about six, or seven. That morning, before going to Mass, I had been told to make some butter. When I had done shaking the bottle and a little ball of butter had taken shape, I had a terrible temptation – I really loved butter! I took it out and licked it, though I didn't eat it. My mother came in just then, and saw me! She really tore me to pieces. AND I had to start the nine Fridays all over again, from the beginning. I remember I cried for a whole week – I felt so humiliated!"

By the end of the First World War – a time of great sacrifice, in which State and Church had both tried hard to mitigate the suffering – Catholics were ready to enter political life. In 1919 a Christian Trade Union was established and the

Sicilian priest Don Luigi Sturzo founded the *Partito Popolare Italiano*, addressing all Catholics who felt *liberi e forti* (that is, they had sufficient courage to display their religious beliefs within the context of the labour movement, which was by then dominated by communist and strongly anticlerical attitudes). At this time Italy was still predominantly a rural society, and the first members of the party were mainly recruited in rural areas. Indeed, one of the party's initial important achievements was a daring agricultural reform, mainly involving the division of the great estates into much smaller pieces of land and promoting their ownership by local inhabitants.

An age-old tradition in rural Italy was the processional tour of the parish agricultural territory, called *Rogazioni* (Rogation days) which lasted typically three to four days, in which everyone took part. Rogation (supplicatory) prayers and songs were chanted by the procession of parishioners and blessings were bestowed on the fields and vineyards at established stages of the tour. Far from being just the perpetuation of an obsolete tradition (of possible pagan origin), the journey through every parishioner's property became the occasion for charitable initiatives in aid of those who obviously could not cultivate their land because of various types of difficulty. This practice is illustrated by the following accounts:

> Santina: "We started out from [one village], then the Mass was celebrated at the church of San Martino. On the following three days we went to [the second village]. Prayers were said – in Latin – and then we recited the Litanies. During the *Rogazioni* it became clear to everyone when people were in some kind of difficulty... you know, maybe patches of land that hadn't been cultivated, revealing that that family had some problem or other. So we would try to lend a hand. If we got to know that there were no men in a family, someone would go and do some digging, and plant or pick vegetables. ...You know, at the time we could only eat what we had grown. ... My dad used to say, 'Help people when they are in need, because when they are OK they can help themselves!'"

> Giovanni: "In our village we had two Rogation weeks in the year. On the day of San Marco (April 25th) we walked up to the Sanctuary, and when we got to the top, the priest would bless the land, the fields and vineyards. Then we would go in church and Mass was celebrated. ... On the way back the procession would walk right through the streets, in the midst of the houses. The next *Rogazione* was on the Ascension – which was celebrated on a Thursday in those days, not like now, when they've moved it to the following Sunday. This procession started on the Monday, then went on for three days, ending Thursday, when we went all the way to the little chapel right at the extreme limit of the village, and from there up the hill to [another village].

"This gave us the opportunity to see if there were people who might have problems such as sickness in the family, or a male member who had died. ... The whole village would rally round to go and help them with the work they couldn't do themselves – like pruning the vines or gathering olives. I'm talking of the years before the war – before 1945. Just think of the difference between then and nowadays! Today you can't find anyone to help you, no, certainly not!"

Interviewer: "So it was as if religious beliefs became translated into ...."

Giovanni: "Helping, helping one another!"

Although examples were given of the shortcomings of particular priests, those who attended church functions had normally been taught by their forebears never to criticise their priests, who – however unworthily – represented Jesus Christ, but to transfer the precepts of love into their activities and relationships of everyday life.

The loss of that sense of close community and of the church's ever-ready presence was evident in many of the comments received. For example, religious processions had been very important and frequent parts of communal life (as many as nine taking place during the course of the year), involving the whole community, carrying beautifully decorated large crucifixes and large tableaus of the religious event or saint being commemorated. Giovanni told us:

"Then we had the processions 'of the four saints': the Guardian Angel, the Assumption, Our Lady of the Rosary and St Catherine. In each we walked in different directions, in order to cover the whole extension of the village. And, lastly, we had two more processions: Corpus Christi, which we still have now, and the Sacred Heart, when the girls all wore a medal – green when they were very young, and red from adolescence upwards."

Maria was proud to tell us that she still had her medals, after all these years.

We asked Giovanni to give us the specific reason for his telling us about all this, and he replied that he wanted us to know "what the village was in those days – how many things – and with what devotion – they used to do them", thus enhancing the difference he sees with the fewer public church events taking place nowadays:

"Yes, in procession they took out that famous *baldacchino* [religious canopy for covering a sacred object] and everyone took part – every single one! Nowadays, if you want someone to carry the Cross in procession you've got to go and search all over for them – and you won't find a single person!"

Even the administration of Extreme Unction to the sick called for great attention to exterior details, as Armando described:

"When the parish priest went out to take someone Holy Communion, he would give a warning by ringing the bells before leaving the church. ... A little procession was formed, where the priest carried an umbrella to protect the ciborium [in which the sacred hosts were kept], and was accompanied by two altar-boys. He used to wear that chasuble, the one with the red embroidery, that's still there in church. On the way, a few villagers would join the group – not many, but about three or four at least. The people did not go into the house, however – they would wait outside. The priest remained a while, on his own, talking to the sick person – if they were not very seriously ill – and then they all went back to church."

Praying and singing (all kinds of songs, but hymns in particular) appeared to be interwoven in everyday activities, part and parcel of rural people's life in those days:

Giovanni: "Everything has changed now. In those days people all knew each other, and would spend a lot of time together. There was no television, nor all the things we have now. ... On Sunday we went to Mass, and then we would get together – the young people especially – and chat about all sorts of things. ... Then, on a Sunday afternoon, we would go to Vespers ... that was another opportunity to meet up. You know, there was no cinema, there was practically nothing – it was as if religious functions were some kind of 'entertainment'. Outside the church, another opportunity for getting together was at the time when beans or maize were gathered. If somebody had a lot, they would invite neighbours to help shelling them, and while they were working they would pray, and sing [*starts to sing*]. ... It's not the same nowadays."

But not all changes taking place in later years were seen negatively. The reforms to the liturgy following the Vatican Council of the 1960s had made the Mass more understandable. In the past the rosary was often recited during Mass so as to protect the majority from distraction while the priest, facing the altar with his back to the congregation, spoke in Latin. The following comments are revealing:

Santina: "Clemente used to say the rosary in church – and sometimes she would fall asleep. On a Sunday she would say the rosary during Mass, but I don't know whether that was a good thing or not. Couldn't she have followed Mass instead?"

Marida: "I think it's better nowadays, with the Mass celebrated in Italian. At least we can understand what we are talking about!"

The core of Christian faith and doctrine – love of God, and one's neighbour – was passed on to the younger generations predominantly by the example of the older members of the family, and community: it was actually through the loving care and teachings of parents, grandparents or some special loved one that beliefs were communicated and kept in loving memory:

> Santina: "We were supposed to say the rosary every evening. I still remember that my Grandad, who died in 1929, taught us to say the rosary together, every night after supper, and afterwards he would tell us stories until Mother sent us all to bed. My Grandad had emigrated to America when he was young and he used to tell us how lucky he had been. … If there is a heaven, he is surely there! Before going to sleep we would say an Our Father, a Hail Mary and then the prayer to the Guardian Angel. Grandad used to teach us to pray for everyone. He would say the intentions, for example 'for all seamen', 'for all people in prison' … because he had a kind thought for anyone who needed help, and he taught us to pray for them. He had been back and forth from America eight times, had married twice and had 22 children. With the money he earned he used to buy plots of land over here, and houses in America, which he used to let to immigrants like himself.
>
> "He used to help our church here quite a lot. For example, he gave a large sum of money towards buying the organ in [a particular village]. … I remember he used to say, 'I bought the organ, but they won't play it for me when I die', because he no longer lived there. So he asked to be taken there for his funeral. … When he was very old, he couldn't walk very well, so he used a stick. My mother used to say to us, 'You must always go to Mass. Your grandfather walked with three legs, but he never missed Mass!'
>
> "I remember also how we were taught to respect older people. The first morsel of food, the first cup of milk, the first glass of water were for Grandad. Up until this day, whatever we know or do was instilled deep down by our family – and nobody can change that."

The presence of grandparents, and sometimes even of parents' siblings with their children in the same family home, are the practical demonstration of the importance that was attributed to one's elders:

> Marida: "Yes, there were 10 of us in my family. Just think of finding a family of 10 nowadays! They can't get on even when there are only two or three members."

> Giovanni: "Yes, well, do you realise what it meant, cultivating this land where water is scarce and the soil is clayey – families with seven or eight children – including the old folk? There were about 10 to

12 members in each, you know. … These properties, far from the houses very often, have nearly all been abandoned now, but in those days the villagers would slave away, planting vegetables, maize and some wheat for bread. Otherwise what was there to eat for so many mouths all the year through? But when I think about the old folk! They were such an important part of the family –the real authorities! They were listened to, and always had a good word of advice to give you. And they were more religious than nowadays. You know, I think it was thanks to them that families stuck together so well: grandfather and grandmother, father, mother and seven to eight children, all living together in mutual love and respect."

This would be the strength that accompanied them throughout the storms and conflicts of life, sometimes regardless of the help and support that they may have found –or not – in their priests. When posed the question whether they had never been tempted to defect from religion, or think differently about the beliefs they had been taught by their families, Santina's answer summarised what many expressed:

"In whom would we place our trust, if not in God?"

From most of the interviewees, one of the issues that emerged most frequently was that of freedom of choice for believers: seen by some as positive, by others as negative. This is also a common theme in current scholarly discourse on the role of the Roman Catholic Church in Italian society (Frisina, 2010). A number of the persons we interviewed saw the Church retrospectively as authoritarian and imposing its practices: one was not free to express one's opinions nor did not have the courage to accept the consequences of doing so. The subsequent attitude was sometimes to practise passively, without too much conviction. Such people feel that today the situation has improved: Christians may be fewer, but they are freer, more coherent and outspoken. For this reason, adhering to the Church provides more satisfaction and gratification. Another set of people sees all this the other way round: in the past there was greater order, rules were set out clearly and had to be observed rigorously; but there was always someone who could enlighten you, who could indicate the path you were supposed to follow, especially through their example of maintaining a sense of community and family and the continuity of both. Today anarchy reigns: everything is indefinite, everyone can do what they want and there is no sense of "unity". Therefore relativity and diversity of intentions tend to create an ungovernable situation.

Conclusion

What are the implications for the UK from these observations of Christian belief among older people in other European societies? There are similarities to be observed, as in the last-mentioned contemporary concern with autonomy of belief and practice, but there are also major differences. In the first place a pan-European perspective should make British people aware that their own historical experience of progressive decline in religiosity is a limited perspective. Second, the interview extracts show how deeply rooted religious traditions can be, that they can be hardy enough to survive severe and long-lasting persecution. Third, and related to this last point, the extracts suggest that religious beliefs are based on much more than intellectual convictions, that they are matters as much of the 'heart' as of the 'head'. Fourth, and perhaps most importantly from the perspective of this book, they illustrate the important role of religious belief in many older people's lives, both in the sustaining memories of the positive religious practices of the past and in the consequent witness they are able to provide to future generations of believers. They also supply further instances (as in Chapter Three) of older people's close attention to deficiencies in religious organisations.

It might be objected that the life experiences that have been discussed have come from countries in Eastern and Southern Europe, whereas the UK has much more in common with neighbouring countries in north-western Europe. This is undoubtedly true, but Europe is a small continent, and becoming smaller, with improved access to travel enabling people to live and to work in more than one part of it and even to commute large distances. As a result cross-cultural influences are on the increase. Just as it is possible to sample a wide variety of different cuisines in many cities and towns of the UK, so the different styles of religious worship on offer are expanding as well. As immigrants become more confident in what they have to offer, they provide new opportunities for the indigenous population.

Eastern European immigration is particularly important in this regard. For example, attendance at Roman Catholic churches is exceeding that of the established Church of England for the first time since the Reformation, despite falling attendance at both churches from within the indigenous population. The Catholic Church is bolstered by immigrants from more religious countries, including from Poland. Furthermore Polish immigrants are challenging current provision of religious services by Catholic churches in the British Isles as they demand a greater intensity of sacramental life (Von Hugel Institute, 2007). As a result of immigration from other countries previously under Soviet influence, Eastern Orthodox churches also have a higher visibility in the UK, Ireland and the rest of Western Europe than ever before. Liturgy that was once seen as exotic and impenetrable has now become open for westerners to experience (Phadraig, 2009).

Immigration is also bringing into the UK people of other than Christian faiths, peoples often with a strong and unbroken association between their sense of community and religious faith. It is interesting that as part of the recent UK ESRC-funded national programme of research on enhancing older people's quality of life, some of the most striking illustrations for the benefits of religion are provided by older British people from minority ethnic groups, where identity and practice remain strong. Despite scoring lower on other indices of quality of life, such as income, housing and environment, these older people scored higher on indices of community and belonging than the indigenous older population. Their religious contributions are both needed and valued (Grewal et al, 2004).

Europe is searching for a new identity in a world where its economic weight is in relative decline. Although this does not mean that it will necessarily return to its Christian origins, it will likely re-evaluate its religious character as it seeks values of sufficient weight to underpin a common culture. The kind of secularism currently being fostered by the European Union – influenced as it is by the principles of the French republic, which demands exclusion of religion from public affairs – may no longer be adequate to the larger Europe of the 21st century (Davie, 2006). The pressures to acknowledge the role of religion are likely to increase rather than decrease. Arguments to recognise the religious rights of Muslims may also lead to an increased confidence on the part of Christians to challenge secularism.

In the short term secular and religious understandings of society are likely to be in increasing conflict, and in everyone's interest it would be advisable to seek to build frameworks which allowed peaceful discourse between the religious and secular camps. More acknowledgement of Christianity's role in the formation of European culture, including its scientific and artistic achievements, is needed. Within the UK, in particular, politicians have to develop more effective policies of dealing with the often competing interests of Christian and Humanist secularist groups. Might not older people themselves, from their lifetimes' experience of conflict, have some part to play in promoting peaceful coexistence? The beginnings can be seen in the willing participation of elders in inter-faith dialogue.

EIGHT

Religious difference and age: the growing presence of other faiths

Peter G. Coleman, Amina Begum and Saba Jaleel

Ageing in a multi-faith Britain

Not only has the UK experienced a decline in religious observance over the last 50 years, it has also witnessed an increase in the diversity of religious, and spiritual, expression. Taken together these phenomena can give the impression that the UK is ceasing to be a Christian country. Within the countryside the medieval churches of small towns and villages demonstrate an ancient Christian heritage, but in the big cities the new religious buildings of Hindu, Muslim, Sikh and other faiths often appear much more alive than the Victorian and early-20th-century Christian churches built in large numbers to minister to an expanding urban population. Such buildings often look forlorn or shabby. Some have been abandoned. Some have been rehabilitated as temples and mosques of other faiths. But it is new building that provides evidence of the confidence of the incoming faiths. As we were writing this chapter Hindus in London were celebrating the completion of a magnificent temple in Wembley, rivalling the near-by football stadium in quality of presence if not in size. This is as good a sign as any of the changing religious character of the UK.

Nor is the change simply one of increasing numbers of immigrants belonging to the other great faiths of the world. A new creativity is at play, particularly in the younger part of the population, which wants to explore what diverse religions and their related spiritual practices offer in terms of mystery, awe, and uplifting experience of transcendence. New forms of spiritual movements are arising, sometimes related to their faiths of origin, but increasingly detached from them and often presented in eclectic and syncretic forms. They reflect the concerns of the new century: for peace and harmony among the nations and peoples within an increasingly interdependent world, where domination of one group by another is seen as unacceptable also in the realm of faith; for peace and harmony also with the environment, where the ecological system becomes increasingly under threat as a result of human expansion and progress. In this context it is not surprising that eastern spiritualities, which have not shown the same tendency as Judaeo-Christian cultures to dominate and control the natural world, find particular favour.

This changing context provides opportunities for young people looking for meanings and values that can underpin their growing need for identity, commitment and belonging. But it also provides new possibilities for older people whose economically productive life is winding down and who have more time for reflection on other potentially more valuable ways of finding meaning in life. There are opportunities to take action together with others in a similar position, as well as with young people, in order to safeguard life in the future. Religious and spiritual movements can answer to these needs.

However, most British people born in the pre-war years still appear uncomfortable with exploring these new possibilities, even when they no longer seem to have much time for the type of Christianity into which they were socialised when young. Partly it is because issues of choosing between different religious traditions and making new starts in spiritual life do not come naturally to generations who were brought up with the idea of loyalty to the tradition one was born into. But it is also because religions and spiritualities tend to be geared to incorporating new young members rather than older ones. This change of attitude will no doubt occur in the near future as the baby boomer generation continues to draw attention to itself.

The immensity of the changes that have already occurred in this area of life can be documented in many ways. The first author of this chapter was involved in two conferences of the Age Concern movement, 27 years apart, which touched on ageing and spiritual need. In 1979 the newly renamed Age Concern England launched an enquiry 'Ageing in the '80s'. The initial discussion document had a special section on 'the spiritual needs of the elderly'. To include a section on spiritual needs was innovative in public welfare policy statements. But in examining the content one can see how things have changed in the last quarter century. In the first place the author of the document clearly identifies 'spiritual' with 'religious', in a way that is no longer possible. She makes a very important anthropological point about religion:

> Religion has traditionally been linked with old people: ancestor worship and the veneration of patriarchs share a common attitude of respect for the old as being somehow more in touch with the world of the spirit – both because they have lived longer and have gained in wisdom, and also because they are reckoned to be nearer the great mystery of death which is seen as the dividing line between the two worlds.

The author goes on:

> Developed Christianity does not seem to have this same veneration for the old as a group set aside, because in Christian terms death is no longer a dividing line between two worlds. For Christians, the world of the future is already here in embryo; and life and death are part

of one pilgrimage to realize that world for all to see. (Age Concern England, 1979)

Again this raises very interesting questions. For example, does Christianity need a theology of age? But what is startling in retrospect is the Christian-centred focus of the document. Other religions are mentioned but not as having a presence in the UK.

A quarter of a century later, when Age Concern took an initiative in the new millennium to draw attention to older people's spiritual and religious needs such a Christocentric view was no longer possible. It is necessary to be aware of the different faiths and spiritualities present in the country. As the final publication (Burke, 2007) shows, this was a far from straightforward project. How does one incorporate the diverse interests now involved in the subject of spirituality, not only the different religions, but the legitimate demands of non-religious interests to be included, and the huge variations among those who make up modern spiritual movements? At the same time it is important to balance the interests both of current older people and of those of us who will be old shortly.

In this chapter we will first examine the place of ageing within some of the great faiths and draw attention to the somewhat different attitudes to age they promote. We will then consider in greater depth one particular faith, Islam – the largest of the incoming faiths – and the importance of sensitivity to the beliefs and practices among the growing numbers of British older Muslims. Faith cannot be dissociated from other areas of life, and we shall illustrate this point by examining the relationship between what older Muslims say about their beliefs in regard to their physical and mental health. This will help emphasise the need for health and welfare professionals to be aware of religious sensitivities. Finally we shall reflect a little on the future, not only on the possibilities of older people's conversion to faiths other than Christianity, but also their role within new spiritual movements.

The world's faiths and conceptions of ageing

A sufficient knowledge and understanding of religion – what is sometimes referred to as 'religious literacy' – can no longer be assumed, even among otherwise well-educated people. Paucity of religious education at school means that a large proportion of the UK population now often has a sketchy and often inaccurate perspective on the main tenets and practices of Christianity, let alone of the other faiths represented within their community.

In the case of gerontologists it is also important to understand the influence that religious beliefs may have on attitudes to ageing. Not all religions view ageing in the same way. Therefore one can expect differences in age-related behaviour, expectations and self-conceptions to be related to a person's religion and depth of identification with it. In the following account we will limit consideration of to the so-called 'Abrahamic' faiths of Judaism, Christianity and Islam, which share a common root, and the interrelated faiths of Hinduism and Buddhism, which have influenced much of Indian, Chinese and other Asian cultures. A fuller account of the world's religions would necessarily include some of the other early religions of the world such as Confucianism, Jainism, Shamanism, Shintoism, Taoism and Zoroastrianism, as well as historically newer forms as Sikhism and Baha'i. Much of course could be written about how each of these major faiths influence the experience of ageing, and what follows is inevitably a personal selection.

The Abrahamic religions

The monotheistic religions of Judaism, Christianity and Islam emerged in succession in the Middle East, but expanded to influence the development especially of European, African and American civilisation. They largely replaced the earlier systems of beliefs in these continents, including the characteristically polytheistic Indo-European religions. Their similarities and differences, both within and between one another, need careful study. They are similar in that they share a common root in the stories of the creation of the world and humankind's relationship with God, and a strong emphasis on belief in one God alone. They are often called 'Abrahamic' because of their shared acknowledgement of the significance to these stories of the figure of Abraham, father of successive leaders of God's chosen people, and his trust in God's direction of his life. But of course there are many other honoured persons and events in these ancient narratives that are shared between these faiths.

But there are also significant differences. Judaism, like Hinduism, but unlike Christianity, Islam and Buddhism, is closely associated with ethnicity. Its scriptures tell of the emergence of a particular race of people, their acceptance of the commandments God has given to them, and their subsequent history through various successes and failures. The Hebrew Scriptures provide some of the most powerful images of old age in western culture (Dulin, 1988). They contain a variety of themes: historical accounts, realistic in their depiction of power and frailty, which demonstrate the importance of family life for all age groups; calls within the prophetic and psalmist writings for greater sensitivity to the needs of elderly people; and within the so-called 'wisdom' writings, such as 'Ecclesiastes', a focus on the personal dimensions of ageing, especially physical deterioration. Taken as a whole they provide a strong moral teaching to society not to neglect the old, and it is probably not coincidental that Jewish homes and care organisations have long had a high reputation both in US and European social services. At the same time, perhaps partly because of these strong injunctions, absence or loss of family care can be a cause of great psychological pain in Jewish communities. This is evident from some key early studies in the social gerontological literature (for example, Hazan, 1980; Francis, 1984). As a distinct religious group older members of the Jewish faith have also had to face the unique challenge of maintaining their faith in God in the face of the Holocaust of European Jews in the Second World War.

Christianity emerged out of Judaism during the period of Roman dominion of Palestine. As a result of its openness to different ethnic groups and the universality of its message, Christianity spread rapidly through the Greek and Roman world, and, despite the persecutions it encountered from the authorities, by the 4th century after Christ it had been adopted as the official religion of the Roman Empire. However, Christianity was characterised by controversy from its earliest days, occasioned by the very subtlety and complexity of its beliefs about the relationship between God and man, as well as by difficulties in reconciling the exercise of authority across different communities (churches) of believers along with the rights of individual conscience. As it grew, unity became increasingly difficult to maintain. Successive schisms took place, the most significant being the division of the western (Catholic) church from the eastern (Orthodox) churches by the early part of the second millennium after Christ, and the separation of Protestant sects from the western Catholic church in the 16th and 17th centuries. The first North American colonies were established by Protestant émigrés from Western Europe, and Protestantism in its initially Calvinistic and later Evangelical forms has given a distinct character to American religion (Noll, 2002). Much of the US literature on religion and ageing also reflects an emphasis on the individual's direct access to God rather than on mediation through the corporate body of believers, the latter being more characteristic not only of Catholicism, in its conception of the Church, but also of Judaism and Islam.

Although the early Christian Scriptures repeat Jewish prescriptions not to neglect the elderly, and particularly show concern for widows, the much stronger emphasis within Christianity on ongoing life with God beyond death diminished any special importance attributed to reaching old age per se. Disregard of ageing may also have been encouraged by the medieval characterisation of Jesus's age of death as 'the perfect age' (Burrow, 1986). As a consequence middle age came to be depicted as the high point of life, whereas the social significance of ageing faded in Europe and America (Cole, 1991). More recently, attempts have been made by Christian theologians to correct this historical neglect, to embrace ageing in all its aspects, to combat the contemporary culture of worship of youth and of autonomy, and to call older people to witness to moral commitments and to their hope in Christ (for example, Hauerwas et al., 2003). However, ageism is still to be found in the Christian churches themselves and is only gradually being confronted. We shall return to this subject in Chapter Nine.

Islam emerged from the desert of the Arabian peninsula on the edge of the Christian world in the seventh century after Christ. To its early eastern Christian opponents it appeared at first as yet another internal heresy to be combated. But with surprising rapidity Islam took over much of the Middle East as well as North Africa, and spread eventually into Asia. The Qur'an also offered a message of universal brotherhood, and belief in an almighty and merciful God who will judge all mankind at the end of time. But at the same time it taught a simpler relationship of man as servant to God and cultivated in practice a stronger sense of social responsibility. Religious precepts were understood as determining all aspects of life, including care of older people (Abdul-Rauf, 1982). Ethical teachings about respect and honour due to older people have been taken more seriously than in Christianity.

Relatively little research has yet been conducted on religion and age within Muslim samples. Nevertheless, interview studies with older Muslims living both inside and outside Muslim countries testify to the huge importance of religion within their lives, its contribution to their quality of life, and development with ageing (Imamoglu, 1999; Ahmadi and Thomas, 2000; Aflakseir and Coleman, 2009). We will consider Islam and ageing in greater depth later in this chapter.

Hinduism and Buddhism

Whereas Judaism, Christianity and Islam, despite their history of reciprocal conflict and persecution, are closely interrelated religions, Hinduism together with Buddhism form a quite distinct way of approaching the transcendent. Hinduism is one of the oldest surviving belief systems in the world and remains vibrant in its homeland of the Indian subcontinent.

Fundamental to Hinduism is its teaching on the stages of life from student to householder to retired person to ascetic (Tilak, 1989). This makes it a very age-friendly religion, for despite the loss of physical vigour that accompanies ageing, the important aim of life is a state of stability and changelessness beyond death. It is old age that stands for maturity, not young adulthood or even middle age. In fact Hinduism is remarkably unconcerned about ageing and death. Its most ancient texts – the RigVeda – speak of death as a passing over to joy. The suffering and losses are key to the liberation experience. They waken people to reality. The resultant virtues of confrontation with finitude, the wise use of declining powers and abilities, and the creative response to limits are increasingly appreciated by western thinkers (Ram-Prasad, 1995). There are therefore positive expectations on the behaviour of people as they become older. Like the Jewish prophets, old Hindu sages provide immensely attractive images and models of ageing.

Buddhism is also of particular interest from a gerontological perspective because its founding story of the Buddha gaining insight is based on confrontation with old age, disease and death, from which he had been protected as young man. Although the Buddhist influence can be felt within later developments in Hinduism, Buddhism deals with these problems quite differently by means of an ascetic renunciation of the world throughout life. It teaches in similar terms about the importance of karma, a key concept in both Hinduism and Buddhism about the automatic consequences of good and bad deeds, and reincarnation through further lives dependent on karma. Ageing itself is viewed as a product of good karma, providing the opportunity for further enlightenment. However, Buddhism puts more emphasis on eventual release from the cycle of rebirth through cultivation of high levels of spirituality.

From its origins in India, Buddhism spread to Tibet, and from there to China and Japan, developing somewhat different characteristics in each culture. Buddhism, unlike other Asian religions, has proved more exportable to other ethnic groups, including westerners. It is popular also in intellectual circles, because of its practical emphasis on developing ways of coping, principally in meditation, in facing the stresses of life, and as a consequence has strong links with contemporary popular psychology (for example, Goleman, 1997). Similarly to Hinduism, Buddhism has created an attractive image and expectation of age, as a stage of life when a person's concerns should be primarily spiritual, concerned with the path of salvation. At the same time it could be criticised as reinforcing passivity in the face of older people's diminished economic and political status.

Neither Hinduism nor Buddhism has been the subject of much empirical research in the context of studies on ageing in the UK, although there is now the beginning of interest. There is some research on older groups of Buddhists in Asian societies with strong social gerontological traditions, such as Singapore, whose mixed population also provides an excellent multi-religious and multi-ethnic context for studying religion and ageing (Mehta, 1997; Jianbin and Mehta, 2003). The similarity between Hinduism and Judaism has already been noted in that religious identification closely overlaps with ethnicity. As noted in the case of Mr Jewell (Chapter Two), family members' falling away from Jewish religious and cultural practice can have corrosive effects on sense of identity and well-being. It has been demonstrated in a study of three generations of Hindu women living in East London how granddaughters' absence of identification with Hinduism is associated with impaired mental health on the part of their grandmothers (Guglani et al, 2000).

These brief accounts of major religions to be found in the UK need to be enlarged by more in-depth consideration of the role they play in older people's lives. This would be a large undertaking and the research literature available is still very limited. In the following section we have decided to focus on Islam, which has become the major alternative faith to Christianity within Europe and which we have begun to research more in a gerontological context. We hope that the following account gives some insight into how membership of a different faith group can influence the experience of ageing.

Experience of ageing in another faith tradition: being an older British Muslim

Islam came to Europe in the seventh century. In the first century of its existence it had already reached along the coasts of Africa and arrived on islands and coasts of the European Mediterranean. A flourishing Islamic culture was created in Spain, which existed until the 'reconquista' by Christian kingdoms in the Middle Ages. In the same period Ottoman Islamic forces began to overrun the Byzantine Empire and other Orthodox Christian nations of South Eastern Europe. Resistance lasted many centuries but Constantinople finally fell to the Ottomans in 1453 and thereafter became the capital of an Ottoman Empire that stretched through large parts of Eastern Europe as well as across the Middle East. By the 17th century Ottoman forces even threatened to overthrow the Hapsburg kingdom of Austria.

However, through the 18th and 19th centuries its power ebbed, and the Ottoman Empire finally collapsed in the aftermath of the First World War. Nevertheless, the hope for universal Islamic rule under a worthy successor to the Prophet Muhammad – a 'caliph' – has never disappeared, nor the aspirations to a political and spiritual unity, which in the Christian world used to be expressed by the concept of 'Christendom'. Moreover, even though fragmented the Muslim world has retained its central Islamic character. As Bernard Lewis states, 'most Muslim countries are still profoundly Muslim, in a way and in a sense that most Christian countries are no longer Christian' (Lewis, 2003: 14). This point is vital to understanding the Muslim presence in the UK and Europe.

Despite the defeats, persecutions and out-migrations of the 19th and 20th centuries, including the recent atrocities against Muslims in the former Yugoslavia, the Islamic presence in south-east Europe has remained and is at its strongest in Albania, Bosnia and Herzegovina, Kosovo, Macedonia, and Montenegro. Within the newly enlarged European Union, Islam has its largest presence in Bulgaria, with 12% of the population being adherents. As much as 10%-15% of the population of Russia is also thought to be Muslim. Tartarstan is a predominantly Islamic enclave with a long history, dating to its previous dominance of Russia in the Middle Ages.

However, within Western and Northern Europe the Muslim presence is relatively new, the result of immigration since the Second World War and particularly since European colonies in Africa and Asia gained independence and previous colonial subjects gained the right to live in their former governing country. In particular, many Muslims from North Africa have settled in France, and from the Indian sub-continent in Britain. Emigration for work in the expanding economies of Europe has also led to an increase in the Muslim population in Central and Northern Europe, for example the large numbers of Turkish 'guest workers' coming to Germany. Currently France, Denmark and the Netherlands have the largest Muslim population in Western Europe (all over 5%), followed by Austria and Switzerland (both 4%), and the UK (3%). By comparison, the largest Jewish population in Europe is in France (1%), and the largest Hindu population is in the UK (0.5%).

Muslims in Britain settled in industrial areas and established communities in certain cities and regions such as Glasgow, Bradford, Birmingham and London. This generation of Muslims tended, as other migrants, to want to live together in the same areas, thus limiting their interaction with the indigenous population. This may be put down to language barriers, a lack of cultural awareness or confidence in a new country, as well as hostility and discrimination from the host population. The largest numbers of Muslims in England and Wales have family origins in Pakistan (43%). They are younger on average than the general population, and there is still a relatively low prevalence of Muslims aged over 65, but increasing gradually as the first migrants grow old.

The importance of fasting

We will illustrate the importance of improving understanding of Islam from two recent studies that we have conducted on health issues among older British Muslims. The first (qualitative) study was on diabetes and the significance of fasting and the second (quantitative) study was on depression and the stigma associated with mental illness. In discussing these subjects it is necessary to understand the subtle but important differences between Muslim and Christian understanding of health. Like Christians, Muslims have an integrated concept of body and soul, but the body is seen primarily as a means for the development of the soul. Persons are therefore encouraged to maintain good health, and will be judged accountable for the way they have looked after the blessing of a healthy body and mind. But the ultimate aim of life is obedience and submission to the will of Allah, and in the practical manifestation of this faith in Him through the five 'pillars' of Islam: testimony, prayer, fasting, charity, and pilgrimage.

For the devout Muslim, as for the devout Christian, this life is a journey. A Muslim's ultimate goal is to reside in Jannah (Paradise) for all of eternity. From this viewpoint, it is apparent that Muslims, as dictated by their faith, should live their lives in preparation for the promised hereafter. Therefore, ill health is seen as a temporary and relatively trivial aspect of a short-term life. In fact the Qur'an makes little reference of physical or mental illness. Its primary focus is on the state of the heart and categorically declares: 'it is only in the mention of Allah that hearts find rest' (Holy Qur'an 13: 28). Muslims therefore turn to the Sunnah, with its accounts of Muhammad's teaching, for more detail regarding physical and mental well-being. The prophet Muhammad taught:

> Never is a believer stricken with discomfort, hardship, illness, grief or even with mental worry that his sins are not expiated for him. (Sahih Al-Bukhari Hadith)

Therefore devout Muslims are expected to turn first to prayer, meditation and 'dhikr', the remembrance of Allah, in the face of illness and disease, before turning to conventional medical treatment. However, with this, there is a balancing statement from the prophet which teaches:

> Seek medical treatment, O servants of Allah, for surely medical treatment is part of God's Providence.

It is important for healthcare professionals to be aware of these alternative views, and of the importance of religious practice, in order to maximise patient compliance.

At the same time the poorer health of Muslims in UK society needs a response. The 2001 Census showed that Muslims fare worse than other religions in relation to self-reported poor health and limiting long-term illness or disability rates. It also revealed that Muslims are the most likely to be living in overcrowded households (32% vs 8% in the general population). But Muslims also have the largest household size in Britain. This correlates to lower rates of social isolation within the Muslim community, which in turn may have a significant effect on depression.

It is also important to note that fasting is considered beneficial to health. This is increasingly recognised in western secular society, but it is difficult for most people in the West, even devout Christians, to understand the enormous significance of fasting for Muslims. Even though fasting was a discipline practised strongly by Christians, and although still an important practice among Eastern Orthodox Christians, it has largely lapsed, not only among Protestants but also Catholics. During the month of Ramadan, the ninth month in the Islamic, lunar calendar, Muslims abstain from eating and drinking from dawn till dusk for the entire month. This is prescribed in the Qur'an:

> Oh you who believe! Fasting is prescribed to you as it was prescribed
> to those before you [i.e. Jews and Christians], so that you may learn
> self restraint.

Not only is fasting seen to elevate a person morally through the acquisition of self-discipline, but it also reminds the whole of society, rich and poor, of the plight of those who are impoverished. Although exemptions are stated in the Qur'an for the young, pregnant and nursing mothers, as well as the old, frail and unwell, since fasting may be detrimental to health, many older people with health weaknesses consider that they should continue fasting as they have always done. For older Muslims fasting is not only a religious obligation but a habitual activity that they have been engaged in since attaining maturity. Breaking it is therefore emotionally painful. This raises particular problems among those with diabetes, a condition that is markedly more prominent among South-Asian Indian peoples, and which requires a regular monitoring of diet.

A small study of 10 older Bangladeshis with diabetes, between the ages of 63 and 75 years, with an average age of 70 years, was able to elicit some of the dilemmas associated with fasting. Two interviews were conducted with each participant, the first to obtain an overview of the person's situation, thoughts and feelings and to establish a good relationship and appropriate rapport, the second to delve more deeply into issues of fasting and spiritual and other reasons for continuing or discontinuing during the period of the fasts.

Continuing to fast provided these older people with a sense of peace and well-being, as the following quotes show:

> "When I do keep it, in my mind comes peace. By the will of Allah I
> am keeping it, and my intention is to keep it all."
>   "All praise to Allah, keeping it yourself is much more rewarding. I
> feel that when I fast I am well and my weight is well."

> "When I was admitted into hospital everyone told me not to fast, but I fasted, without problems."

This also applied to those who could not fast because it was detrimental to their health. They wished to be able to fast again. For some not fasting threatened their identity as a Muslim, as a 'servant of Allah':

> "I'm happy that I didn't have to break them [the fasts]. Now if I was to fall ill during Ramadan, then I'd have to break them. So I am happy that I can carry out my obligations."

One person who was also on dialysis because of kidney failure had struggled with these issues over many years:

> "I asked the scholars. They have also said that if saline is going inside my stomach then it is going to my whole body and because of that if I fast it isn't valid. I didn't fast for two years, I gave to charity. But after that I thought, yes I am upset that my fasts aren't valid, but on the other hand it doesn't affect me if I fast. So I couldn't satisfy my heart, so I have been fasting. ... I haven't gone down that route of whether I can or cannot. You see when it isn't affecting my health then I don't see the harm in keeping them."

Another person, also on dialysis, repeated the same point:

> "The fact that when I fast, I've never – I don't feel dizzy – I feel better. Then why should I break my fasts?"

The strong family and community character of Islam was also reflected in participants' comments. One interviewee reported that it upset him that he was the only one eating while his family abstained from food during Ramadan. This is when all Muslims globally are fasting together and coming together to break their fasts daily. There is a feeling of unity and belonging that some may feel is too difficult and sad to let go.

> "In the house no one is eating. My sons and daughters, everyone is [fasting]. ... I'm the only one eating. I feel really bad. I don't even feel like eating."

Similar comments were made by others:

> "I don't feel good. Everyone's fasting and I am not, because of my illness."

Other members of the family shared in this sadness. As one participant's wife said:

> "If we don't fast then we feel uneasy inside. If you break fast, do you know what it is like? There is sadness inside."

It was also clear from this project that the strength of older Muslims' attitudes on this subject was not understood by half of the doctors with whom they came into contact. They were particularly disappointed that their doctors only saw themselves as administering medication and did not know about matters pertaining to religion:

> "The doctor tells me not to fast, not to pray, but that isn't his business. These are my duties that I will have to answer to Allah about. I know the doctor will tell me that it is for my own health, but who knows that if I don't fast I will not get many other illnesses?"

This particular participant clearly felt that by keeping her fasts and following her religious duties her health would be safeguarded and other illnesses avoided. Indeed, four out of the 10 participants did not inform their doctor that they had intentions to fast:

> "What's the point of telling? They are of one way of life and we are of another way of life. If you tell them, it is not as if they will understand. They'll say, 'Don't do it'. If they were Muslim then you could say."

Interestingly, the remaining six who did tell their doctor still continued to fast, or at least attempted to, despite being advised against it. They were more inclined to value the Imam's (religious leader's) advice.

Those who did not fast indicated lowering of well-being during Ramadan. Fasting was such an essential part of their religion that it had become an intrinsic part of their life. Some compensated by performing the night prayers during Ramadan, a particularly demanding requirement to get up during the night to pray, usually for over an hour. Clearly this is an area where more discussion is needed between religious leaders and health professionals so that consistent advice is given about how to manage fasting with diabetes, for example not eating too much to compensate for fasting and not taking medication irregularly. There also needs to be more awareness of the consequences of changing drug routines abruptly. For example a patient could be on a long-acting hypoglycaemic medicine that might lead to hypoglycaemia while abstaining from food all day.

Attitudes to depression and faith

Depression is another prevalent condition among older people that raises particular issues for Muslims. As already stated, Islam teaches that all illnesses can be a means of expiation of minor sins. This also includes depression. Islamic belief dictates that the state of the heart is key to the balance of man's essence. The Qur'an repeatedly asserts that life is a test. It accepts that the trials and tribulations of life are hard to bear, but it also reminds the believer that these trials are surmountable and temporary.

The greatest challenge for Muslims is the idea of submitting themselves to the will of Allah. This means that they entrust all of their affairs to a supreme being that is believed to be all-forgiving and all-knowing. This is well illustrated by the famous saying by Umar ibn Khattab, the prophet Muhammad's disciple, who states:

> Go easy on yourself, for the outcome of all affairs is determined by God's decree. If something is meant to go elsewhere, it will never come your way, but if it is yours by destiny, from you it cannot flee.

The idea behind these sayings, teachings and beliefs is that man should not worry about the negative and saddening events of life, such as grief and loss, pain and remorse, or guilt and sorrow; rather they should put their faith in God, who will reward them for their patience and perseverance.

This fundamental belief influences perception of the risk factors that govern depression. For example, from an Islamic perspective, social isolation may be viewed as a test from God, one that must be approached with patience, the greatest height of spiritual development that a Muslim can attain. Muslims should busy themselves with remembrance of God and His love for them. The same would apply to living with disability or grief from the loss of a loved one. Furthermore, these beliefs may affect a Muslim person's psychological coping style and serve as a positive coping mechanism.

It should be noted that Islamic teachings are also rich with preventative measures that are only now being emphasised in primary medical care in the West. This includes the importance of exercise, which some studies claim to be as effective as antidepressant medication, and the necessity to perform prayer, the reward for which is greater if done in congregation, thus tackling the detrimental effects of social isolation and lack of social support.

As already indicated in the case of diabetes, the very nature of the Islamic faith requires all those interacting with it to understand that it could perhaps transcend all other values that a Muslim may hold. It is precisely because of this that healthcare professionals may experience difficulties when treating Muslim patients. Islam is not just what a patient holds dear in their personal and private life; rather, in theory, it affects their every action and decision, including their thoughts on medical diagnoses and treatment, and ultimately patient compliance.

We conducted a quantitative survey of older people aged over 65 years to investigate the association between religiosity and resilience to depression among Muslims living in Glasgow and London. The sample of 67 we collected (33 males and 34 females) were predominantly of Pakistani origin, identified via elderly day-care centres and word-of-mouth, and interviewed in Urdu and Punjabi. Three quarters of the sample felt they had a long-term illness or disability. We used a Qur'an-based questionnaire to examine their strength of belief (Jana-Masri and Priester, 2007) as well as the Royal Free interview for religious and spiritual beliefs (King et al, 2001), already used in our studies mentioned in Chapters Three and Four, and the Hospital Anxiety and Depression Scale.

As expected, there was a strongly significant relationship between the measure of depression and whether or not participants felt they had an illness or disability, but an even stronger relationship between their degree of religiosity and absence of depressive symptoms. The latter association remained strong within a regression analysis that also controlled for gender, living alone and disability level. It was evident that large numbers of participants with high strength of religiosity showed resilience in face of adverse factors such as having a long-term illness or disability. This also applied to some persons who had relatively low social support.

More in-depth qualitative investigation is needed to explore these relationships further, and in particular provide more insight into the Muslim viewpoint on depression. For many of the participants in this study depression appeared to be simply a matter of cause and effect. Women, for example, explained that depression for them was caused by their husbands speaking harshly to them, their children not being obedient, or having to look after a large extended family. They saw depression as a very short-lived and controllable 'glitch' in their lives, or the lives of others.

In previous chapters (Two and Three) we have given some consideration to the idea of 'fate' held by older people of a Christian background. Interviewing Muslims shows the need for further investigation of this key concept. Although Muslims do not accept the notion of fatalism, they do, however, resign to the idea that God is their sovereign master who has chosen to endow them with free will. There are no 'accidents' in the universe. Such beliefs perhaps grant Muslims armour against depression. If one can externalise feelings of distress, grief and sadness, it takes away some of the burden. Most participants, both male and female, commented readily on fate and the will of God, referring to the already mentioned teaching of Umar ibn Khattab not to dwell on the trials and tribulations of this world as they are all in the "hands of God". They regularly referred to prayer and religious assistance in the event of depressive symptoms.

Nevertheless there was a feeling of guilt amongst some participants who acknowledged that depression could be a 'real' cause of ill health. It was seen as admitting defeat to something that should instead be regarded as 'the will of God'. This was associated with feelings of blasphemy and sin, in that believers should submit to the will of God and not fall into despair. They had been given the resources to do so in the teachings of the Qur'an and Sunnah.

These and other studies (for example Hussain and Cochrane, 2003) have demonstrated the importance of cultural competence in dealing with illness, and particularly mental illness, with people of other religions. There are various reasons, for example, why depression, and also the risk of suicide, may be presented differently both by the person concerned as well as by co-religionist friends and family (Pritchard and Amanullah, 2007). Doctors and other health professionals need to understand these factors in order to be sensitive to the needs of patients from other faiths than their own (Leavey and King, 2007).

Widening spiritual opportunities for the UK's older population

The UK, together with many other Western European countries, has developed into a multi-faith society over a relatively short period of time. In 1971, at the time of the first interviews with older people reported in Chapter Two, the combined Muslim, Sikh and Hindu population of England and Wales had not yet reached 1% of the total. By 2001 it was approaching 5%. The change in visible presence is even better documented by the rise in the total number of officially registered mosques, which had only just reached double figures by 1971 but had increased exponentially to approaching one thousand by the end of the century (British Religion in Numbers, website of the University of Manchester, www.brin.ac.uk). These trends are expected to continue. The UK's ethnic minority population is calculated to rise to 20% by 2051. Of course a large part of this increase will be of Christians from Asia, Africa and the Caribbean. But in some European countries, such as Austria, Switzerland and Sweden, Muslims will come to play an increasingly important part, perhaps reaching one in five of the population by the middle of the century.

From the perspective of faith, a more significant statistic from European surveys is that Muslims under 25 are as devout as those over 55. Indeed Muslim youth are often stricter in their religious allegiance than their elders (Kaufmann, 2010). It is worrying for the UK that Muslims here have the most anti-western attitudes in Europe – even though British non-Muslims have relatively tolerant views of Islam and Muslims (Pew Research Centre, 2006). Increased attention to Islam will likely also benefit Christianity. Similarities as well as differences will become more evident. Indeed, as Kaufmann (2010) predicts, cooperation across religious divides may well increase in order to combat what the different faiths agree are excessively liberal public policies.

The low religious literacy of the British population needs particular attention. This has implications at different levels of educational provision, in school of course, but also at higher levels of professional formation. For example, undergraduate medical students are taught about particular faith-based issues related to medical practical, such as the refusal of Jehovah's Witnesses to undergo blood transfusions. But it can be argued that even more time and resources should be allocated to the teaching of medicine in the context of religion and culture, that this would improve awareness and consequently better healthcare services for ethnic minorities, as well as for neglected subgroups within the indigenous population. Increased attention to the relationship between spirituality and health would benefit the whole population. At the present time there is a paradox within British healthcare in that nurses have been disciplined for praying with patients, although increased emphasis is being placed on spiritual care as an integral part of nursing. Such issues can only be resolved by providing more opportunities for spiritual choice without infringing personal liberties.

Some degree of conflict, however, seems inevitable, as present western society is also marked by a rise in expression of militant atheistic humanism. As the subject of religion has risen in the media and in public consciousness, opposing secular attitudes have also hardened and become more strident. The popularity in the UK of Richard Dawkins' book *The God Delusion* (2006), and in the US of Christopher Hitchens' book *God is not Great* (2007), reflects the threat felt by many about the resurgence of religious authority, especially in the educational realm. But religions also benefit from this debate, as more explicit consideration of atheism helps to put into relief the nature and functions of religion and religious belief. As we illustrated in Chapter Six, it is not possible to accurately assess the influence of religious belief without examining how people manage without it, and whether Humanism or other principled approaches to life can provide similar benefits.

As a result of globalisation, the nature and content of religious and non-religious belief is ceasing to be a predictable attribute of location or ethnic grouping. Although current generations of older people still tend to see themselves as religious and Christian (Voas and Crockett, 2005), this is likely to change in the near future with the ageing of the baby boomers, who first favoured the term 'spirituality'. But since levels of religious knowledge and education are much poorer in these soon-to-be-old generations, interesting questions arise about whether they can be persuaded to reconsider the Christianity they rejected when they were young, often on only superficial acquaintance.

There will also be increasing opportunities for older as well as younger people to learn about and convert to other faiths. The taboo on conversion to religions outside of one's culture of origin is lessening. In the case of religions such as Christianity, Islam and Buddhism there is no barrier imposed by the religion itself. All are multiracial. Islam has recently attracted increasing numbers of both male and female converts, including prominent figures, such as Cat Stevens in the world of music. The number of people choosing a different religious or spiritual path in adulthood, and even late life, is likely to increase. In fact, as social inhibitions to conversion are removed, the latter period of life from middle age onwards is likely to become the time for exploration of alternative spiritual teaching.

This does not necessarily mean conversion to a new religion. Increasing numbers of people in the West do not see the need to attach themselves to a particular religion in order to lead more spiritual lives. There is a growing phenomenon of 'spirituality shopping', where people take what suits them from a consideration of a variety of religious traditions. These include pre-Christian native (pagan) religions, but also the religions of the East, such as Hinduism and Buddhism. The baby boomer generation is strongly represented in studies of 'new age' spirituality. Paul Heelas and Linda Woodhead's study of holistic spirituality in the Kendal area of North England found that 55% of all those active in the milieu were aged between 40 and 59 years, the majority being women (Heelas and Woodhead,

2005). Increasing concerns for persons at this stage of life tend to be related to matters of health and fitness, and holistic spirituality fits in well with their needs. Whether these involvements will increase further with advanced age is not yet clear. It could be that greater concern with issues of meaning may lead to more serious consideration of a wide range of alternative religious and spiritual pathways.

The growing volatility in religious and spiritual discourse has in the late 20th century tended to separate the present older generation from younger cohorts. Getting the former to speak about spiritual beliefs outside of the context of specific religious beliefs is not easy, and the suggestion of distancing from religious allegiance is more anxiety-provoking than releasing. They may be dissatisfied with the Christian religion that they were taught as children but are not yet making use of alternative spiritual opportunities. It is therefore all the more important that they are not neglected by their churches of origin.

NINE

Ageing and the future of belief

Peter G. Coleman

The changing context of belief

The return of religion to the public agenda has been one of the major surprises of the new century. However, older people seem not to have benefited so far from this increased attention to belief and its implications. In the UK itself religion, spirituality and belief have rarely achieved coverage in conferences and publications on the needs of older people or gained much from the increasing funds given to research on ageing by the British research councils. It might be claimed that religious older people are no longer the majority of their age group. But there is increasing recognition that minorities need protection from discrimination. Again, it might be argued that religious older people are not stigmatised or disadvantaged in the ways that, for example, black and gay minorities still are. But this may no longer be true. Persons of strong religious convictions tend increasingly to be seen as alien to the UK's liberal and secular contemporary culture. To express or to discuss religious views in public has long been discouraged, partly for understandable reasons stemming from still painful historical memories of inter-religious conflict. But such restrictions may also function now more for the ease of the non-religious majority in the population.

One of the benefits of the debate – at times strident – in the contemporary media between atheists and religious believers is that it breaks this taboo, and promotes reflection on matters of ultimate value such as the meaning of life and death. It also encourages genuine enquiry into the nature of religious belief. This is especially important, as religious knowledge within the UK has sunk to appalling levels, even with regard to Christianity, which is central to the UK's historical and cultural heritage. As Grace Davie has pointed out, we live at present in a paradoxical situation of the increasing salience but declining comprehension of religion (Davie, 2000). This tension can only be resolved by a greater effort on the part of civil society to try to understand the religious elements within it, and on the part of religious groups to communicate and create opportunities for discussion with the rest of the population.

But how important will be the subject of religion and ageing in the long run? The UK has experienced a long period of religious decline, which has also affected the older population. If these trends continue, future generations of older people are likely to be even less religious than at present. Indeed, from a reading of the work of some social researchers who have charted religious affiliation in the UK over the last century, one may obtain an impression that the process of decline is almost natural or inevitable. Moreover, a trajectory of generational decline in attendance at worship has also been found among British ethnic minorities (Crockett and Voas, 2006). This suggests that there is something about the character of UK society and culture that encourages religious disenchantment.

However, processes, even long-lasting ones, have not only beginnings but also endings. Only in the eyes of those who believe in the 'rightness' of the trend does religious decline seem 'natural'. Indeed, there is now evidence for increasing religiousness on the part of young Muslims living in Europe, particularly among those in higher education (Phalet et al, 2010). This change may well reflect the stigmatising of Muslims following the 2001 terrorist attack on New York and the consequent response of the US and British governments. If so, this is again an example of how historical events can influence individual beliefs. But Islam may be increasingly feared in the western world not only because of the terrorist threat from particular Islamic groupings, but also at a more profound level because it threatens the global capitalist system. Islam proclaims a return to a conception of the stewardship of the natural world subject to revelation from God rather than exploitation of natural resources according to solely rational and economic principles (Evans, 2011). It is not inconceivable that Islamic principles could win a future struggle of hearts and minds.

Moreover, it is not only Islam that may become more influential in the UK. There are areas of Europe where Christianity maintains a strong presence, and the world as a whole is not becoming less Christian or indeed less religious. Compared to the so-called developing world recent Western European history lacks inspiring examples of Christian action. Nor is there drama to match the experience of Christians under Soviet persecution (see Chapter Seven) or the continuing deaths of Christian witnesses in other parts of the world. But the growth of international communication means that sources of inspiration are no longer local or restricted to one's own culture. In this respect religious and spiritual beliefs also benefit greatly from globalisation.

Ageing and meaning

Because of the paucity of gerontological material in this field in the UK, this book has been an exercise in assembling evidence from a very narrow database. Most of the data on older people's beliefs has been collected by researchers at the University of Southampton, and most of the samples interviewed have been relatively small ones, and often concentrated on older people living alone, for example in sheltered housing schemes. But it is hoped that the evidence from these studies provides a stimulus for more representative and more detailed research, both of a quantitative and qualitative character. Nevertheless, the very activity of surveying this material has brought out some important points.

In the first place it has highlighted the need for finding new or better answers to questions about existential meaning when growing old, if previous customs and beliefs no longer seem valid. Negative perceptions of ageing are being successfully combated at present, but only by providing opportunities for people to continue previous work-oriented lifestyles for longer. However, although the experience of ageing is changing, the inevitable association with death as its end goal cannot be avoided. The meaning of life at the limits of viability will remain a disturbing presence and the role of religious and other spiritual rationales for continued living in the last stages will continue to be relevant. The challenges from existential questions at all crisis points throughout life find their culmination in old age. They are not of limited 'academic' interest. How older people actually find answers to these questions of meaning and purpose so as to sustain their daily lives are important topics for social research, and have huge implications for provision for those living in states of frailty and debility.

The evidence from the interviews recorded in this book show how older people recall instances where they have employed religious means of coping in the past to their advantage, and continue to build on them as they face new challenges in later life. Mrs Ditton in Chapter Two provided a striking example of reliance on God as well as on her own resources. She was not particularly religious, at least according to her own understanding of being religious, but she no doubt would have agreed with St Augustine's advice: 'pray as though everything depended on God, work as though everything depended on you'. Religions not only give advice on how to act, they also provide resources and practices that can be of special use in times of need. There is now substantial scientific evidence on the benefits of religion for older people in times of illness and also of bereavement (Wink and Scott, 2005; Coleman, 2010), but relatively little attention has been given to the means by which they are gained. The cases described in Chapter Five not only illustrate the power of religious practice in circumstances of bereavement, but also provide insight into how these benefits are obtained.

However, we cannot assume that religion is unique in enhancing meaning at critical points of life. As the cases presented in Chapter Six illustrate, it is possible for well-considered life principles to support individuals in a variety of late life trials. Most of the people interviewed described themselves as Humanists and belonged to organisations that supported like-minded people to live according to secular moral principles. But one of the losses of modern society is the decline in membership of groups that meet regularly to share their common interests. Decline in church membership is partly explainable in terms of the general trends away from group identification and towards more individualised patterns of living (Putnam, 2000). The consequent isolation is being compensated to some extent by electronic membership of 'friends' groups, but this does not fully make up for the decline in physical togetherness in space and time.

Politicians have begun to address this loss of identification with one's own locality. Such a perspective highlights the neglected value of churches in sustaining 'parish' life. Despite their decline in membership they remain a major basis for providing local services and creating community life, hitherto neglected by government (Davis et al, 2008). Church leaders have reacted positively to the growing prospects that faith groups may become regarded by political leaders as resources rather than problems. It will be interesting to see how religious organisations respond to the challenges to provide more in the way of welfare services, including those for older people, and whether alternative local humanistic service provision will also emerge.

A second important point our interviews have demonstrated is that older people can speak in instructive ways about issues of personal belief and commitment if given time and encouragement. They clearly would like to be given more opportunity to communicate what they think about spiritual provision. Often their silence is the result of lack of practice in speaking about existential meaning and of neglect by those, including religious ministers, who should care about these matters but often choose not to enquire. Interviewing and other forms of communication with older people about their spiritual beliefs are the focus of Chapter Three. The material presented there also underlines the fact that older people are not just passive recipients of what religious organisations tell them. As has been found in many other areas of service provision, older people want to be consulted more than we often assume. They can resent being taken for granted, and this applies to their beliefs and commitments as well. Religious organisations must evolve more dynamic policies for involving their older members in decisions about church life, including liturgical change. There has undoubtedly been some decline in pastoral standards in this area – noticed even by the non-religious (for example Mrs Shields in Chapter Four), and even some blatant ageism in the way older people have been provided for. Education in ministry with older people has been given a low priority up to recently.

Rob Merchant (2003) and James Woodward (2008) among others have argued that religious ministry to older people has to be seen as a major feature of church life within an ageing population. New opportunities for evangelism will emerge as the baby boomer generation of the 50s and 60s enter retirement. Although they will have been less religiously socialised when young, this in itself may be an advantage as they may be more prepared to explore what religion offers. Fortunately there is now a corresponding expansion of interest in pastoral work with older people, and not only in North America. Within the UK in recent years, and also in Australia, there has been a series of notable publications addressing these issues (Jewell, 1999; MacKinlay, 2001; Merchant, 2003; Jewell, 2004; MacKinlay, 2006; Woodward, 2008; MacKinlay, 2010).

One of most developed areas of pastoral work with older people occurs within hospital chaplaincy services. In-patients in hospital are mainly middle aged and older, and chaplaincy services have begun to develop particular skills in communicating with a predominantly non-churchgoing population (Cobb, 2005; Speck, 2005). They are available to deal with the existential questions that naturally arise as a result of major illness and the accompanying threat to life. Although secularists have challenged the inclusion of such an apparently religious service within state-funded health services, the reality is that it is in fact a 'spiritual' service (in the broad sense of spiritual) and is available to all hospital patients. Chaplains are able to distinguish between the solely 'spiritual' and the 'religious' services that they provide. Admittedly in other areas of chaplaincy provision, for example in higher education, secular chaplains have been included as part of the team; this in time may also occur within the health service.

Pastoral care for persons with dementia and their caregivers is of special importance. Indeed, dementia poses a principal challenge to modern man's perception of the meaning and value of life. Typically persons with dementia have been neglected at all levels of service provision, and this has led to nihilistic attitudes and a general pessimism about quality of life with dementia that encourages choices for assisted dying. Fortunately these views are now being challenged vigorously (Nuffield Council on Bioethics, 2009). An overemphasis on rationality and continuous memory as criteria for personhood within the western philosophical tradition has contributed to this neglect. Yet Christianity in its essence teaches a relational concept of the person in the image of the Trinitarian God who cannot be understood outside the concept of community, belonging and relatedness (Allen and Coleman, 2006; Hudson, 2010). The new recovery of respect for the person with dementia in the UK, which was stimulated by the work of Tom Kitwood (1997), is also indirectly the product of religious thinking, specifically through the influence of Martin Buber's *I and Thou* (Buber, [1923] 1970). Sustaining the sense of relationship and retaining memory on behalf of the other person are central to present understanding of good dementia care practice.

Ageing and spiritual exploration

We should all welcome an increased openness to questions about the meaning of life and death. Keeping death in focus is not necessarily morbid. In fact it should heighten awareness of new opportunities for living more fully. Older people, in the words of T. S. Elliott, 'should be explorers'. Ageing brings increased time for reflection in which to explore further the beliefs that have already been acquired and to consider new alternative ways of thinking, feeling and being. Forty years ago we were interviewing older people such as Mrs Parsons (see Chapter Two) who were actively exploring their beliefs, and, as the response to our recent surveys (see Chapter Three) have indicated, many older people want to be recognised as questioning their faith. For the baby boomer generation, ageing is likely to be even more a time of challenging assumptions. Gerontological publications are at last engaging with this central aspect of being human (Biggs, 1999; Randall and Kenyon, 2001; Gullette, 2004; Edmondson and von Kondratowitz, 2009).

More recognition also needs to be given to spiritual seeking as central to religious life. It is not the enforced ingestion and repetition of a body of doctrine that counts as belief but its reworking in imagination, and this is always a personal matter. Besides, religious beliefs cannot ultimately be encapsulated in words because they refer to a reality beyond human language. They are better lived and expressed in real-life experiences and commitment. The imagination is free and its deployment is an essential step to developing and re-affirming belief, a point made by John Henry Newman in the 19th century as Christian belief came under challenge in Britain (Gallagher, 2010). The involvement of the heart together with the head does not detract from the validity of belief. Rather it demonstrates its human character.

As the growing interest in spirituality indicates, there is a desire to live in a way that recognises the importance of the 'sacred' and the need to search for it. One particularly interesting trend is the increase in journeys to the many long-established religious pilgrimage sites throughout Europe, as well as the continued attraction of visiting cathedrals and other major religious buildings (Davie, 2006). The rise in pilgrimage is particularly striking, as it involves young as well as older people, and is contrary to the secularisation trend (Hermkens et al, 2009). Because pilgrimage involves travel and usually living together in community, it brings people of different generations together in recognition of their common humanity and search for spiritual goals in life. It also makes understandable and less alien the major investment in pilgrimage made by traditional religious cultures, particularly Islam of course, but also Christianity.

One of the, perhaps surprising, themes of this book has been globalisation, with regard to both its positive and negative consequences. Religion was not only the link to the supernatural realm but was also the binding force within a community. Religious heterodoxy and apostasy was therefore perceived as threatening, and severe restrictions were put in place to prevent it. In many countries, particularly in the Muslim world, that is still true today. But there have also been societies that learned to live well and stably with the existence within them of different religious communities. The Ottoman Empire, for example, although giving precedence to Islam, was multi-faith in character and throughout most of its history more tolerant than most other European Christian empires.

We live now in a world of diversity, but where that diversity is increasingly present everywhere. Different ethnic and faith groups still tend to live separately from one another, although intermingling has become greater as practitioners of different religions travel, work and play together in the broader society. In some ways globalisation has negative consequences by increasing the likelihood of individual isolation, but in other ways it promotes good qualities such as tolerance of others and openness to new experience. We live in a less united but 'bigger' society, and we have to find a way of making it flourish.

In Europe persons are freer to choose what to believe than they have ever been before. Although old age is a time of life for exploration it is also a time for coming to some conclusions. Contemporary older people now have the added challenge of giving witness to their beliefs in a more complex society. They need to explain why they have come to the particular position they have while still being tolerant of other valid pathways. This dilemma is evident also in Erik Erikson's definition of the quality of late life to which he gave the name 'integrity'. It combined acceptance and defence of one's own life's values with 'comradeship with the ordering ways of distant times and different pursuits' (Erikson, 1963: 260). Erikson also made clear that development even in old age involves a dialectic between two poles. Doubt is not something to be ashamed of, but part of the life of a believer – a fact that is witnessed to by many writers on spirituality from St Augustine in the 4th century to Miguel de Unamuno in the 20th:

> Those who believe they believe in God, but without passion in the heart, without anguish of mind, without uncertainty, without doubt and even at times without despair, believe only in the idea of God, not in God himself. (de Unamuno, [1913] 1954: 193)

This book started with a distinction between belief and knowledge. Both are related to truth, a concept we humans do not want to abandon. Yet it is the reality of the human condition that, despite advances in knowledge, ultimate truth about the meaning and purpose of life remains unattainable by human means alone. It can only be resolved by divine revelation to which many of the great faiths claim privileged access. Religious belief means continuing to engage with that revelation. Atheists and agnostics on the other hand choose to create their own meaning and purpose in life. In that sense they also create their own beliefs.

In commenting on the inclusion of spirituality in its 1979 report (already mentioned in Chapter Eight), Age Concern England stated:

> All people, young or old, need to have their beliefs taken seriously. But for the old this is particularly difficult because their relative isolation and vulnerability makes it all too easy for those who seek to help them to ignore their beliefs, while trying to meet their physical and social needs.

Unfortunately this statement still remains true today. It is hoped that this book has shown the value, and also the great interest, in considering older people's beliefs and has encouraged more attention to be paid to them.

References

Abdul-Rauf, M. (1982) 'The ageing in Islam', in F. Tiso (ed) *Aging: Spiritual perspectives*, Lake Worth, FL: Sunday Publications, pp 171-82.

Aflakseir, A. and Coleman, P.G. (2009) 'The influence of religious coping on the mental health of disabled Iranian war veterans', *Mental Health, Religion and Culture,* vol 11, no 2, pp 175-90.

Ahmadi, F. and Thomas, L. E. (2000) 'Gerotranscendence and life satisfaction: studies of religious and secular Iranians and Turks', *Journal of Religious Gerontology,* vol 12, pp 17-41.

Age Concern England (1979) *Ageing into the '80s: Discussion document*, London: Age Concern England.

Allen, F.B. and Coleman, P.G. (2006) 'Spiritual perspectives on the person with dementia: identity and personhood', in J. Hughes, S. Louw and S. Sabat (eds) *Dementia: Mind, meaning and the person,* Oxford: Oxford University Press, pp 205-21.

Allen, R.E. (1990). *The concise Oxford dictionary of current English*, 8th edn, Oxford: Oxford University Press.

Andrews, M. (1991) *Lifetimes of commitment. Aging, politics, psychology,* Cambridge: Cambridge University Press.

Atchley, R.C. (2009) *Spirituality and aging,* Baltimore: John Hopkins.

Atkinson, R. (1991) *The life story interview (Qualitative research methods series no 44),* London: Sage.

Bäckström, A., Davie, G., Edgardh, N. and Pettersson, P. (eds) (2010) *Welfare and religion in 21st century Europe: Volume 1 Configuring the connections,* Farnham: Ashgate.

Baumeister, R.F. (2002) 'Religion and psychology: introduction to the special issue', *Psychological Inquiry,* vol 13, pp 165-7.

Becker, G., Xander, C.J., Blum, H.E., Lutterbach, J., Momm, F., Gysels, M. and Higginson, I.J. (2007) 'Do religious or spiritual beliefs influence bereavement? A systematic review', *Palliative Medicine,* vol 21, pp 207-17.

Biggs, S. (1999) *The mature imagination: Dynamics of identity in midlife and beyond,* Buckingham: Open University Press.

Blazer, D. and Palmore, E. (1976) 'Religion and aging in a longitudinal panel', *The Gerontologist,* vol 16, pp 82-5.

Brown, C.G. (2001) *The death of Christian Britain,* London: Routledge.

Browning, W.R.F. (2004) *Dictionary of the Bible,* Oxford: Oxford University Press.

Buber, M. ([1923]1970) *I and thou,* translated by W. Kaufman, New York: Touchstone Books.

Burke, G. (2007) *Spirituality: roots and routes: A secular reflection on the practice of spiritual care.* London: Age Concern England.

Burrow, J.A. (1986) *The ages of man: A study in medieval writing and thought,* Oxford: Clarendon Press.

Carrette, J. and King, R. (2005) *Selling spirituality*, London: Routledge.

Cobb, M. (2005) *The hospital chaplain's handbook: A guide for good practice*, Norwich: Canterbury Press.

Cole, T. (1991) *The journey of life: A cultural history of aging in America*, Cambridge: Cambridge University Press.

Coleman, P.G. (1972) *The role of the past in adaptation to old age*, PhD Thesis, University of London.

Coleman, P.G. (1986) *Ageing and reminiscence processes: Social and clinical implications*, Chichester: Wiley.

Coleman, P. G. (2002) 'Doing case study research in psychology', in A. Jamieson and C. R. Victor (eds) *Researching ageing and later life*, Buckingham: Open University Press, pp 135-54.

Coleman, P. G. (2010) 'Religion and age', in D. Dannefer and C. Phillipson (eds) *International handbook of social gerontology*, London: Sage, pp 164-76.

Coleman, P.G. and McCulloch, A.W. (1985) 'The study of psychosocial change in late life: some conceptual and methodological issues', in J.M.A. Munnichs, P. Mussen, E. Olbrich, and P.G. Coleman (eds) *Life-span and change in a gerontological perspective*, New York: Academic Press, pp 239-55.

Coleman, P.G. and McCulloch, A.W. (1990) 'Societal change, values and social support: exploratory studies into adjustment in late life', *Journal of Aging Studies*, vol 4, pp 321-32.

Coleman, P.G. and Mills, M.A. (2004) 'Memory and preservation of religious faith in an atheistic society: accounts of the practice of religion in the former Soviet Union', in A. Portelli (ed) *Proceedings of the International Oral History Association*, Rome: IOHA.

Coleman, P.G. and O'Hanlon, A. (2004) *Ageing and development: Theories and research*, London: Edward Arnold.

Coleman, P.G. and Podolskij, A. (2007) 'Identity loss and recovery in the life stories of Soviet World War II Veterans', *The Gerontologist*, vol 47, pp 52-60.

Coleman, P.G., Ivani-Chalian, C. and Robinson, M. (1993) 'Self-esteem and its sources: stability and change in later life', *Ageing and Society*, vol 13, pp 171-92.

Coleman, P.G., Ivani-Chalian, C. and Robinson, M. (2004) 'Religious attitudes among British older people: stability and change in a 20 year longitudinal study', *Ageing and Society*, vol 24, pp 167-88.

Coleman, P.G., McKiernan, F., Mills, M.A. and Speck, P. (2002) 'Spiritual belief and quality of life: the experience of older bereaved spouses', *Quality in Ageing and Older Adults*, vol 3, no 1, pp 20-6.

Coleman, P.G., McKiernan, F, Mills, M. and Speck, P. (2007) 'In sure and uncertain faith: belief and coping with loss of spouse in later life', *Ageing and Society*, vol 27, pp 869-90.

Coleman, P.G., Carare, R.O., Petrov, I., Forbes, E., Saigal, A., Spreadbury, J.H., Yap, A. and Kendrick, T. (2011) 'Spiritual belief, social support, physical functioning and depression among older people in Bulgaria and Romania', *Aging & Mental Health*, vol 15, no 3, pp 327-33.

Coyle, A. (2008) 'Qualitative methods and the (partly) ineffable in psychological research on religion and spirituality', *Qualitative Research in Psychology*, vol 5, pp 56-67.

Crockett, A. and Voas, D. (2006) 'Generations of decline: religious change in 20th century Britain', *Journal for the Scientific Study of Religion*, vol 45, no 4, pp 567-84.

D'Arcy, M.C. (1945) *The nature of belief*, London: Sheed & Ward.

Davie, G. (1994) *Religion in Britain since 1945: Believing without belonging*, London, Blackwell

Davie, G. (2000) 'Religion in modern Britain: changing sociological assumptions', *Sociology*, vol 34, no 1, pp 113-28.

Davie, G. (2002) *Europe: the exceptional case: Parameters of faith in the modern world*, London: Darton, Longman and Todd.

Davie, G. (2006) 'Religion in Europe in the 21st century: the factors to take into account', *Archives of European Sociology*, vol 47, no 2, pp 271-96.

Davies, C. (2004) *The strange death of moral Britain*, New Brunswick, NJ: Transaction.

Davis, F., Paulhaus, E. and Bradstock, A. (2008) *Moral but no compass: Church, government and the future of welfare*, Chelmsford: Matthew James Publishers.

Dawkins, R. (2006) *The God delusion*, London: Bantam Books.

Dein, S. and Stygall, J. (1997) 'Does being religious help or hinder coping with chronic illness? A critical literature review', *Palliative Medicine*, vol 11, pp 291-8.

de Unamuno, M. ([1913] 1954) *The tragic sense of life*, translated by J.E. Crawford Fitch, New York: Dover Publications.

Dillon, M. and Wink, P. (2007) *In the course of a lifetime: Tracing religious belief, practice, and change*, Berkeley, CA: University of California Press.

Dulin, R.Z. (1988) *A crown of glory: A Biblical view of aging'*, New York: Paulist Press.

Edmondson, R. and von Kondratowitz, H.-J. (eds) (2009) *Valuing older people. A humanist approach to ageing*, Bristol: The Policy Press.

Erikson, E.H. ([1950] 1963) *Childhood and society*, London: Penguin.

Eurobarometer (2005) *Social values, science and technology. Report 225*, Brussels: European Commission.

Evans, A. (2011) 'The limits of tolerance: Islam as counter hegemony?', *Review of International Studies*, vol 37 (in press).

Exline, J.J. and Rose, E. (2005) 'Religious and spiritual struggles', in R.F. Paloutzian and C.L. Park (eds) *Handbook of the psychology of religion and spirituality*, New York: Guilford Press, pp 315-30.

Fawcett, T.N. and Noble, A. (2004) 'The challenge of spiritual care in a multi-faith society experienced as a Christian nurse', *Journal of Clinical Nursing*, vol 13, pp 136-42.

Firth, S. (1999) 'Spirituality and age in British Hindus, Sikhs and Muslims', in A. Jewell (ed) *Spirituality and ageing*, London: Jessica Kingsley, pp 158-74.

Fishman, D.B. (1999) *The case for pragmatic psychology*, New York: New York University Press.

Fowler, J.W. (1981) *Stages of faith*, New York: Harper & Row.

Francis, D. (1984) *Will you still need me, will you still feed me, when I'm 84?'*, Bloomington IN: Indiana University Press.

Frisina, A. (2010) 'What kind of church? What kind of welfare? Conflicting views in the Italian case', in A. Bäckström, G. Davie, N. Edgardh, and P. Pettersson (eds) (2010) *Welfare and religion in 21st century Europe: Volume 1 Configuring the connections,* Farnham: Ashgate, pp 147–66.

Froese, P. (2008) *The plot to kill God. Findings from the Soviet experiment in secularization,* Berkeley: University of California Press.

Fry, P.S. (2001) 'The unique contribution of key existential factors to the prediction of psychological well-being of older adults following spousal loss', *The Gerontologist,* vol 41, pp 69–81.

Gallagher, M.P. (2010) *Faith maps: Ten religious explorers from Newman to Joseph Ratzinger,* London: Darton, Longman and Todd.

Gall, T. L. and Cornblat, M. W. (2002) 'Breast cancer survivors give voice: a qualitative analysis of spiritual factors in long-term adjustment', *Psycho-Oncology,* vol 11, pp 524–35.

Gillies, J. and Neimeyer, R.A. (2006) 'Loss, grief, and the search for significance: toward a model of meaning reconstruction in bereavement', *Journal of Constructivist Psychology,* vol 19, pp 31–65.

Goleman, D. (1997) *Healing emotions: Conversations with the Dalai Lama on mindfulness, emotions and health,* Boston: Shambhala.

Greeley, A.M. (2003) *Religion in Europe at the end of the second millennium: A sociological profile,* London: Transaction.

Greeley, A.M. (2004) 'Religious decline in Europe?', *America. The National Catholic Weekly,* vol 190, no 7 (www.americamagazine.org).

Grewal, I., Nazroo, J., Bajekal, M., Blane, D. and Lewis, J. (2004) 'Influences on quality of life: a qualitative investigation of ethnic differences among older people in England', *Journal of Ethnic and Migration Studies,* vol 30, pp 737–61.

Guglani, S., Coleman, P.G. and Sonuga-Barke, E.J.S. (2000) 'Mental health of elderly Asians in Britain: a comparison of Hindus from nuclear and extended families of differing cultural identities', *International Journal of Geriatric Psychiatry,* vol 15, pp 1046–53.

Gullette, M.M. (2004) *Aged by culture,* Chicago: University of Chicago Press.

Gutmann, D.L. (1987) *Reclaimed powers: Towards a new psychology of men and women in later life,* New York: Basic Books.

Gutmann, D.L. (1997) *The human elder in nature, culture and society,* Boulder, CO: Westview Press.

Hauerwas, S., Stoneking, C.B., Meador, K.G. and Cloutier, D. (eds) (2003) *Growing old in Christ,* Grand Rapids, MI: William B. Eerdmans.

Hazan, H. (1980) *The limbo people: A study of the constitution of the time universe among the aged,* London: Routledge.

Heelas, P. (1996) *The New Age movement,* Oxford: Blackwell.

Heelas, P. and Woodhead, L. (2005) *The spiritual revolution: Why religion is giving way to spirituality,* Oxford: Blackwell.

Henry, J.P. (1988) 'The archetypes of power and intimacy', in J.E. Birren, and V.L. Bengtson (eds.) *Emergent theories of aging,* New York: Springer, pp 269-98.

Hermans, H.J.M. and Hermans-Jansen, E. (1995). *Self-narratives: The construction of meaning in psychotherapy,* New York: Guilford.

Hermkens, A.K., Jansen, W. and Notermans, C. (eds) (2009) *Moved by Mary. The power of pilgrimage in the modern world,* Farnham: Ashgate.

Hill, P.C. and Hood, R.W. (1999) *Measures of religiosity,* Birmingham, AL: Religious Education Press.

Hitchens, C.E. (2007) *God is not great: How religion poisons everything,* New York: Warner Books.

Holloway, M. (2007) *Negotiating death in contemporary health and social care,* Bristol: The Policy Press.

Hogan, M. (2010) *The culture of our thinking in relation to spirituality,* New York: Nova Science Publishers.

Houtman, D. and Mascini, P. (2002) 'Why do churches become empty, while New Age grows? Secularization and religious change in the Netherlands', *Journal for the Scientific Study of Religion,* vol 41, no 3, pp 455-73.

Howse, K. (1999) *Religion and spirituality in later life: A review,* London: Centre for Policy on Ageing.

Hudson, R. (2010) 'Orthodox faith: a lively spirit for older people', in E. MacKinlay (ed) *Ageing and spirituality across faiths and culture,* London: Jessica Kingsley, pp 152-166.

Hussain, F.A. and Cochrane, R. (2003) 'Living with depression: coping strategies used by South Asian women, living in the UK, suffering from depression', *Mental Health, Religion & Culture,* vol 6, no 1, pp 21-44.

Idler, E.L., Kasl, S.V., and Hays, J.C. (2001) 'Patterns of religious practice and belief in the last year of life', *Journal of Gerontology: Social Sciences,* vol 56B, pp S326-34.

Imamoglu, E.O. (1999) 'Some correlates of religiosity among Turkish adults and elderly within a cross-cultural perspective', in L.E. Thomas and S.A. Eisenhandler (eds) *Religion, belief, and spirituality in late life,* New York: Springer, pp 93-110.

James, W. (1902) *The varieties of religious experience,* Cambridge, MA: Harvard University Press.

Jana-Masri, A. and Priester, P.E. (2007) 'The development and validation of a Qur'an-based instrument to assess Islamic religiosity: the religiosity of Islam scale', *Journal of Muslim Mental Health,* vol 2, no 2, pp 177-88.

Jewell, A. (ed) (1999) *Spirituality and ageing,* London: Jessica Kingsley.

Jewell, A. (ed) (2004) *Ageing, spirituality and well-being,* London: Jessica Kingsley.

Jianbin, X. and Mehta, K.K. (2003) 'The effects of religion on subjective *aging* in Singapore: An interreligious comparison', *Journal of Aging Studies,* vol 17, pp 485-502.

Jones, C. (1991) 'Qualitative interviewing', in G. Allan and G. Skinner (eds) *Handbook for research students in the social sciences,* London: The Falmer Press.

Jones, C., Wainwright, G. and Yarnold, E. (eds) (1986) *The study of spirituality,* London: SPCK.

Kalish, R.A. and Reynolds, D.K. (1976) *Death and ethnicity: A psychocultural study.* Los Angeles, CA: University of Southern California Press.

Kanev, P. (2002) 'Religion in Bulgaria after 1989: historical and socio-cultural aspects', *South East Europe Review,* vol 5, pp 75-96.

Kaufmann, E. (2010) *Shall the religious inherit the earth? Demography and politics in the twenty-first century',* London: Profile Books.

Kay, A.C., Gaucher, D., McGregor, I. and Nash, K. (2010) 'Religious belief as compensatory control', *Personality and Social Psychology Review,* vol 14, no 1, pp 37-48.

Kennedy, M. (2000) 'Christianity and child sexual abuse – the survivor's voice leading to change', *Child Abuse Review,* vol 9, no 1, pp 124-41.

Kenny, A. (2006) *What I believe,* London: Continuum.

King, M., Speck, P., and Thomas, A. (2001) 'The Royal Free interview for religious and spiritual beliefs: developments and standardisation', *Psychological Medicine,* vol 25, pp 1125-34.

Kirby, S.E., Coleman, P.G. and Daley, D. (2004) 'Spirituality and well-being in frail and non-frail older adults', *Journal of Gerontology: Psychological Sciences,* vol 59B, pp P123-9.

Kirkpatrick, L.A. (2004) *Attachment, evolution and the psychology of religion,* New York: Guilford Press.

Kitwood, T. (1997) *Dementia reconsidered: The person comes first,* Buckingham: Open University Press.

Klass, D., Silverman, P.R. and Nickman, S.L. (1996) *Continuing bonds: New understandings of grief,* London: Taylor & Francis.

Koenig, H.G., Kvale, J.N. and Ferrel, C. (1988a) 'Religion and well-being in later life', *The Gerontologist,* vol 28, pp18-28.

Koenig, H.G., George, L.K. and Siegler, I.C. (1988b) 'The use of religion and other emotion-regulating coping strategies among older adults', *The Gerontologist,* vol 28, pp 303-10.

Koleva, D. (2007) 'The memory of socialist public holidays: between colonization and autonomy', in U. Brunnbauer and S. Troebst (eds) *Zwischen Amnesie und Nostalgie. Die Erinnerung an den Kommunismus in Sudosteuropa,* Cologne: Bochlau, pp 185-98.

Krause, N. (1995) 'Religiosity and self-esteem among older adults', *Journal of Gerontology: Psychological Sciences,* vol 50B, pp P236-46.

Krause, N. (2006) 'Religious doubts and psychological well-being: a longitudinal nvestigation', *Review of Religious Research,* vol 47, pp 287-302.

Krause, N., Ingersoll-Dayton, B., Ellison, C.G. and Wulff, K.M. (1999) 'Aging, religious doubt, and psychological well-being', *The Gerontologist,* vol 39, pp 525-33.

Krause, N., Liang, J., Bennett, J., Kobayashi, E., Akiyama, H. and Fukaya, T. (2010) 'A descriptive analysis of religious involvement among older adults in Japan', *Ageing and Society,* vol 30, no 4, pp 671-96.

Kynaston, D. (2007) *Austerity Britain 1945–51,* London: Bloomsbury.

Kynaston, D. (2009) *Family Britain 1951–57,* London: Bloomsbury.

Lambert, J-L. (2005) 'Orthodox Christianity, Soviet atheism and "animist" practices in the Russianized world', *Diogenes,* vol 52, no 1, pp 21-31.

Leavey, G. and King, M. (2007) 'The devil is in the detail: partnership between psychiatry and faith-based organisations', *British Journal of Psychiatry,* vol 191, pp 97-8.

Levin, J.S. (ed) (1994) *Religion in aging and health,* Thousand Oaks, CA: Sage.

Levin, J.S.; and Tobin, S.S. (1995) 'Religion and psychological well-being', in M.A. Kimble, S.H. McFadden, J.W. Ellor and J.J. Seeber (eds) *Aging, spirituality and religion: a handbook,* Minneapolis, MI: Fortress Press.

Lewis, B. (2003) *The crisis of Islam. Holy war and unholy terror,* London: Weidenfeld & Nicolson.

Lynch, G. (2007) *The new spirituality: An introduction to progressive belief in the twenty-first century,* London: I.B. Tauris.

MacKinlay, E. (2001) *The spiritual dimension of ageing,* London: Jessica Kingsley.

MacKinlay, E. (2006) *Spiritual growth and care in the fourth age of life,* London: Jessica Kingsley.

MacKinlay, E. (ed) (2010) *Ageing and spirituality across faiths and culture,* London: Jessica Kingsley.

Marcoen, A. (2005) 'Religion, spirituality and older people', in M.L. Johnson, V.L. Bengtson, P.G. Coleman, and T.B.L. Kirkwood (eds) *The Cambridge Handbook of Age and Ageing,* Cambridge: Cambridge University Press, pp 363-70.

Marshall, C. and Rossman, G. (2006) *Designing qualitative research,* Thousands Oaks, CA: Sage.

McAdams, D. P. (1993) *Stories we live by: Personal myths and the making of the self,* New York: William Morrow.

McClain-Jacobson, C., Rosenfeld, B., Kosinski, A., Pessin, H., Cimino, J. E. and Breitbart, W. (2004) 'Belief in an afterlife, spiritual well-being and end-of-life despair in patients with advanced cancer', *General Hospital Psychiatry,* vol 26, pp 484-6.

McCulloch, A.W. (1985) *Adjustment to old age in a changing society,* PhD Thesis, University of Southampton

McCullough, M.E., Enders, C.K., Brion, S.L. and Jain, A.R. (2005) 'The varieties of religious development in adulthood: a longitudinal investigation of religion and rational choice', *Journal of Personality and Social Psychology,* vol 89, no 1, pp 78-89.

McFadden, S.H. (1996) 'Religion and spirituality', in J.E. Birren (ed) *Encyclopedia of gerontology, Volume 2,* San Diego, CA: Academic Press, pp 387-97.

McFadden, S.H. (2005) 'Points of connection: gerontology and the psychology of religion', in R.F. Paloutzian and C.L. Park (eds) *Handbook of the psychology of religion and spirituality,* New York: Guilford Press, pp 162-76.

McFadden, S.H. and Levin, J.S. (1996) 'Religion, emotions and health', in C. Magai and S.H. McFadden (eds) *Handbook of emotion, adult development and aging,* San Diego: Academic Press, pp 349-65.

Mehta, K.K. (1997) 'The impact of religious beliefs and practices on aging: a cross-cultural comparison', *Journal of Aging Studies*, vol 11, pp 102-14.

Merchant, R. (2003) *Pioneering the third age. The church in an ageing population*, Carlisle: Paternoster Press.

Mills, M.A. and Coleman, P.G. (2002) 'Lebensrückblicksinterventionen bei älteren Menschen. Ein psychodynamischer Ansatz', in A. Maercker (ed) *Alterspsychotherapie und Klinische Gerontopsychologie*, Berlin: Springer, pp 359-76.

Mills, M.A., Coleman, P.G., McKiernan, F. and Speck, P. (2002) '"Relational" research: the recruitment and retention of older participants for qualitative studies', *ESRC Growing Older Programme*, Newsletter, Issue 5, p 2.

Moberg, D.O. (ed) (2001a) *Aging and spirituality: Spiritual dimensions of aging theory, research, practice and policy*, New York: The Haworth Press.

Moberg, D.O. (2001b) 'Research on spirituality', in D.O. Moberg (ed.) *Aging and spirituality: Spiritual dimensions of aging theory, research, practice and policy*. New York: The Haworth Press, pp 55-69.

Mowat, H. (2008) *The potential for efficacy of healthcare chaplaincy and spiritual care provision in the NHS (UK): A scoping review of recent research*, Aberdeen: Mowat Research Ltd.

Nelson, C. J., Rosenfeld, B., Breitbart, W. and Galietta, M. (2002) 'Spirituality, religion, and depression in the terminally ill', *Psychosomatics*, vol 43, no 3, pp 213-20.

Noll, M.A. (2002) *America's God. From Jonathan Edwards to Abraham Lincoln*, New York: Oxford University Press.

Norris, P. and Inglehart, R. (2004) *Sacred and secular: Religion and politics worldwide*, Cambridge: Cambridge University Press.

Nuffield Council on Bioethics (2009) *Dementia: Ethical issues*, London: Nuffield Council on Bioethics.

Paley, J. (2007) 'Spirituality and secularization: nursing and the sociology of religion', *Journal of Clinical Nursing*, vol 17, pp 175-86.

Pargament, K.I. (1997) *The psychology of religion and coping: Theory, research, practice*, New York: Guilford Press.

Petrov, I. C. (1996) 'Feelings and attitudes towards the changes during social and economic transition: a study on autonomous elderly subjects in Sofia', *Romanian Journal of Gerontology and Geriatrics*, vol 17, pp73-82 and vol 18, pp 76-85.

Pew Research Center (2006) *The great divide: How westerners and Muslims view each other*, Washington, DC: Pew Research Center.

Phadraig, M.N.G. (2009) 'Religion in Ireland: no longer an exception', *Research Update*, no 64 (www.ark.ac.uk).

Phalet, K., Baysu, G. and Verkuyten, M. (2010) 'Political mobilisation of Dutch Muslims: religious identity salience, goal framing, and normative constraints', *Journal of Social Issues*, vol 66, no 4, pp 759-79.

Polivka, L. (2000) 'Postmodern aging and the loss of meaning', *Journal of Aging and Identity*, vol 5, pp 225-35.

Population Reference Bureau (2010) *World population data sheet,* Washington, DC: Population Reference Bureau.

Pritchard, C. and Amanullah, S. (2007) 'An analysis of suicide and undetermined deaths in 17 predominantly Islamic countries contrasted with the UK', *Psychological Medicine,* vol 37, no 3, pp 421-30.

Putnam, R.D. (2000) *Bowling alone: The collapse and revival of American community,* New York: Simon & Schuster.

Ram-Prasad, C. (1995) 'A classical Indian philosophical perspective on ageing and the meaning of life,' *Ageing and Society,* vol 15, pp 1-36.

Randall, W.L. (2009) 'Transcending our stories: a narrative perspective on spirituality in later life', *Critical Social Work,* vol 10, no 1.

Randall, W.L. and Kenyon, G.M. (2001) *Ordinary wisdom. Biographical aging and the journey of life,* Westport, CT: Praeger.

Roberts, E. and Shukman, A. (eds) (1996) *Christianity for the twenty-first century: the life and work of Alexander Men,* London: SCM Press.

Sadler, E. (2009) *Exploring the role of spirituality in successful ageing,* PhD Thesis, University of London.

Sarbin. T.R. (1986) 'The narrative as a root metaphor for psychology', in T.R. Sarbin (ed) *Narrative psychology: the storied nature of human conduct,* New York: Praeger.

Scheepers, P. and Schilderman, H. (2010) 'Religious sources of solidarity', presentation at end of programme conference at University of Cambridge, June 2010, on *Re-emergence of religion as a social force,* NORFACE (www.relemerge.org).

Seabrook, J. (1980) *The way we are,* London: Age Concern England.

Sedikides, C. (2010) 'Why does religiosity persist?', *Personality and Social Psychology Review,* vol 14, no 1, pp 3-6.

Sedikides, C. and Gebauer, J.E. (2010) 'Religiosity as self-enhancement: A meta-analysis of the relation between socially desirable responding and religiosity', *Personality and Social Psychology Review,* vol 14, no 1, pp 17-36.

Sheldrake, P. (1992) *Spirituality and history: Questions of interpretation and method.* New York: Crossroads.

Sheldrake, P. (ed) (2005) *The new SCM dictionary of Christian spirituality,* London: SCM Press.

Speck, P. (2005) 'Spirits not included: is there an evidence base to support the inclusion of spiritual care in clinical practice?', *Nursing Management,* vol 12, no 6, pp 28-31.

Speck, P., Mills, M.A. and Coleman, P.G. (2006) *Knowledge and attitudes towards ageing: service provision and care as a factor for well-being for a new generation of elderly people within a faith community,* Report of research findings for the Nuffield Foundation, University of Southampton.

Spreadbury, J.H. (2010) *The role of religious and spiritual belief and practice in coping and adjusting to spousal bereavement in later life,* PhD thesis, University of Southampton.

Strauss, A. and Corbin, J. (1998) *Basics of qualitative research: grounded theory, procedures and techniques,* Newbury Park, CA: Sage.

Taylor, D (2001) *Tell me a story: The life-shaping power of our stories*, St Paul's, MN: Bog Walk Press

Tearfund (2007) *Churchgoing in the UK*, Teddington, Middlesex: Tearfund.

Tilak, S. (1989) *Religion and aging in the Indian tradition*, Albany, NY: State University of New York Press.

Tobin, S.S. (1991) *Personhood in advanced old age: Implications for practice*, New York: Springer.

Tornstam, L. (1996) 'Caring for elderly – introducing the theory of gerotranscendence as a supplementary frame of reference for the care of elderly', *Scandinavian Journal of Caring Sciences*, vol 10, pp 144-50.

Tornstam, L. (1999) 'Later-life transcendence: a new developmental perspective on aging', in L.E. Thomas and S.A. Eisenhandler (eds) *Religion, belief and spirituality in late life*, New York: Springer, pp 178-201.

Vitz P.C. (1990) 'The use of stories in moral development: new psychological reasons for an old education method', *American Psychologist*, vol 45, pp 709-20.

Voas, D. (2010) 'Extending and enhancing the International Social Survey Programme (ISSP) 2008 module on religion', presentation at end of programme conference at University of Cambridge, June 2010, on *Re-emergence of religion as a social force*, NORFACE (www.relemerge.org).

Voas, D. and Crockett, A. (2005) 'Religion in Britain: neither believing nor belonging', *Sociology*, vol 39, pp 11-28.

Von Hugel Institute (2007) *The ground of justice:. The report of a pastoral enquiry into the needs of migrants in London's Catholic community*, Cambridge: Von Hugel Institute.

Wadsworth, M.E.J. and Freeman, S.R. (1983) 'Generation differences in beliefs: a cohort study of stability and change in religious beliefs', *The British Journal of Sociology*, vol 34, no 3, pp 416-37.

Walsh, K., King, M., Jones, L., Tookman, A. and Blizard, R. (2002) 'Spiritual beliefs may affect outcome of bereavement: prospective study', *British Medical Journal*, vol 324, pp 1551-4.

Ware, K. (1997) *The Orthodox Church*, London: Penguin.

WHOQOL SPRB Group (2006) 'A cross-cultural study of spirituality, religion and personal beliefs as components of quality of life', *Social Science & Medicine*, vol 62, pp 1486-97.

Wilkinson, P. J. and Coleman, P. G. (2010) 'Strong beliefs and coping in old age: a case based comparison of atheism and religion', *Ageing and Society*, vol 30, no 2, pp 337-61.

Wink, P. and Scott, J. (2005) 'Does religiousness buffer against the fear of death and dying in late adulthood?', *Journal of Gerontology: Psychological Sciences*, vol 60B, pp 207-14.

Woodhead, L. (2004) *A very short introduction to Christianity*, Oxford: Oxford University Press.

Woodward, J. (2008) *Valuing age. Pastoral ministry with older people*, London: SPCK.

Wuthnow, R. (1998) *After heaven: Spirituality in America since the 1950s,* Berkeley, CA: University of California Press.

Zappen, J (2000) 'Mikhail Bakhtin (1895-1975)', in M.G. Moran and M. Ballif (eds) *Twentieth-century rhetoric and rhetoricians: Critical studies and sources,* Westport CT: Greenwood Press.

Index

Note: Entries preceded by ★ indicate pseudonyms of case study participants.

V

Voas, D. 28, 76

W

Walsh, K. 80
war 21–2, 50
welfare provision 114–15
Wink, P. 61–2
women
  decreasing belief in later life 64, 69–71
  increasing belief in later life 67–9
  and religion 12, 14–15, 19–20
Woodhead, L. 15, 154
Woodward, J. 2–3, 160
World War One 17, 21–2, 130
World War Two 21, 50

Y

young people
  bad behaviour 19, 20
  church attendance 61
  Islam 153, 158
  Russia 116, 119
  spiritual belief and non-religiosity 12, 14,
    139, 140